LANDLORDS' RIGHTS AND DUTIES IN FLORIDA

Tenth Edition

Mark Warda
Attorney at Law

SPHINX® PUBLISHING
AN IMPRINT OF SOURCEBOOKS, INC.®
NAPERVILLE, ILLINOIS
www.SphinxLegal.com

Published by: **Sphinx® Publishing, An Imprint of Sourcebooks, Inc.®**

Naperville Office
P.O. Box 4410
Naperville, Illinois 60567-4410
630-961-3900
Fax: 630-961-2168
www.sourcebooks.com
www.SphinxLegal.com

This publication is designed to provide accurate and authoritative information in regard to the subject matter covered. It is sold with the understanding that the publisher is not engaged in rendering legal, accounting, or other professional service. If legal advice or other expert assistance is required, the services of a competent professional person should be sought.

From a Declaration of Principles Jointly Adopted by a Committee of the
American Bar Association and a Committee of Publishers and Associations

This product is not a substitute for legal advice.

Disclaimer required by Texas statutes.

Library of Congress Cataloging-in-Publication Data
Warda, Mark.
  Landlords' rights and duties in Florida / by Mark Warda.-- 10th ed.
    p. cm.
  Includes index.
  ISBN 1-57248-491-8 (pbk. : alk. paper)
  1. Landlord and tenant--Florida--Popular works. I. Title.

KFF117.Z9W37 2005
346.75904'34--dc22   2005027280

Printed and bound in the United States of America.
BG — 10 9 8 7 6 5 4 3 2 1

CONTENTS

Tenant's Bankruptcy
Landlord's Appeal
Satisfaction of Judgment

Making a Claim
Amount
Hearings
Defenses
Liens
Distress for Rent and Replevin

Withholding Access
Liens

USING SELF-HELP LAW BOOKS

Before using a self-help law book, you should realize the advantages and disadvantages of doing your own legal work and understand the challenges and diligence that this requires.

The Growing Trend

Rest assured that you will not be the first or only person handling your own legal matter. For example, in some states, more than 75% of the people in divorces and other cases represent themselves. Because of the high cost of legal services, this is a major trend, and many courts are struggling to make it easier for people to represent themselves. However, some courts are not happy with people who do not use attorneys and refuse to help them in any way. For some, the attitude is, "Go to the law library and figure it out for yourself."

We write and publish self-help law books to give people an alternative to the often complicated and confusing legal books found in most law libraries. We have made the explanations of the law as simple and easy to understand as possible. Of course, unlike an attorney advising an individual client, we cannot cover every conceivable possibility.

Cost/Value Analysis

Whenever you shop for a product or service, you are faced with various levels of quality and price. In deciding what product or service to buy, you make a cost/value analysis on the basis of your willingness to pay and the quality you desire.

When buying a car, you decide whether you want transportation, comfort, status, or sex appeal. Accordingly, you decide among choices such as a Neon, a Lincoln, a Rolls Royce, or a Porsche. Before making a decision, you usually weigh the merits of each option against the cost.

When you get a headache, you can take a pain reliever (such as aspirin) or visit a medical specialist for a neurological examination. Given this choice, most people, of course, take a pain reliever, since it costs only pennies, whereas a medical examination costs hundreds of dollars and takes a lot of time. This is usually a logical choice because it is rare to need anything more than a pain reliever for a headache. But in some cases, a headache may indicate a brain tumor, and failing to see a specialist right away can result in complications. Should everyone with a headache go to a specialist? Of course not, but people treating their own illnesses must realize that they are betting on the basis of their cost/value analysis of the situation. They are taking the most logical option.

The same cost/value analysis must be made when deciding to do your own legal work. Many legal situations are very straightforward, requiring a simple form and no complicated analysis. Anyone with a little intelligence and a book of instructions can handle the matter without outside help.

But there is always the chance that complications are involved that only an attorney would notice. To simplify the law into a book like this, several legal cases often must be condensed into a single sentence or paragraph. Otherwise, the book would be several hundred pages long and too complicated for most people. However, this simplification necessarily leaves out many details and nuances that would apply to special or unusual situations. Also, there are many ways to interpret most legal questions. Your case may come before a judge who disagrees with the analysis of our authors.

Therefore, in deciding to use a self-help law book and to do your own legal work, you must realize that you are making a cost/value analysis. You have decided that the money you will save in doing it yourself outweighs the chance that your case will not turn out to your satisfaction. Most people handling their own simple legal matters never have a problem, but occasionally people find that it ends up costing them more to have an attorney straighten out the situation than it would have if they had hired an attorney in the beginning. Keep this in mind while handling your case, and be sure to consult an attorney if you feel you might need further guidance.

Local Rules   The next thing to remember is that a book which covers the law for the entire nation, or even for an entire state, cannot possibly include every procedural difference of every jurisdiction. Whenever possible, we provide the exact form needed; however, in some areas, each county, or even each judge, may require unique forms and procedures. In our state books, our forms usually cover the majority of counties in the state or provide examples of the type of form which will be required. In our national books, our forms are sometimes even more general in nature but are designed to give a good idea of the type of form that will be needed in most locations. Nonetheless, keep in mind that your state, county, or judge may have a requirement, or use a form, that is not included in this book.

You should not necessarily expect to be able to get all of the information and resources you need solely from within the pages of this book. This book will serve as your guide, giving you specific information whenever possible and helping you to find out what else you will need to know. This is just like if you decided to build your own backyard deck. You might purchase a book on how to build decks. However, such a book would not include the building codes and permit requirements of every city, town, county, and township in the nation; nor would it include the lumber, nails, saws, hammers, and other materials and tools you would need to actually build the deck. You would use the book as your guide, and then do some work and research involving such matters as whether you need a permit of some kind, what type and grade of wood is available in your area, whether to use hand tools or power tools, and how to use those tools.

Before using the forms in a book like this, you should check with your court clerk to see if there are any local rules of which you should be aware or local forms you will need to use. Often, such forms will require the same information as the forms in the book but are merely laid out differently or use slightly different language. They will sometimes require additional information.

Changes in the Law   Besides being subject to local rules and practices, the law is subject to change at any time. The courts and the legislatures of all fifty states are constantly revising the laws. It is possible that while you are reading this book, some aspect of the law is being changed.

It is just as likely, however, that an area of law has not changed in decades. We try to keep our cases as current as possible, but a reference to a 1926 case, for example, may in fact be the latest and best reference for a certain point of law. It is also possible that a case decided just months ago has already been overturned by a higher court. Feel confident to rely on the cases we give you, but remember that the points they are making can change, and it is always best to do additional research.

In most cases, the change will be of minimal significance. A form will be redesigned, additional information will be required, or a waiting period will be extended. As a result, you might need to revise a form, file an extra form, or wait out a longer time period; these types of changes will not usually affect the outcome of your case. On the other hand, sometimes a major part of the law is changed, the entire law in a particular area is rewritten, or a case that was the basis of a central legal point is overruled. In such instances, your entire ability to pursue your case may be impaired.

To help you with local requirements and changes in the law, be sure to read the section in Chapter 1 on "Doing Further Research."

Again, you should weigh the value of your case against the cost of an attorney and make a decision as to what you believe is in your best interest.

● ● ● ● ●

A new addition to this book is a *Table of Authorities*. A Table of Authorities is a listing of all the cases cited throughout this book. It lists the topic the case addresses, the page it can be found on, and the case citation. Throughout the text, court cases are noted by the book symbol 📖.

You can find the case that the 📖 represents by turning to the Table of Authorities. Cases that are explained in greater detail are also referenced in the text of this book with citations included. (See "Doing Further Research" in Chapter 1 for more detailed information regarding case citations.)

INTRODUCTION

Florida's landlord/tenant laws are like a double-edged sword. If a landlord does not know about them or ignores them, he or she can lose thousands of dollars in lost rent, penalties, and attorney's fees. However, a landlord who knows the law can use the procedures to simplify life and to save money. Knowledge is power, and knowing the laws governing rentals will give you the power to protect your rights and to deal with problems effectively.

Laws are written to be precise, not to be easily readable. This book explains the law in simple language so that Florida landlords can know what is required of them and know their rights under the law. If you would like more details about a law, you can check the statutes in Appendix B or research the court cases as explained in Chapter 1.

Nearly every year the Florida legislature passes new laws regulating landlord/tenant relations, and the courts of the state write more opinions defining the rights of landlords and tenants. To keep this book current and useful, this tenth edition includes recent statutory and case law changes.

The Florida Bar, under orders by the Florida Supreme Court, prepared some forms for use by landlords, landlords' agents, and paralegals, and we have included these approved forms in this book. However, these forms do not cover every situation, so we have created additional forms to fit landlords' needs.

No book of this type can be expected to cover every situation that may arise. Laws change and different judges have different interpretations of what the laws mean. Only your lawyer, reviewing the unique characteristics of your situation, can give you an opinion of how the laws apply to your case. But this book can give you the legal framework to avoid costly mistakes.

When following the procedures in this book, it should be kept in mind that different counties have different customs, and some judges have their own way of doing things. So the requirements in your area may differ somewhat from those outlined in this book. Clerks and judge's assistants cannot give you legal advice, but often they can tell you what is required in order to proceed with your case. Before filing any forms, ask if your court provides its own forms or has any special requirements.

I   LAWS THAT GOVERN RENTAL PROPERTY

Florida landlord/tenant law consists of both statutes passed by the legislature and legal opinions written by judges. The statutes usually address specific issues that have come up repeatedly in landlord/tenant relations. The judicial opinions interpret the statutes and decide what the law is in areas not specifically covered by statutes.

Unfortunately, statutes sometimes conflict, and different judges do not always interpret them in the same way. So a landlord can be caught in a *catch-22* situation with conflicting *right* answers. Even an experienced lawyer cannot always find an easy solution.

Fortunately, this is a rare situation. If it happens to you, your two choices are to fight the issue in a higher court or to give in and do what is demanded. Most small landlords cannot afford a long court battle, so the only practical solution is to give in. For this reason it is usually better to work out a settlement with a tenant than to let an issue go to a building inspector or before a judge. (This will be explained in more detail later in the book.)

When reading the law contained in judges' opinions, be sure to note from which court the opinion originated. If it is not from your district, it might not be binding on your case. Supreme Court of Florida opinions apply to all courts in Florida, but District Court of Appeal opinions only apply to the district in which they sit. Circuit Court appeals of County Court cases only are binding in the circuit in which that court sits, and County Court opinions are not binding in other courts. However, while another court may not have to follow the ruling of a court below, all of these cases may be used as rationale by other county courts.

Florida's *Landlord-Tenant Act* is divided into three parts, covering nonresidential, residential, and self-storage space tenancies. An interesting fact is that most of the nonresidential sections have been in effect since the 1800s and originally applied to all tenancies. However, these sections were limited to nonresidential tenancies when Florida adopted a new residential Landlord-Tenant Act in 1973. Consequently, the nonresidential statute is much more antiquated and refers to such things as the tenant's "bedclothes," which do not make sense in a nonresidential tenancy.

Many principles of landlord/tenant law apply to both kinds of tenancies. When a specific law applies to only residential or nonresidential tenancies will be noted in the text. You can also know the difference because the nonresidential sections are numbered from 83.001 to 83.251, the residential from 83.40 to 83.682, and the self-storage space from 83.801 to 83.809.

Applicability of the Residential Act

The residential portion of the Landlord-Tenant Act applies to most residential tenancies but does not apply to hotels; motels; rooming houses; religious, educational, geriatric, or medical facilities; transient rentals; condominium owners; or, proprietary leases in cooperatives. It also does not apply to contracts to purchase property.

Purchase Contracts In a contract for sale of property that provided the Landlord-Tenant Act would apply in the event of default, the court held this invalid and said that rules for foreclosing a mortgage would apply. 📖

De Facto Purchase Agreements 📖 Where an agreement was titled "Real Estate Lease" but was in fact a twelve-year purchase agreement, a court held that the Landlord-Tenant Act did not apply and a foreclosure was necessary to remove the buyer.

(Buyer's Advantage Finance Co. Inc. v. Morse, 4 Florida Law Weekly Supplement (FLW Supp.) 475 (Co.Ct. Santa Rosa 1997).)

One possible way to use landlord/tenant law in a purchase or option situation would be with a *land trust*. If the purchaser signs a lease with the trustee for possession of the property and a separate purchase or option agreement with the beneficiary of the trust for purchase of the beneficial interest, the arrangement may allow use of landlord/tenant law for an eviction. No case is known to have ruled on this issue, but one case allowed a similar situation. 📖

Mobile Home When a mobile home *and* lot are rented, Florida Statutes, Section 723.002 states that the Landlord-Tenant Act applies. When a lot is rented to the owner of a mobile home, then Chapter 723 (the Landlord-Tenant Act) applies. 📖 If the unit rented is a "recreational vehicle" in a recreational vehicle park (as defined in Florida Statutes, Section 513.01), then the tenant is a transient guest and can be removed like a nonpaying hotel guest. 📖

Vacant Land. One Florida court has held that this chapter does not apply to vacant land onto which a tenant moves a mobile home to use as a residence. 📖

Boat At least one case has allowed a landlord to evict a boat from a marina using the residential landlord/tenant procedure, because the boat was being used as a residence. However, the landlord did not follow the exact notice requirement, so he lost the case. 📖

Applicability of the Nonresidential Act

The nonresidential landlord/tenant laws apply to nonresidential tenancies, to residential tenancies that do not fall into the definition of the residential act, and to any other tenancies that are not covered by the mobile home park or self-storage laws.

Commercial The nonresidential act applies to nearly all rentals of commercial property, but at least one case has held that it does not apply to stalls in markets such as flea markets. 📖

Residential in Fact The nonresidential act could apply to tenancies that are, in fact, residential but which do not fall under the definition of the residential or mobile home chapters.

Florida Statutes, Section 83.001, states that it applies to nonresidential tenancies "and all tenancies not governed by part II of this chapter." This would indicate that it could cover residential tenancies if they did not fit into the definition of residential tenancies in part II.

📖 It has been held that the residential tenancy rules do not apply to land rented to a person who placed a mobile home on it. (*Russo v. Manfredo*, 35 Fla.Supp.2d 23 (Cir.Ct. Citrus Co. 1989).)

📖 The residential tenancy laws do not apply to occupancy under a contract of sale. Therefore, if a party was renting a property under a contract of sale, this section of landlord/tenant law might apply. However, one appeals court has ruled otherwise. (*Casavan v. Land O'Lakes Realty, Inc.*, 542 So.2d 371 (Fla. 5 DCA 1989).)

Rules of the Division of Hotels and Motels

Under Florida Statutes, Chapter 509, the Division of Hotels and Motels of the Department of Business Regulation has the power to regulate the rental of apartment buildings of five units or more. The division says that any five units or homes on a contiguous piece of property comes under their jurisdiction, but the statute excludes buildings that have less than five units. (Fla. Stat., Sec. 509.013(4)(b)4.)

Owners of buildings that come under the jurisdiction of the Division of Hotels and Motels are required to be registered with them and are subject to their rules, which are contained in the Florida Administrative Code, Chapters 61C-1 and 61C-3. These can be photocopied at a law library or obtained from the Department of Business and Professional Regulation. Their number is 850-487-1395.

Rules of the Florida Department of Legal Affairs

The Florida Department of Legal Affairs at one point issued rules purporting to cover residential tenancies. They were repealed. Future attempts to regulate landlord/tenant relations should be considered questionable because two courts have ruled that the Florida statutes covering deceptive trade practices, under which the rules are promulgated, do not apply to mobile home or real estate transactions. 📖

Nursing Homes and Related Facilities

Nursing homes and related facilities are not covered by the landlord/tenant statute. Florida has special statutes regulating "Nursing Homes, Assisted Living Facilities, Home Health Care Facilities, Adult Day Care Centers, Hospices, and Adult Foster Homes." These are found in Florida Statutes, Chapter 400.

Local Laws

In some areas, local governments have passed various rules regulating landlords. For example, in one area it is a crime for a landlord not to have a walk-through inspection both before and after the tenancy. Be sure to check with both your city and county governments for any local laws.

Federal Laws

Federal laws that apply to rental of real estate include discrimination laws such as the *Civil Rights Act*, the *Americans with Disabilities Act*, and lead-based paint rules of the Environmental Protection Agency. (These are explained in Chapter 2 of this book.)

The United States Department of Housing and Urban Development (HUD) has a handbook that explains the rules applicable to public housing and other HUD programs.

Know Your Rights

Do not assume that every law is constitutional or that every government employee is right. You may have to bring your case to a higher court to get all of the rights you are entitled to. In one case, some tenants who were being evicted filed a complaint with a state civil rights commission. The commission held a hearing at which it both represented the tenants and ordered the landlords to pay the tenants $40,000 in damages and not to evict the tenants. The daughter of one of the landlords filed a suit against the commission, and the court held that the landlords had been denied several constitutional rights. The commission agreed to pay the landlords $100,000.

Doing Further Research

This book contains a summary of most of the court cases and statutes that affect landlord/tenant law in Florida. However, you may want to research your predicament further by reading the entire statute section or court case. To do this, you should use the statute section number or case citation. Florida Statute citations appear in this book as "Fla. Stat., Sec. ##.##." All of Florida's landlord/tenant statutes are included in Appendix B.

As described in the Using Self-Help Law Books section, court cases are noted by the following book symbol 📖. Where you see the 📖, a point of law being made is supported by a court decision. You can find the citation for that decision in the Table of Authorities found in Appendix A. Other cases are summarized throughout the text, with their citations being given with the summary and in the Table of Authorities. Case citations include the name of the case, the volume and page of the reporter, the court, and the year. For example, *Clark & Lewis v. Gardner*, 109 So. 192 (Fla. 1926) means that the case is found in volume 109 of the Southern Reporter on page 192, and that it is a 1926 case from the Florida Supreme Court. The notation "(Fla. 3 DCA 1964)" means the case was decided in Florida's third district court of appeals. The notation "(11th

Cir. App. Div. 1987)" means in a circuit court acting as an appeals court from county court in the 11th circuit, and "(Co.Ct. Broward 1996)" means a county court in Broward county.

Good Faith Obligation

Every residential rental agreement and duty under the landlord/tenant law requires *good faith,* which is defined as "honesty in fact." Any sort of dishonesty or trickery could cause a loss of valuable rights. (Fla. Stat., Sec. 83.44). While this requirement is not in the nonresidential act, any lack of good faith in a nonresidential tenancy would likely have just as bad consequences for the perpetrator.

Fictitious Names

As of 1991, anyone doing business in Florida under a name other than his or her own personal or corporate name must register the name with the Secretary of State. (Fla. Stat., Sec. 865.09.) This applies to landlords who use management company names or apartment building names. A corporation that does business under its own name does not have to register. The procedure is to advertise the name once in a local newspaper and then to file a form with the Secretary of State with the filing fee (currently $50).

Registration lasts for five years and expires on December 31st of the fifth year. It may be renewed for $50. If a business is sold, the old registration may be assigned and the name re-registered for $50.

Sales and Use Tax

Florida sales and use tax applies to certain types of rentals. Technically, all rentals are subject to the tax, unless they are exempt. Some of the exemptions include the following.

- ✪ Transient rentals of over six months. (Fla. Stat., Sec. 212.03(1).) To qualify, a landlord should get written leases of longer than six months from each tenant.

- ✪ Permanent places of residence. (Fla. Stat., Sec. 212.03(7)(c).) To qualify, at least half the rental units must rent for over three months.

- ✪ Rentals to full-time students. (Fla. Stat., Sec. 212.03(7)(a).)

- ✪ Agricultural, recreational, condominium recreational, airport, port facilities, qualified production facilities, movie theatre concessionaires, and those exempt under F.A.C. 12A-1.070(19)(c). (Fla. Stat., Sec. 212.031(1)(a).) See the statute for more details.

- ✪ Property already subject to parking, dock, or storage space tax. (Fla. Stat., Sec. 212.031(1)(a).)

This means that generally all commercial rentals and transient rentals of six months or less are taxed, while all permanent residential rentals are exempt.

The tax is paid by the tenant to the landlord in addition to the rent. This should be spelled out clearly in the lease.

- ✪ Since 1989, when a commercial lease does not state who pays the tax, the tenant must pay the tax in addition to the rent. 📖

- ✪ If a tenant pays rent by performing services or trading some piece of property, the tax is still due.

Each property manager or owner who collects the tax must first obtain a tax number from the Florida Department of Revenue and then make payments to the state of the taxes collected. These payments are made monthly, quarterly, or semi-annually, depending on the amount collected. Property managers of facilities that are exempt from the tax must still register with the state and file a declaration each year that the property is exempt.

You can register to collect the tax at this website:

www.myflorida.com/dor/eservices/apps/register

You can also download the registration form at:

www.myflorida.com/dor/forms/download/!sales.html

Or you can call 800-352-3671 and ask that the form be sent to you.

There is a $5 registration fee. As compensation of your time in collecting the tax for the state of Florida, you are allowed to keep 2.5% of the tax collected (if you file on time).

Towing Vehicles

Florida Statutes, Section 715.07 controls when vehicles can be towed from private property. The term "vehicle" includes any mobile item that normally uses wheels, whether motorized or not. The law includes many rules for the towing company, but the important rules for landlords are the following.

- ✪ In most cases, in order to tow vehicles from your property, you must have signs with the proper wording and correct-sized letters.

- ✪ The sign rules do not apply to single family homes or when you personally informed the vehicle's owner.

- ✪ If you do not follow the rules, you can be liable to the vehicle's owner for damages and attorney's fees.

- ✪ Municipalities can have stricter laws than the state statute, so check with your police department.

2 CREATING THE LANDLORD/TENANT RELATIONSHIP

The best way to avoid problems with tenants is to make the right decisions when creating the relationship. This means choosing the right tenant, using the right lease, and avoiding any violations of the laws that apply. This chapter explains how to do that.

Screening Prospective Tenants

The first step in avoiding legal problems with tenants is to carefully choose who will be your tenant. As long as you do not discriminate based on categories such as race, sex, and age (see pages 12–16), you can be selective as to whom you rent your property. A tenant who has had the same apartment and job for the last five years will probably be a better tenant than one who has been evicted several times.

You should get a written application from all prospective tenants. Besides allowing you to check their past record as a tenant, the information can be helpful in tracking them down if they disappear owing you rent or damages. (see form 1, p.167.) Be sure that the form you use does not ask illegal questions such as those concerning an applicant's nationality.

You should check the *defendant index* of the court records (not just the *official records*) of your county or the last county the applicants lived in to see if they have ever been evicted or sued. It would also be wise to check the *plaintiff index* to see if they have ever sued a landlord. In some counties these indexes are combined.

You should check with a prior landlord to see if he or she would rent to them again. Do not bother checking with their present landlord. He or she may lie just to get rid of them. Be sure the people you talk to are really landlords. Some tenants use friends who lie for them.

There are some companies that, for a fee, will investigate tenants, including employment, previous landlords, court cases, and their own files of *bad tenants*. Some landlords require a nonrefundable application fee to cover such an investigation. CBI/Equifax offers a Tenant Apartment Protection Service. Call 800-685-1111, or check your phone book under Credit Reporting Agencies.

Discrimination

Since Congress passed the *Civil Rights Act of 1968*, it has been a federal crime for a landlord to discriminate in the rental or sale of property on the basis of race, religion, sex, or national origin. In addition, Florida passed its own anti-discrimination statute in 1983, which makes such acts a state crime and adds the additional category of handicapped persons. In 1988, the United States Congress passed an amendment to the Civil Rights Act that bans discrimination against both the handicapped and families with children. Except for apartment complexes that fall into the special exceptions, such as those designated senior living facilities, all rentals must now allow children in all units.

Civil Rights Act of 1968

Under the Civil Rights Act of 1968, any policy that has a discriminatory effect is illegal. (United States Code (U.S.C.), Title 42, Section 3631.) This means that even if you do not intend to discriminate, if your policy (such as requiring a certain income level) has the effect of discriminating, you can be liable. Failure to attend a hearing or to produce records can subject you to up to a year in prison or a $1000 fine.

Penalty. A victim of discrimination under this section can file a civil suit, a HUD complaint, or request the U.S. Attorney General to prosecute. Damages can include actual losses and punitive damages of up to $1000.

Limitation. The complaint must be brought within 180 days.

Exemptions. This law does not apply to single-family homes if:

- ✪ the owner owns three or less;

- ✪ there is no more than one sale within twenty-four months;

- ✪ the person does not own any interest in more than three at one time; and,

- ✪ no real estate agent or discriminatory advertisement is used.

It also does not apply to a property that the owner lives in if it has four or less units.

Coercion or Intimidation. If coercion or intimidation is used to effectuate discrimination, there is no limit to when the action can be brought or the amount of damages that can be received. For example, firing a real estate agent who rented to African-Americans was found intimidating enough to warrant unlimited damages. 📖

Civil Rights Act, Section 1982
The Civil Rights Act, *Section 1982* is similar to the previously discussed statute but whereas Section 3631 applies to any policy that has a discriminatory effect, this law applies only when it can be proved that the person had an intent to discriminate. (U.S.C., Title 42, Section 1982.)

Penalty. Actual damages plus unlimited punitive damages.

In 1992, a jury in Washington, D.C. awarded civil rights groups $850,000 in damages against a developer who only used Caucasian models in rental advertising. The Washington Post now requires that 25% of the models in the ads it accepts be African-American to reflect the percentage of African-Americans in the Washington area.

Limitation. None.

Exemptions. None.

Civil Rights Act 1988 Amendment
The 1988 Amendment to the Civil Rights Act, also known as the *Fair Housing Act*, bans discrimination against the handicapped and families with children. (U.S.C., Title 42, Sec. 3601.) Unless a property falls into one of the exemptions,

it is illegal under this law to refuse to rent to persons because of age or to people with children. While landlords may be justified in feeling that children cause damage to their property, Congress has ruled that the right of families to find housing is more important than the rights of landlords to safeguard the condition of their property, and ensure the peace and quiet of other tenants.

Regarding the disabled, the law allows them to remodel the unit to suit their needs as long as they return it to the original condition upon leaving. It also requires new buildings of four units or more to have electrical facilities and common areas accessible to the disabled.

Penalty. $10,000 for first offense; $25,000 for second violation within five years; and up to $50,000 for three or more violations within seven years. Unlimited punitive damages in private actions.

> A federal appeals court ruled that if a party who is discriminated against because of his her race does not have any actual monetary damages, he or she is not entitled to punitive damages. Punitive damages can be awarded without monetary damages when a person is denied constitutional rights, but not under the Fair Housing Act. (*Louisiana Acorn Fair Housing v. LeBlanc*, 211 F.3d 298 (5th Cir. 2000).)

Limitation. Complaint must be brought within two years for private actions.

Exemptions. This law does not apply to single-family homes if the owner owns three or less; if there is no more than one sale within twenty-four months; if the person does not own any interest in more than three at one time; and if no real estate agent or discriminatory advertisement is used. (A condominium unit is not a single-family home, so it is not exempt.) The law also does not apply to a property that the owner lives in if it has four or less units. There are also exemptions for dwellings in state and federal programs for the elderly, for complexes that are solely used by persons 62 or older, and for complexes where at least 8% of the units are rented to persons 55 or older.

Americans with Disabilities Act

The *Americans with Disabilities Act* (ADA) requires that *reasonable accommodations* be made to provide the disabled with access to commercial premises and forbids discrimination against them. This means that the disabled must be able to get to, enter, and use the facilities in commercial premises. It requires that if access is *readily achievable* without *undue burden* or *undue hardship*, changes must be made to the property to make it accessible.

The law does not clearly define important terms like "reasonable accommodations," "readily achievable," "undue burden," or "undue hardship," and does not even explain exactly who will qualify as handicapped or disabled. The law includes people with emotional illnesses, AIDS, dyslexia, and past alcohol or drug addictions, as well as hearing, sight, and mobility impairments.

Under the ADA, if any commercial premises are remodeled, then the remodeling must include modifications that make the premises accessible. All new construction must also be made accessible.

What is reasonable will usually depend upon the size of the business. Small businesses will not have to make major alterations to their premises if the expense would be an undue hardship. Even large businesses would not need shelving low enough for people in wheelchairs to reach so long as there is an employee to assist the person.

However, there are tax credits for businesses of less than thirty employees and less than one million dollars in sales that make modifications to comply with the ADA. For more information on these credits, obtain IRS forms 8826 and 3800 and their instructions. Get them online at **www.irs.gov**.

Some of the changes that must be made to property to make it more accessible to the disabled are:

- ✪ installing ramps;

- ✪ widening doorways;

- ✪ making curb cuts in sidewalks;

- ✪ repositioning shelves;

- ✪ repositioning telephones;

- ✪ removing high pile, low-density carpeting; and,

- ✪ installing a full-length bathroom mirror.

Both the landlord and the tenant can be liable if the changes are not made to the premises. Most likely, the landlord would be liable for common areas and the tenant for the area under his or her control.

Penalty. Injunctions and fines of $50,000 for the first offense or $100,000 for subsequent offenses.

Exemptions. Private clubs and religious organizations are exempt from this law, and the ADA does not apply to residential property.

Florida Discrimination Law

The Florida Discrimination Law is very similar to the federal statutes. (Fla. Stat., Sec. 760.20-.37.) The reason for a duplicate state statute is to give victims of discrimination a state remedy that may be easier to pursue than a federal one. This statute does not, however, require apartment owners to make all areas accessible to the handicapped.

Military Personnel

Section 83.67 was amended in 2003 to forbid discrimination against military personnel. This was part of a bill allowing military personnel out of their lease agreements. (see Chapter 9.)

Florida HIV Law

Under Florida Statutes, Section 760.50, it is illegal to discriminate against persons with HIV. One tenant who was evicted by his landlord was awarded $5,000 plus attorney's fees against a landlord who was found to have discriminated against him because he had AIDS. 📖 Under Florida Statutes, Section 689.25, HIV or AIDS status does not have to be disclosed in a real estate transaction.

Local Laws

Landlords should check their city and county ordinances before adopting a discriminatory policy such as an adult-only complex. A Dade County ordinance prohibits even federally subsidized housing for the elderly because it is discriminatory.

Agreements to Lease

What are your rights if a tenant agrees to rent your unit but then backs out? An agreement to enter into a lease may be a valid and binding contract even if a lease has not yet been signed. 📖

As a practical matter, it will probably not be worth the time and expense to sue someone for breaching an oral agreement to lease. Whether or not a landlord could keep a deposit after a prospective tenant changed his or her mind would depend upon the facts of the case and the understanding between parties. Writing "nonrefundable" on the deposit receipt would work in the landlord's favor.

Leases and Rental Agreements

There are different opinions as to whether or not a landlord should use a lease with a set term, such as one year, or an open ended agreement. Some argue that they would rather not have a lease so they can get rid of a tenant at any time. The disadvantage is that the tenant can also leave at any time, which means the unit may be vacant during the slow season.

Rental Agreements

In all cases, even month-to-month tenancies, there should be a written agreement between the parties. If the landlord does not want to tie up the property for a long period of time, he or she can use a **RENTAL AGREEMENT** that states that the tenancy is month-to-month, but that also includes rules and regulations that protect the landlord. (see form 6, p.177.)

Lease

A lease is a rental agreement for a set term. It can be as short as a few weeks or as long as several years.

Required Clauses

The minimum elements that a lease must contain to be valid are:

- ✪ name of lessor (landlord) or agent;

- ✪ name of lessee (tenant);

- ✪ description of the premises;

- ✪ rental rate;

- ✪ starting date; and,

- ✪ granting clause ("Lessor hereby leases to Lessee…").

(There have been cases in which a lease has been valid when one or more of these terms has been omitted if there was an objective means to determine the missing term. Such exceptions are beyond the scope of this book, and it is best that all the required terms are present.)

Management Disclosure

At or before the beginning of a residential rental, the landlord must disclose to the tenant either his or her name and address or the name and address of his or her agent. The agent, if any, retains authority until the tenant is given written notice of a change of agent. (Fla. Stat., Sec. 83.50(1).) In most cases the landlord's name and address in the lease or rental agreement is sufficient and no other notice need be given. If an agent collects rent after he or she is discharged and absconds with the money, it is the landlord's loss if the landlord did not inform the tenants in writing that the agent no longer had authority to collect rents.

Termination Clause

Section 83.575, added to the Landlord-Tenant Act in 2003, allows a landlord to require a tenant to give notice to a landlord before vacating the premises at the end of a lease term. The notice cannot be required more than sixty days in advance. The lease can require the tenant to pay liquidated damages if the tenant fails to give such notice.

Radon Clause

Whenever a building is leased or sold in Florida, at least one document must contain the following clause. (Fla. Stat., Sec. 404.056(5).)

> **RADON GAS: Radon is a naturally occurring radioactive gas that, when it has accumulated in a building in sufficient quantities, may present health risks to persons who are exposed to it over time. Levels of radon that exceed federal and state guidelines have been found in buildings in Florida. Additional information regarding radon and radon testing may be obtained from your county public health unit.**

Placing this clause in a lease can help protect the landlord against suits from tenants who may claim injury from radon gas. Landlords who omit this clause risk liability.

Lead Paint Disclosure

Notice must be given to tenants of rental housing built before 1978 that there may be lead-based paint present and that it could pose a health hazard to children. This applies to all housing except housing for the elderly or zero-bedroom units (efficiencies, studio apartments, etc). It also requires that a pamphlet about lead-based paint, titled *Protect Your Family From Lead in Your Home* be given to prospective tenants. The recommended **DISCLOSURE OF INFORMATION ON**

LEAD-BASED PAINT AND/OR LEAD-BASED PAINT HAZARDS form is included in this book as form 8.

More information and copies of the pamphlet can be obtained from the National Lead Information Center at 800-424-5323. The information can also be obtained at: **www.nsc.org/issues/lead**. You are also required to make disclosures to the tenants when you do any work on the property that disturbs more than two square feet of paint.

Suggested Clauses The following clauses are not required by any law, but are suggested by the author to avoid potential problems during the tenancy:

- ✪ security and/or damage deposit;

- ✪ last month's rent;

- ✪ use clause (limiting use of the property);

- ✪ maintenance clause (spelling out who is responsible for which maintenance);

- ✪ limitation on landlord's liability;

- ✪ limitation on assignment of the lease by tenant;

- ✪ clause granting attorney's fees for enforcement of the lease;

- ✪ clause putting duty on tenant for own insurance;

- ✪ late fee and fee for bounced checks;

- ✪ limitation on number of persons living in the unit;

- ✪ in a condominium, a clause stating that the tenant must comply with all rules and regulations of the condominium;

- ✪ requirement that if locks are changed, the landlord is given a key (forbidding tenants to change locks may subject the landlord to liability for a break-in);

- ✪ limitation on pets;

✪ limitation on where cars may be parked (not on the lawn, etc.);

✪ limitation on storage of boats, etc. on the property;

✪ in a single-family home or duplex, a landlord should put most of the duties for repair under Florida Statutes, Section 83.51 on the tenant;

✪ in commercial leases there should be clauses regarding the fixtures, insurance, signs, renewal, eminent domain, and other factors related to the business use of the premises; and,

✪ to protect the landlord if it is necessary to dispose of property left behind by a tenant, a clause cited in Florida Statutes, Section 83.67(3) should be in the lease. (See "Property Abandoned by Tenant" in Chapter 8.)

For an explanation and analysis of each of the different clauses used in residential and commercial leases and suggestions on how to negotiate, see *Essential Guide to Real Estate Leases*, available through Sourcebooks, Inc.

Oral Leases   A lease of property for *less than one year* does not have to be in writing to be valid. Oral leases have been held up in court. However, written leases are recommended even for tenancies less than one year.

📖 *Proof.* To prove an oral lease of one year, the evidence must be "clear, full and free from suspicion." (*Eli Einbinder, Inc. v. Miami Crystal Ice Co.*, 317 So.2d 126 (Fla. 3 DCA 1975).)

📖 *Part Performance.* When a landlord gave a tenant the key to the premises and the tenant paid rent, improved the property, and stopped looking for other locations, partial performance of the contract made it unnecessary for it to be in writing. (*Poinciana Properties Ltd. v. Englander Triangle, Inc.*, 437 So.2d 214 (Fla. 4 DCA 1983).)

Problem Clauses

If a judge feels that a rental agreement is grossly unfair, he or she may rule that it is *unconscionable* and unenforceable. (Fla. Stat., Sec. 83.45.) In such a case, the judge may ignore the entire lease or may enforce only parts of it. Therefore, making your lease too strong may defeat your purpose. There is not much guidance as to what may or may not be unconscionable, so what the judge believes reasonable will prevail.

📖 A cost of living adjustment in the rent was found not to be unconscionable. (*Bennett v. Behring Corp.*, 466 F. Supp. 689 (1979).)

Waivers of Liability or Rights
If either of the following clauses are included in a lease, it is void and unenforceable, and a party suffering damages because of the clause may recover money from the landlord for any losses so caused. (Fla. Stat., Sec. 83.47.)

✪ A clause waiving the rights, remedies, or requirements of the Florida Landlord/Tenant Law.

✪ A clause limiting the liability of the landlord to the tenant or of the tenant to the landlord, arising under law.

Hidden Clauses
If a lease contains a clause limiting a landlord's liability, or otherwise falls outside standard lease terms, it should not be buried in the lease. It should be pointed out, and initialed by the tenant. Otherwise, its enforceability could be questioned in court, and it could be found *unconscionable*.

Water Beds
If a flotation bedding system (water bed) does not violate the building codes, a landlord cannot prohibit it in his or her building. (Fla. Stat., Sec. 83.535.) A lease clause prohibiting it would be unenforceable. However, Florida law requires a tenant to carry insurance on the water bed to cover personal injury and property damage, which names the landlord as the loss payee. Such a requirement should also be in the lease to avoid misunderstandings later.

Waivers in Commercial Leases
In a commercial lease, a tenant may waive rights that may not be waived in a residential lease. A commercial lease spells out nearly all of the rights and obligations of the parties. The statutes concerning landlord/tenant law are very limited in scope, so it is important to spell everything out carefully in the lease.

Notice. The right to a three-day notice may be waived in a commercial lease. However, some type of notice of termination is necessary. If a lease provides for notice on default longer than three days, then that would be controlling and the landlord would have to give whatever notice is required by the lease. 📖

Default. The three options that a landlord has when a tenant defaults (see Chapter 9, "Remedies for Breach") may be waived in a lease if the lease specifies the rights of the landlord. 📖

Limiting Similar Businesses

Provisions in a lease that limit the landlord's right to lease to similar businesses should be strictly construed. A lease providing that a tenant would be the only appliance store in a shopping center will not prevent a landlord from leasing to a department store that also sells appliances.

Options

Both residential and nonresidential leases may contain clauses that grant the tenant an option to extend the lease for another term or several terms. Often these options provide for an increase in rent during the renewal periods.

Some general rules regarding renewal options to keep in mind include the following.

✪ An option to renew a lease is valid and enforceable, even if not all of the terms are spelled out. 📖

✪ Some terms may be left open for future negotiation or arbitration, but when no terms are stated, the court can assume that the terms will be at the same terms as the original lease. 📖

✪ Leases that can be renewed indefinitely are not favored by the courts and when doubt exists as to the terms, they may be limited to one renewal term. 📖

✪ If a lease contains a notification clause for vacating, a renewal option may go into effect if a tenant vacates without the required notification.

Options to Purchase

If a lease contains an option to purchase, it will usually be enforceable exactly according to its terms.

📖 When a tenant continued renting the property as a tenant-at-will after his lease expired, the court ruled that his option to purchase the property expired at the end of the lease. (*Gross v. Bartlett*, 547 So.2d 661 (Fla. 2 DCA 1989).)

Forms

The landlord should be careful to choose a good lease form. Some forms on the market do not comply with Florida law and can be dangerous to use.

Florida Bar Forms

In 1992, the Florida Bar, under orders by the Florida Supreme Court, created three lease forms. These are for a single-family home/duplex, an apartment in a complex, and a unit in a condominium or cooperative. The purpose of the forms is to allow property managers and other nonlawyers to fill them out for people without the risk of being charged with practicing law.

In 1998 and 1999, the Florida Supreme Court deleted and then reinstated the "Residential Lease—Single Family Home and Duplex" from the approved forms, and asked the Florida Bar to revise it. In 2000, the Florida Supreme Court approved the revised lease form submitted by the Florida Bar, but also continued to approve the 1992 version of the form. Curiously, the court stated, "We express no opinion as to whether these approved lease forms comport with current law." The court added that the chief judge of each circuit is authorized to prepare instructions that are supplemental to the Florida Bar's instructions.

Both lease forms are included with the court opinion. (*Florida Bar Re Revision to Simplified Forms, Pursuant to Rule 10-2.1 (a) of the Rules Regulating the Florida Bar*, Case No. SC92023.) While most attorneys would prepare or recommend a simple lease of two or three pages, these forms are ten pages each. Besides the usual information, they include long explanations of Florida law including lists of tenants' rights and landlords' obligations. The court option including the leases can be found at **www.floridasupremecourt.org/decisions/pre2004/bin/92023.pdf**.

Forms in this Book

Forms 4, 5, and 6 in this book are leases developed and used by the author. They are free of legalese and intended to be easily understandable by both parties. You may also need to use forms 8 and 9 as explained elsewhere in the text.

Signatures

If you do not have the proper signatures on the lease, you could have problems enforcing it or evicting the tenants. If the property is owned by more than one person, it is best to have all owners sign the lease.

In most cases, it is best to have all adult occupants sign the lease so that more people will be liable for the rent. But in inexpensive rentals in which evictions are frequent, having just one person sign will save a few dollars in fees for *service of process*.

Initials   Some landlords have places on leases for tenants to place their initials. This is usually done next to clauses that are unusual or very strongly pro-landlord. This might be helpful because in one case a judge refused to enforce a clause that was "buried" on page two of the lease, even though the judge admitted it was highlighted. Even initials might not help if a judge really does not like a clause. 📖

Witnesses   No witnesses are required for a lease of one year or less. A lease of over one year is not valid without two witnesses to the Landlord's signature. (Fla. Stat., Sec. 689.01.) If a party accepts the benefits of a lease, even if it is not properly witnessed, that party may be *estopped* from contesting the lease's validity. 📖

Notary   A lease does not need to be notarized to be valid.

> **Warning:** A landlord should not allow his or her signature on a lease to be notarized because the lease could then be recorded in the public records. This could cloud his or her title to the property and cause a problem when the property is sold.

Backing Out of a Lease

There are circumstances in which a party can back out of a lease. However, these circumstances are limited and subject to misconceptions.

Rescission   Contrary to the beliefs of some tenants, there is no law allowing a rescission period for a lease. Once a lease has been signed by both parties, it is legally binding on them.

Fraud   If one party fraudulently misrepresents a material fact concerning the lease, the lease may be unenforceable. 📖

Impossible Purpose   If the lease states that the premises are rented for a certain purpose and it is impossible to use the premises for that purpose, then the lease may not be enforceable.

    📖   When property was rented for a moving and storage business and the zoning laws made it illegal to operate the business on the premises, the landlord could not sue the tenant for failing to pay the rent. (*La Rosa v. G.S.W.*, 483 So.2d 472 (Fla. 3 DCA 1986).)

    📖   When the tenant could not operate his business because of difficulty in getting insurance, this was found to be not enough to make it impossible to use the property, and the tenant had to pay the rent. (*Home Design Center - Joint Venture v. County Appliances of Naples, Inc.*, 563 So.2d 767 (Fla. 2 DCA 1990).)

Illegal Purpose   If a lease is entered into for an illegal purpose, then it is void and unenforceable by either party. An example of void leases includes situations in which the property, which is the subject of the lease, is not owned by the landlord. 📖

3 HANDLING SECURITY DEPOSITS

This chapter applies only to residential tenancies. (Florida does not have statutes governing nonresidential deposits.)

Amount

Unlike some states, Florida does not have a law limiting the amount of security deposit a landlord may require. What to charge must be made based on the practical consideration of what is the most you can get without scaring away possible tenants.

Bank Account

All types of damage, rent, pet, and other tenant advance deposits, must be kept in a separate account "for the benefit of the tenant" unless a surety bond is posted. (Fla. Stat., Sec. 83.49(1).) The separate account may be interest bearing or noninterest bearing, and the landlord cannot pledge the money, use it in any way, or mix it with his or her own money.

📖 When a tenant sued a landlord over a security deposit and asked for punitive damages because he had not kept it in a separate account, a county court held that the tenant was not entitled to punitive damages. (*Williams v. Scrima*, 18 Fla. Supp. 2d 72 (Co.Ct. Palm Beach Co. 1986).)

If the landlord posts a surety bond for the amount of the deposit, or $50,000, whichever is less, the funds may be commingled with his or her own, but tenants must be paid 5% interest on their deposits. If a landlord (or his or her agent) rents properties in five or more counties, a bond may be posted with the Secretary of State. (Fla. Stat., Sec. 83.49(1)(c).)

These provisions will probably be a surprise to most landlords. Very few landlords or tenants are aware of these rules and even fewer understand them. Because of the expenses of a surety bond, the small landlord is stuck with the separate account alternative. However, tenants come and go, and with deposits of only several hundred dollars, banks are not pleased with the opening and closing of accounts with each new tenant. The landlord technically cannot commingle even $10 of his or her own in the account to keep it open.

As a practical matter, a $5 or $10 deposit of a landlord's own money to keep an account open during periods when there were no security deposits on hand would probably not be considered an actionable violation of the statute. In fact, it appears that most small Florida landlords do not keep the funds separate, and this is seldom brought up by tenants.

Notice

Under Florida Statutes, Section 83.49(2), landlords must give notice to tenants within thirty days of receiving a deposit of how the deposit is held, as follows:

✪ Within thirty days of receipt of a deposit, written notice must be given in person or by mail to the tenant, which includes the following (a **NOTICE OF HOLDING SECURITY DEPOSIT** can be used for this purpose (see form 11, p.187);

  • name and address of the depository;

- whether it is in a separate account or commingled with the landlord's funds;

- if it is commingled, whether it is in a Florida interest-bearing account; and,

- a copy of Florida Statutes, Section 83.49(3).

If any of the above information changes, a new notice must be given within thirty days. The interest, if any, must be paid or credited to the tenant at least once a year. All of the information required in the notice can also be included in the lease the tenant signs when starting the tenancy.

Interest

The deposits do not have to be placed in an interest-bearing account, but if they are, the tenant must be given either 75% of the interest paid or 5% interest (at the landlord's option). Considering the current low interest rates, it won't be worth the bookkeeping for most landlords to use an interest bearing account. But for landlords with hundreds of properties or if rates rise, it might be profitable.

In those cases in which interest must be paid to a tenant, it must be either paid or credited against the rent at least once a year. No interest need be paid to a tenant who wrongfully terminates his or her tenancy prior to the end of the term. (Fla. Stat., Sec. 83.49(9).)

Most tenants do not even know they are entitled to interest on their deposit, but occasionally a vacating tenant will demand interest. A landlord who has not followed the separate account rule is better off paying it and avoiding a suit that could cost attorney's fees.

Keeping the Deposit

Unless the landlord follows the notice requirements, he or she cannot keep the security deposit no matter how much damage the tenant has done. (Fla. Stat., Sec. 83.49(3).) The landlord must return the tenant's security deposit together with interest, if any, within fifteen days of the day the tenant vacated the premises.

Thirty-Day Notice

If the landlord wishes to keep any part of the security deposit, he or she must send the following notice by certified mail to the tenant's last known address within thirty days of the date that the tenant vacated the unit. (see form 20, p.205.)

THIS IS NOTICE OF MY INTENTION TO IMPOSE A CLAIM FOR DAMAGES IN THE AMOUNT OF $_____ UPON YOUR SECURITY DEPOSIT, DUE TO _____ [state any reasons]. IT IS SENT TO YOU AS REQUIRED BY §83.49(3), FLORIDA STATUTES. YOU ARE HEREBY NOTIFIED THAT YOU MUST OBJECT IN WRITING TO THIS DEDUCTION FROM YOUR SECURITY DEPOSIT WITHIN FIFTEEN (15) DAYS FROM THE TIME YOU RECEIVE THIS NOTICE OR I WILL BE AUTHORIZED TO DEDUCT MY CLAIM FROM YOUR DEPOSIT. YOUR OBJECTION MUST BE SENT TO _____ [landlord's address].

If, as happens in many cases, the damages exceed the deposit, then you should show this in the notice. You can sue the tenant in small claims court for the balance, but this is rarely worth the expense.

If you try to send the tenant the balance of a deposit but cannot find the tenant, then the money is considered abandoned and is supposed to be turned over to the State of Florida.

If this notice is not sent as required, the deposit must be returned to the tenant, even if the tenant caused damage to the premises. If the tenant must sue for return of his or her deposit, the landlord will have to return the deposit and pay the tenant's attorney's fees.

- If the tenant sues the landlord for the deposit and the landlord sues the tenant for damages, the court could order the landlord to return the deposit and pay the tenant's attorney's fees immediately and then hold a trial for the damages later, at which time the tenant can spend the money and be judgment proof. (*Durene v. Alcime*, 448 So.2d 1208 (Fla. 3 DCA 1984).)

- When the tenant won his security deposit back and the landlord won recovery for damages, the landlord had to pay both his and the tenant's attorney's fees. (*Malagon v. Solari*, 566 So.2d 352 (Fla. 4 DCA 1990).)

📖 When the parties bitterly fought over a security deposit for over a year, and the file grew to nine volumes of depositions, motions, notices, and documents, the tenant ended up settling for a return of $1,525.00, and the tenant's attorney was awarded $20,000.00 in attorney's fees. On appeal, this amount was reduced to "only" $5,000.00 (plus $1,100.00 in costs). (*Missilian v. Zimmerman and Permulter*, 22 Fla. Supp. 2d 185 (11th Cir. App. Div. 1987).)

Early Termination by Tenant

If the tenant vacates the premises prior to the end of the term of the lease, he or she must give at least seven-days notice of leaving early or the landlord does not have to send the notice. The tenant's notice can be sent by certified mail or personally delivered, and it must include an address at which the tenant can be reached. Failure to give the notice is not a waiver on any rights the tenant may have to the security deposit. A landlord is well-advised to send the **NOTICE OF INTENTION TO IMPOSE CLAIM ON SECURITY DEPOSIT** (see form 20, p.205) even if the tenant fails to send his or her notice to avoid any problems in case the tenant lies about giving notice.

📖 A Miami court ignored the statute and said that even when the tenant did not give the seven-days notice, the landlord still had to give the fifteen-days notice. (*Rollo v. Armesto*, 6 FLW Supp. 398 (11th Cir. App. Div. 1999).)

Forwarding Address

If the tenant has not left a forwarding address, the notice must be sent to the property address even though you know the tenant is gone. (The tenant might have given a forwarding address to the post office.) If you would like to know the tenant's new address, you can write "ADDRESS CORRECTION REQUESTED" on the front of the envelope and the post office will send you the address for a small fee.

📖 Where a landlord did not know the tenant's new address but did know the tenant's attorney, the landlord was still correct in mailing the certified notice to the vacated property. (*Newman v. Gray*, 4 FLW Supp. 271 (CC 11th Cir. Dade 1996).)

Objection to Deductions

If the tenant does not object to the amount claimed in the notice within fifteen days of receipt of the notice, then the landlord may deduct the amount claimed and must then remit the balance to the tenant within thirty days of the date the notice was first sent. If the tenant objects, he or she would have to file a suit against the landlord.

To make it more tempting to the tenant, the landlord should include a check for the balance of the deposit, if any, with the notice. The landlord might want to write on the back of the check, "Accepted in full payment of claims against security deposit." However, this might make a tenant want to sue immediately. A check without this language might be cashed by the tenant who plans to sue later but never gets around to it.

Wear and Tear   The landlord may deduct *damages* from a security deposit, but may not deduct normal *wear and tear*. What is normal is subjective and only a judge or jury can decide. A hole in a wall is clearly not normal. An apartment needing painting after a tenant lived there ten years is normal. You have to use your best judgment of what is regular wear and tear or what is excessive. If you have any doubts, you should get a second opinion from a disinterested person or an attorney. A landlord making a claim on a deposit should always take pictures of the damage.

If a security deposit claim goes to court, it is also good to have receipts for the repairs that were done. However, a court will probably allow a landlord to do the work him- or herself and charge a reasonable value of the work. Getting a written estimate before doing the work yourself may be helpful for larger repairs.

> A Florida court allowed a landlord to charge a former tenant for the cost of a real estate agent's fee for finding a new tenant for a rental unit. (*McLennan v. Rozniak*, 15 Fla. Supp. 2d 42 (Palm Beach 1985).)

Some leases have clauses that allow a landlord to keep the entire deposit or a certain portion of it if the tenant leaves before the lease is up. When the clause has been considered a *liquidated damages* clause, it has usually been upheld. However, when it has been considered a penalty, it has been thrown out. It is not possible to say for certain whether a clause will be considered one or the other because judges have a wide leeway in their rulings. Usually the decision depends upon who the judge considers the good guy and the bad guy in the case.

Special Rules

In addition to all of the rules previously discussed in this chapter regarding security deposits, there are some special rules of which you should be aware.

Real Estate Brokers   If there is a conflict with the rules of Chapter 475 regarding what real estate brokerage licensees must do with deposits, Florida Statutes, Section 83.49(3)(d) prevails and licensees must follow these rules.

Hotels and Motels   These security deposit rules do not apply to transient rentals by hotels and motels. (Fla. Stat., Sec. 83.49(4).) Any person who is licensed under Section 509.241 (public lodging and food service establishments) who does not comply with this law (if it applies) may lose his or her license or be fined. (Fla. Stat., Sec. 83.49(8).) Since the law does not apply to transient rentals, this would only apply to hotels or motels that rented to permanent residents or to those without another place of residence.

Public Housing   These security deposit rules do not apply to instances (other than for rent stabilization) in which the amount of rent or deposit, or both, is regulated by laws or rules of a public body. This includes public housing authorities and federal housing programs including Section 202, Sections 221(d)(3) and (4), Section 236 or Section 8 of the *National Housing Act*. (Fla. Stat., Sec. 83.49 (4).)

Except for the requirement of a Notice of Claim on Security, these rules do not apply to public housing under Florida Statutes, Chapter 421. (Fla. Stat., Sec. 83.49(4).)

Municipal Housing Authorities   According to an opinion of the Florida Attorney General, municipal housing authorities do not have authority to require security deposits. (Op. Atty. Gen. 078-104.)

Renewals   If a rental agreement is renewed, the security deposit is considered a new deposit. This means that when a lease is renewed, a new notice as explained on pages 28 and 29 must be sent. (Fla. Stat., Sec. 83.49(6).)

Sale of the Property   Upon sale of the property or change of the rental agent, all deposits and interest must be transferred to the buyer or agent together with an accurate accounting. (Fla. Stat., Sec. 83.49(7).)

Bank Seizure   When a bank seizes an account containing security deposits belonging to tenants for debts owed by landlord, either the landlord or the tenant can take court action against the bank for return of the deposits. 📖

4 RESPONSIBILITY FOR MAINTENANCE

Responsibility for maintenance is another area in which the landlord needs to spell out exactly what is expected from each party and make sure that the law is being followed.

Nonresidential Rentals

Florida statutes do not specify who is responsible for maintenance in nonresidential rentals. All of the responsibilities should be spelled out in the lease.

If the lease puts the responsibility for maintenance on the landlord and the premises are "wholly untenantable," Florida Statutes, Section 83.201 allows the tenant to withhold rent and gives the landlord twenty days to complete the repairs.

📖 When a unit was uninhabitable at the beginning of the lease, the tenant was allowed to recover the fair rental value from the landlord for the time up to when the repairs were completed. (*Zais v. CF West Florida, Inc.,* 505 So.2d 577 (Fla. 4 DCA 1987).)

Residential Apartments

The landlords' duties of maintenance are included in Florida Statutes, Section 83.51(1). Under this law, the landlord must comply with health, housing, and building codes. If there are no codes, the landlord must "maintain the roofs, windows, screens, doors, floors, steps, porches, exterior walls, foundations, and all other structural components in good repair and capable of resisting normal forces and loads and the plumbing in reasonable working condition."

Under Florida Statutes, Section 83.51(2), unless the landlord and tenant agree that these shall be the tenant's responsibility, the landlord must make *reasonable provision* for:

✪ exterminations of rats, mice, roaches, ants, wood-destroying organisms, and bedbugs;

> NOTE: *When the premises must be vacated for extermination, the tenant must vacate for up to four days upon being given seven days written notice. The landlord is not liable for damages but must prorate the rent and not charge for the days that tenant is unable to stay in the premises. The landlord does not have to pay for the tenant to stay at a hotel.*

✪ locks and keys;

✪ clean and safe condition of common areas;

✪ garbage removal and outside receptacles; and,

✪ functioning facilities for heat during winter, running water, and hot water.

Some specific areas of additional consideration under the statute include the following.

✪ These rules do not apply to mobile homes owned by tenants. (Fla. Stat., Sec. 83.51(2)(d).)

✪ The landlord may require the tenant to pay for garbage removal, water, fuel, or utilities. (Fla. Stat., Sec. 83.51(2)(e).)

✪ The landlord is not responsible for conditions that are caused by the tenant, the tenant's family, or guests. (Fla. Stat., Sec. 83.51(4).)

Single-Family Homes and Duplexes

Florida law offers special exceptions for single-family homes and duplexes. The only requirements specifically in the law are that the landlord comply with building, housing, and health codes (Fla. Stat., Sec. 83.51(1)) and supply working smoke detectors. (Fla. Stat., Sec. 83.51(2)(b).) However, these duties can be put on the tenant if it is so agreed in the lease.

Constitutional Conflict

There is a problem with Florida Statutes, Section 83.51 of which landlords should be aware. In stating that landlords must comply with "building, housing, and health codes," it has been argued that the legislature has included "any law, ordinance, or governmental regulation concerning health, safety, sanitation, or fitness for habitation, or the construction, maintenance, operation, occupancy, use, or appearance of any dwelling unit."

This language is so broad and vague that it includes any minor regulation by a municipality, and Section 83.56(1) allows a tenant to withhold rent for a violation.

✪ In Coral Gables, the colors of the buildings must be approved by the Board of Architects. If the color of a building was not approved, a tenant could argue that this gives him the right to withhold rent.

✪ The Division of Hotels and Restaurants has applied its rules to apartment houses and required a landlord to clean a tenant's bathroom when the tenant kept using the toilet after it malfunctioned.

✪ Even though Section 83.51(4) states that a landlord is not responsible for conditions caused by the tenant's own negligence, the Division of Hotels and Restaurants has ignored this and made its own rules under Section 83.51(1).

✪ Section 26-26 of the Code of the City of Miami requires landlords of furnished rentals to provide "housecleaning equipment," and many tenants demand vacuum cleaners.

✪ In Dade County, a vegetable garden has been cited as a sanitary nuisance.

In all of these cases, the tenant could withhold rent because there was a violation.

It has been pointed out by John J. Boyle, an attorney in the Miami area, that Section 83.51 may be unconstitutional. Anyone faced with problems in this area should have his or her attorney obtain a copy of Boyle's book, *Landlord's Remedies in Florida*, published by D&S Publishing, or Boyle's CLE materials for good arguments and case law in this area.

Code Violations

Landlords should be aware that governmental bodies can levy fines of hundreds of dollars a day for minor violations. Ignoring notices of violation can be expensive.

Whenever you receive a governmental notice, you should read it very carefully and follow it to the letter. One landlord who sold his property and thought the problem was solved was fined $11,000 ($500 a day for the last twenty-two days he owned the property) for a violation. After you correct a violation, be sure that the governmental body that sent the notice gives you written confirmation that you are in compliance.

Warranty of Habitability

In recent years, the centuries-old theories of landlord/tenant law have been replaced with new obligations on landlords to protect their tenants. One of these new obligations is the *implied warranty of habitability*, which has been accepted in over forty states. Under this doctrine, any time a dwelling unit is turned over to a tenant, the tenant is automatically given a warranty by the landlord that the premises are in safe and habitable condition and will remain so during the term of the lease.

📖 The case of *Mansur v. Eubanks* officially made the doctrine of habitability the law in Florida. In this case, the tenants gave a $25 deposit and started moving things into the premises. They turned on the gas outside the dwelling and when they went inside, they smelled gas. A resulting explosion seriously injured one of the tenants. The court ruled that the landlord was liable for the tenant's injuries. (*Mansur v. Eubanks*, 401 So.2d 1328 (Fla. 1981).)

📖 In another case, a landlord did not repair a broken hot water heater for three days and was liable for $775,000.00 in damages when a woman carrying boiling water to the bathtub spilled it on her grandson. (*Bennett M. Lifter, Inc. v. Varnado*, 480 So.2d 1336 (Fla. 3 DCA 1985).) This case showed that the duty of the landlord is not just to turn over a safe dwelling unit, but to *keep* it safe.

In a single-family home or duplex, a landlord can attempt to protect him- or herself by stating in the lease that the tenant is responsible for maintaining the premises. This cannot be done in larger buildings.

✪ If a lease states that a tenant is responsible for maintenance, then the landlord should not voluntarily do repairs. Otherwise, the landlord can be held responsible for the safety of the premises. If something comes up that the tenant cannot handle and the landlord would rather do it, he or she should have the tenant sign an agreement that the landlord will repair this one item one time, but that the landlord assumes no other responsibilities.

✪ Although Florida Statutes, Section 83.51 allows the landlord and tenant to agree that the tenant shall have the duty of maintenance, Section 83.47 states that a lease cannot limit a landlord's liability. Where the line will be drawn between these two statutes is not yet known.

Tenants' Responsibilities

Under Florida Statutes, Section 83.52, at all times the tenant must:

✪ comply with all building, housing, and health codes;

✪ keep his or her part of the premises clean and sanitary;

✪ remove his or her garbage in a clean and sanitary manner;

✪ keep all plumbing fixtures in the unit (or used by him or her) clean and sanitary and in repair;

NOTE: *Although the law clearly puts this obligation on tenants, the Division of Hotels and Motels has required landlords to clean up bathrooms that tenants have soiled by allowing the toilet to back up. The rationale of the Division is that, while the law allows the landlord to evict a tenant for sanitary problems, the ultimate responsibility is on the landlord.*

✪ use and operate in a reasonable manner all electrical, plumbing, sanitary, heating, ventilating, air conditioning, and other facilities and appliances, including elevators;

✪ not destroy, deface, damage, impair, or remove any part of the premises or property therein belonging to the landlord nor permit any person to do so; and,

✪ conduct him- or herself and require other persons on the premises to conduct themselves in a manner that does not unreasonably disturb his or her neighbors or constitute a breach of the peace.

Lead Paint Notice

Under rules of the Environmental Protection Agency, if any repairs are done to the property during a tenancy and more than two square feet of lead paint is disturbed, notice must be given to the tenants and the landlord must obtain a receipt from the tenant for the notice. (The notice and receipt are included as form 9 in this book.) The following rules also apply:

✪ any work by plumbers, painters, electricians, and others is included;

✪ the tenants must be given the pamphlet *Protect Your Family From Lead in Your Home*;

✪ if the work is done on common areas of the building, all tenants must be notified; and,

✪ emergency renovations and repairs are excluded.

5 | LANDLORDS' LIABILITIES

The law of responsibilities for injuries and crime on rental property has changed considerably over the last couple decades. The law for hundreds of years that landlords are not liable has been overturned, and landlords are now often liable, even for conditions that are not their fault.

Injuries on the Premises

The landlord has a duty to inspect and repair *common areas* in a rental building with more than one unit. This does not apply to a single-family home. In a duplex, a landlord may state in the lease that the tenants assume the duty to take care of the common areas. 📖

The general rule is that a landlord is not liable for injuries on parts of the premises that are *not under his or her control* except in the following circumstances:

- ✪ when there is a danger known to the landlord;

- ✪ when there is a violation of law in the condition of the premises;

✪ when there is a preexisting defect in construction;

✪ when the landlord undertakes repairing the premises or is required by the lease to do the repairs;

✪ when the landlord did a negligent act; or,

✪ when the premises were a nuisance at the time of the making of the lease or would become one upon tenant's expected use of the premises. ▭

Cases Holding a Landlord Not Liable

The following are cases that held that a landlord would not be liable for injuries. It must be kept in mind that the holdings in some of the earlier cases may have been modified by the rulings in later cases.

▭ When no one knew about a hole under a concrete slab that broke when a tenant stepped on it, the landlord was not liable since the tenant was in a position to know about the danger. (*Zubowicz v. Warnock*, 149 So.2d 890 (Fla. 2 DCA 1963).)

▭ When a landlord rented a single-family home to a tenant and a salesman slipped on a painted concrete step wet with rainwater, there was no liability since there was no concealment—even though it was the landlord who originally painted the step. (*Wingard v. McDonald*, 348 So.2d 573 (Fla. 1 DCA 1977).)

▭ When a tenant was responsible for doing maintenance at his own cost, the landlord was not liable for the tenant's fall on the carpet. (*Stolzenberg v. Forte Towers South, Inc.*, 430 So.2d 558 (Fla. 3 DCA 1983).)

▭ A landlord was not liable for the death of a patron at a bar when the landlord's only interest in the premises was to receive the rent and to receive a reversion of the premises and the liquor license at the end of the lease. (*Santiago v. Allen*, 449 So.2d 388 (Fla. 3 DCA 1984).)

▭ When a tenant saw that a chair was being used to hold a door open but tripped over it when she was momentarily distracted, the landlord was not liable because it was not a dangerous condition, and there was sufficient light and space beside it to get by. (*Schoenbach v. VMS Realty, Inc.*, 503 So.2d 382 (Fla. 3 DCA 1987).)

📖 When a child was injured by falling from a tree onto broken glass at an apartment complex, the landlord was not liable because there was no evidence to show that the landlord knew the glass was there or how long the glass had been there. (*Haynes v. Lloyd,* 533 So.2d 944 (Fla. 5 DCA 1988).)

📖 When employees of a tenant were injured by a gas explosion in a commercial rental unit, the landlord was not liable because he had turned possession of the premises over to the tenant. (*Veterans Gas Co. v. Gibbs,* 538 So.2d 1325 (Fla. 1 DCA 1989).)

📖 When the daughter of a tenant's guest ran through a sliding glass door, the landlord was not liable since he was not in possession of the premises, had no duty to ascertain that the glass was not safety glass, and had no duty to put decals on the glass. (*Fitzgerald v. Cestari,* SC, No. 75,538, Nov. 8, 1990.)

📖 When a woman went into an office building to look for a telephone and slipped on an overripe mango that had fallen from a tree near the entrance, the landlord was not liable because she was not an *invitee,* but only an *uninvited licensee.* In English, this means that since the building owner had no interest in her coming into the building, he was not liable. If she were coming in to visit one of the businesses, the landlord could have been liable. (*Iber v. R.P.A. International Corp.,* 585 So.2d 367 (Fla 3 DCA 1991).)

Cases Holding a Landlord Liable

The following cases are examples of when a landlord was held liable for injuries to a tenant or a guest.

📖 When a landlord continues to do repairs on the premises after turning them over to the tenant, he or she may be liable for injuries on the premises. (*McDonald v. Wingard,* 309 So.2d 192 (Fla. DCA 1975).)

📖 The fact that the landlord used to have carpet in the elevator was evidence that it was negligent not to have carpet when an elderly tenant slipped on the linoleum floor. (*Firth v. Marhoeffer,* 406 So.2d 521 (Fla. 4 DCA 1981).)

📖 When a child being cared for by the tenant was bitten by the tenant's pit bull, landlord was liable because the landlord should have known about the dog and could have terminated the tenancy. (*Vasquez v. Lopez*, 509 So.2d 1241 (Fla. 4 DCA 1987).)

📖 When a tenant's son was bitten by a neighbor's pit bull, a court held that the landlord could be held liable even if its management company only found out a day or two earlier about the dog. (*Giaculli v. Bright*, 584 So.2d 187 (Fla. 5 DCA 1991).)

Landlords' Warranty of Habitability

In 1981, the Florida Supreme Court reversed centuries of landlord/tenant law by adopting the theory of the landlord's warranty of habitability for residential property. This was explained in more detail in the previous chapter. The landlord's warranty of habitability does not apply to nonresidential rentals.

Protection from Liability for Injuries

The basis for liability in these cases is that the landlord breached a duty to keep the premises safe. If a landlord puts the duty to keep the premises safe on the tenant, there will be less likelihood that the landlord can be held liable. Florida Statutes, Section 83.51 allows a landlord to put certain duties of maintenance on the tenant in a single-family dwelling or duplex. A nonresidential lease can probably do the same. But in a multifamily building, the landlord cannot get out of the burden of making sure the premises are safe at all times.

📖 A landlord cannot immunize him- or herself against liability for his or her own negligent actions. (*John's Pass Seafood Co. v. Weber*, 369 So.2d 616 (Fla. 2 DCA 1969).)

The result of all this is that the landlord is the insurer of the safety of tenants and must therefore carry adequate insurance to cover any liability. Many landlords raise their rents to compensate for this additional insurance expense.

Crimes against Tenants

Another area where liability of landlords has been greatly expanded is in the area of crimes against tenants. The former theory of law was that a person cannot be held liable for deliberate acts of third parties. This had been the theory for hundreds of years but has recently been abandoned in favor of a theory that a landlord must protect tenants from crimes.

Basis for Liability

The theory has been stated to be that when the landlord can foresee the possibility of criminal attack, the landlord must take precautions to prevent it. But some have said that this means any time an attack is possible, the landlord must protect the tenant. This would include nearly every tenancy, especially in urban areas. New Jersey has gone so far as to hold landlords strictly liable for every crime committed on their property whether or not they knew there was a risk or took any precautions. This liability for crime, unlike the warranty of habitability, applies to both residential and commercial tenancies. However, it has not been extended to single-family homes, yet.

  📖 When owners of an apartment complex knew about the "sexually aberrant and bizarre behavior" of a tenant's child, they were liable when that child committed a sexual assault upon another child. (*Lambert v. Doe*, 453 So.2d 844 (Fla. 1 DCA 1984).)

  📖 When a landlord failed to provide adequate locks pursuant to Florida Statutes, Section 83.51(2)(a), the landlord was liable when tenant was raped by an intruder. (*Paterson v. Deeb*, 472 So.2d 1210 (Fla. 1 DCA 1985).)

  📖 When a landlord temporarily provided an armed guard on premises, this was used as evidence that the landlord knew of a dangerous condition and could be liable for the rape and murder of a tenant. (*Holley v. Mt. Zion Terrace Apartments, Inc.*, 382 So.2d 98 (Fla. 3 DCA 1980).)

  📖 When an apartment manager shot tenants during a dispute over an eviction, the landlord was liable for damages. (*Gonpere Corp. v. Rebull*, 440 So.2d 1307 (Fla. 3 DCA 1983)); compare however, a similar case in which an apartment manager knifed a tenant who was asking for hot water—the landlord was not liable because the event was not foreseeable or in furtherance of the landlord's interests. (*Perez v. Zazo*, 498 So.2d 463 (Fla. 3 DCA 1986).)

📖 When a tenant in an office building was mugged by an intruder, the landlord was held liable based in part on the fact that the landlord "should have known" of the dangers in the building and taken measures to protect commercial tenants. (*Green Cos. v. DiVincenzo*, 432 So.2d 86 (Fla. 3 DCA 1983).)

Protection from Liability for Crimes

The law is not clear in Florida as to just how far courts will go in holding landlords liable for crimes against tenants. A clause in a lease that makes a tenant responsible for locks and security may provide some protection to landlords in some situations, especially in single-family homes and duplexes.

In apartment complexes where crime is common, landlords may be required to provide armed guards or face liability. Again, insurance is a must and this additional cost will have to be covered by rent increases.

Crimes by Tenants against Nontenants

Courts in Florida have not yet held landlords liable for crimes by tenants against nontenants. It is, however, happening elsewhere in the country, so landlords should be careful not to get in a situation where tenants are using the property for illegal activities.

6 CHANGING THE TERMS OF THE TENANCY

During the course of a tenancy, circumstances can change for either the land-lord or the tenant. While it is not possible to cover every possible change that may arise, there are some common situations of which you should be aware.

Assignment or Sublease by Tenant

As a general rule, unless it is prohibited in a lease, a landlord cannot stop a tenant from assigning his or her lease to someone else or from subletting all or a portion of the premises.

An *assignment* is when a tenant assigns all of his or her interest in a lease to another party who takes over the tenant's position. A *sublease* is when the tenant enters into a new agreement with a third party who deals solely with the tenant. The original tenant is then the sublessor and the new tenant is the sub-lessee. Often the term "assignment" is used when describing either situation, even though there are differences.

Validity   If a lease is for over a year, an assignment of that lease would not be valid unless it had two witnesses. (Fla. Stat., Sec. 689.01.)

Liability   If a lease contains a covenant to pay rent and the landlord does not release the tenant upon the assignment, then the landlord may sue the original tenant if the new tenant defaults. 📖

Waiver   If a landlord knowingly accepts rent from an assignee or a sublessee of a lease, then the landlord waives his or her right to object to the assignment. But if the landlord was unaware of the assignment it does not constitute a waiver. 📖

Approval   Some leases provide that a lease may only be assigned with the approval of the landlord. However, these clauses are not always enforced.

> 📖 Where a lease required written consent to subleases, a court allowed subleases without written consent since the landlord acquiesced in the subleases and did not contest them until the parties got into litigation. (*Holman v. Halford*, 518 So.2d 442 (Fla. 1 DCA 1988).)

> 📖 Where a lease said that a landlord could not unreasonably withhold consent to an assignment but that the landlord could terminate the lease upon notice of the assignment, the court found the clauses repugnant to each other and struck the second one, denying the landlord's right to terminate the lease. (*Petrou v. Wilder*, 557 So.2d 617 (Fla. 4 DCA 1990).)

Sale of Property by Landlord

A landlord has the right to sell property covered by a lease, but the new owner takes the property subject to the terms of the existing leases. In most cases, a landlord is relieved of his or her obligations under a lease upon sale of the property. 📖

The new owner cannot cancel the old leases or raise the rent while the leases are still in effect (unless the leases have provisions allowing the landlord to do so).

> 📖 The new owner must do any repairs to the property that the old owner would have had to do under the terms of the lease. (*City of St. Petersburg v. Competition Sails*, 449 So.2d 852 (Fla. 2 DCA 1984).)

> 📖 When the purchaser of a property sent a tenant a notice that his month-to-month tenancy was terminated and that he would be evicted, the tenant moved out and sued the landlord for wrongful eviction. The landlord said that he did not know that the tenant had a written lease,

but the jury awarded the tenant $7,000.00 in damages. (*Ruotal v. Ottati*, 391 So.2d 308 (Fla. 4 DCA 1980).)

When selling property, a landlord must specify in the sales contract that the sale is subject to existing leases. Otherwise, the buyer may sue for failure to deliver the premises free and clear of other claims. At closing, the leases should be assigned to the buyer.

Foreclosures   When property is purchased at a foreclosure sale, the leases of the tenants are terminated if they were signed after the date of the mortgage and if the tenants were joined as parties to the suit. 📖

Raising the Rent

If a tenancy is for a set term (such as a one-year lease) at a specified rent, then the landlord cannot raise the rent until the term ends unless the lease allows for this. If the tenancy is month-to-month, then the landlord would be able to raise the rent if he or she gives notice at least fifteen days prior to the end of the month. This is based upon the law that the landlord can cancel the tenancy by giving fifteen-days notice. To raise the rent in a month-to-month tenancy, you can use the **NOTICE OF CHANGE OF TERMS**. (see form 15, p.195.)

In such a case, the tenant would probably not have to give fifteen-days notice if he or she decided not to stay at the end of the month. This is because by raising the rent the landlord would be terminating the previous tenancy and making the tenant an offer to enter into a new tenancy at a different rental rate.

Modifying the Lease

If you agree to modify the terms of your lease with a tenant, you should put it in writing. If you do not and you allow a tenant to do things forbidden in the lease, you may be found to have waived your rights. A simple **AMENDMENT TO LEASE/RENTAL AGREEMENT** modification form is included in this book. (see form 12, p.189.)

7 PROBLEMS DURING THE TENANCY

During the course of a tenancy, any number of problems can arise. Some of these problems are caused by the tenant, but some are caused by the landlord. You should be aware of some of the common problems that can arise and know what to do to lessen their impact.

Landlords' Access to the Premises

Under the historic principles of landlord/tenant law, which still apply to non-residential tenancies, the landlord has no right to enter the premises unless it is given to the landlord in the lease. Under Florida's residential landlord/tenant law, the landlord does have a right to access, and the tenant cannot unreasonably withhold consent for the landlord to enter the dwelling unit. (Fla. Stat., Sec. 83.53.) The landlord may enter the premises to make repairs between 7:30 a.m. and 8:00 p.m. if at least twelve hours notice is given. The landlord may also enter to:

❂   inspect the premises;

❂   make necessary or agreed repairs, decorations, or improvements;

✪ supply agreed services; or,

✪ exhibit the dwelling to prospective or actual purchasers, mortgagees, tenants, workmen, or contractors.

However, the landlord may enter for the reasons in the previous paragraph only under the following circumstances:

✪ with the consent of the tenant;

✪ in case of emergency;

✪ when the tenant unreasonably withholds consent; or,

✪ if the tenant is absent from the premises for one-half of the rental period without notice.

The landlord may enter the premises at any time if it is necessary to protect the premises. The landlord must not abuse the right of access or use it to harass the tenant.

Violations by the Tenant

Often the biggest problems during the tenancy are ones caused by tenants.

Rent Due Date   In a residential tenancy, unless otherwise stated in a lease, rent is due at the beginning of each rent payment period (Fla. Stat., Sec. 83.46(1)), and in a non-residential tenancy the rule is the opposite; meaning, unless a lease or rental agreement states that rent must be paid in advance, it does not have to be paid until the end of the term. (This is because hundreds of years ago feudal tenants paid a share of their crops at the end of the season as rent.) 📖

Mailing of rent. If a lease says that rent is due on a certain date, it is not good enough if the tenant mailed it on that date. In some situations (such as paying income tax) the mailing date is important, but not when the lease clearly states when the rent is due. 📖

Vacating Early   If the tenant breaches the lease by vacating the property before the expiration of the lease, the landlord may do one of three things:

1. terminate the lease and take possession of the property for his or her own account (relieving the tenant of further liability);

2. take possession of the premises for the account of the tenant and hold the tenant liable for the difference in rent due under the lease and the rent eventually received; or,

3. let the unit sit vacant and sue the tenant for the full rent as it comes due. (Fla. Stat., Sec. 83.595.) 📖

The law in this area is very complicated. The Florida Supreme Court's decisions have caused confusion in the appellate courts, and many landlords have lost in their attempts to collect damages from tenants. Before taking action regarding large sums of money, a landlord should consult an attorney and request that the attorney review the latest cases in this area as well as the latest publications on landlord/tenant law.

Suing for Rent. The problem in most of the cases in which landlords have lost their suits against tenants is that they have tried to terminate the lease and sue for the rent, combining option (1) with option (2). When this is done, the courts have usually found that the landlord accepted a surrender of the premises and lost all rights to sue for damages.

📖   If a landlord wishes to terminate the lease, then instead of suing for accelerated rent, the landlord should sue for breach of contract. (*Hudson Pest Control Inc. v. Westford Asset Management, Inc.*, 622 So.2d 546 (Fla. 5 DCA 1993).)

If the landlord wishes to sue the tenant for rent for the period up to the point when a new tenant is found, or for future rent, he or she should not terminate the tenancy, but use option (2) and take possession for the account of the tenant.

📖   When a landlord evicts a tenant, some courts have held that this terminates the rental agreement (option (1)) and precludes a suit for future rent. However, a recent decision has made it clear that even when a tenant is evicted, the landlord can choose option (2) and sue the tenant for future rent. (*Colonial Promenade v. Juhus*, 541 So.2d 1313 (Fla. 5 DCA 1989).)

The usual problem in the court cases is a misinterpretation of the landlord's intent. To avoid this, the landlord should analyze the options and make his or her intent clear either in the form of a certified letter to the tenant or in the allegations of the landlord's complaint.

Some other points that a landlord should know about include the following.

- ✪ Where the landlord has many vacant units, he or she can elect option (3) and just sue the tenant for the rent due without trying to rent the unit.

- ✪ If the landlord expects to rent the unit out at a lower rate, then it should be made clear that he or she is taking possession for the account of the tenant and will hold the tenant liable for the difference.

- 📖 When a tenant broke the lease and the landlord sued for the rent for the period before it was rerented, the court held that the landlord was renting the property for the account of the tenant and that the tenant could get credit for the higher rent the landlord was receiving from the new tenant. (*Gould v. Vitiello*, 526 So.2d 1018 (Fla. 2 DCA 1988).)

- 📖 Unless the lease provides that the balance owed under a lease can be accelerated upon default, the landlord cannot sue for the rent until it comes due. (*National Advertising Co. v. Main Street Shopping Center*, 539 So.2d 594 (Fla. 2 DCA 1989).)

- 📖 When a lease stated that the landlord's remedy, in the event of tenant's breach, was to terminate the lease and to relet the premises on account for the tenant, the landlord lost the right to use other remedies usually available and could not sue for rent as it came due. (*Linens of Paris, Inc. v. Cymet*, 510 So.2d 1021 (Fla. 3 DCA 1987).)

Bad Checks   The procedure for collecting on bad checks is contained in Florida Statutes, Section 68.065. It provides for a service charge based on the amount the check was written for, ranging from $25 to $40 or 5% of the amount of the check (whichever is greater), and for triple damages (or a minimum of $50). The procedure is to send a notice by certified mail and then file suit on the check. However, if a tenant cannot immediately pay the check, the landlord would be better advised to immediately start the eviction rather than sue on the bad check.

There is also a criminal law against writing a bad check found in Section 832.07. You may get your sheriff to prosecute the tenant. However, you must comply with certain requirements, such as checking the identification of the maker of the check and not accepting a post-dated check.

Damage to the Premises

If the tenant does intentional damage to the premises, the landlord can terminate the tenancy (see Chapter 8) and can also get an *injunction* against the tenant. (Fla. Stat., Sec. 83.681.) This can be done by filing a complaint with the county or circuit court. For an injunction to be issued, the damage must be over twice the amount of the security deposit or $300, whichever is greater.

Lease Violations

Before taking action for a lease violation, the landlord must decide whether the breach is *curable* or *incurable*. If it is curable, then the tenant must be given seven days to fix the problem. If it is incurable, then the landlord may immediately terminate the tenancy. However, in deciding that a breach is incurable, the landlord takes a risk that if the tenant fights it, the court will say it was curable and the landlord will have to pay the tenant's attorney's fees.

- ✪ Examples of noncompliance that are incurable are destruction, damage, or misuse of the landlord's or other tenant's property by intentional act or continued unreasonable disturbance. (Fla. Stat., Sec. 83.56(2)(a).)

- ✪ Examples of noncompliance that the tenant should be allowed to cure are unauthorized pets, guests, or vehicles; parking in an unauthorized manner; or failing to keep the premises clean and sanitary. (Fla. Stat., Sec. 83.56(2)(b).) In one case, a tenant's son's harassment and hitting of another tenant's son was held to be curable. 📖

If the violation is curable, the landlord must give the following notice to the tenant. (see form 22, p.209.)

> YOU ARE NOTIFIED THAT YOU HAVE VIOLATED YOUR RENTAL AGREEMENT AS FOLLOWS: _____
> _____.
> DEMAND IS HEREBY MADE THAT YOU REMEDY THIS NON-COMPLIANCE WITHIN SEVEN DAYS OF RECEIPT OF THIS NOTICE OR YOUR LEASE SHALL BE DEEMED TERMINATED AND YOU SHALL VACATE THE PREMISES UPON TERMINATION. IF THIS SAME CONDUCT OR CONDUCT OF A SIMILAR NATURE IS REPEATED WITHIN TWELVE MONTHS, YOUR TENANCY IS SUBJECT TO TERMINATION WITHOUT YOUR BEING GIVEN AN OPPORTUNITY TO CURE THE NONCOMPLIANCE.

If the violation is not curable or if the tenant repeats a noncompliance after receiving the notice, then the landlord may terminate the tenancy.

Violations by the Landlord

While it is usually the tenant that violates a lease, there is certain conduct by a landlord that will also constitute violation.

Retaliatory Conduct

In 1983, the Florida legislature passed a law prohibiting landlords from "retaliating against a tenant." (Fla. Stat., Sec. 83.64.) It can be argued that the law is too vague but it would be expensive to take the argument to court. The best strategy is to read the following rules carefully and avoid any conduct that might look like a violation.

Under Florida Statutes, Section 83.61(1), a landlord must not discriminatively do any of the following acts in retaliation against a tenant:

- ✪ raise rent;

- ✪ reduce services; or,

- ✪ threaten court action.

The key is the word *discriminatively*. It is okay to raise all rents but you cannot raise one tenant's rent to retaliate against that tenant.

  📖 When a tenant sued a landlord for damage to his personal property from water leaks, and the landlord chose not to renew the tenant's lease, the court held that the landlord did not violate either the landlord/tenant retaliatory eviction law or the anti-discrimination law (Chapter 760). (*Chancellor v. Garrett*, 2 FLW Supp. 125 (Escambia Co. 1993).)

The conduct of a tenant that a landlord may not retaliate against, under Florida Statutes, Section 83.64(1), is unlimited but specifically includes:

  ✪ tenant complaints to governmental agencies about code violations;

  ✪ tenant participation in tenant's organizations; and,

  ✪ tenant complaints to landlord about maintenance.

To defend an eviction, a tenant may say that the landlord is retaliating. However, the law states that it is not a defense if the landlord brings a good faith action for nonpayment of rent, violation of the rental agreement, or violation by the tenant of the landlord/tenant laws.

  📖 When a tenant admitted to breaching his or her lease by having unauthorized pets, moving a rug to the garage, and other violations, he or she was not allowed to use the retaliatory eviction defense. (*Salmonte v. Eilertson*, 526 So.2d 179 (Fla. 1 DCA 1988).)

Interrupting Utilities

Under Florida Statutes, Section 83.67, a landlord who terminates or interrupts utilities such as water, heat, light, electricity, gas, elevator, garbage collection, or refrigeration can be held liable for three month's rent for each violation, plus the tenant's court costs and attorney's fees. This can be frustrating to a landlord whose tenant is intentionally wasting utilities to hurt the landlord. The correct response in such a situation would be to get an emergency restraining order under Florida Statutes, Section 83.681.

  📖 A court ruled that although the statute seems to say that any interruption of utilities entitles a tenant to three months rent, it could not possibly mean that, since that would be absurd and unreasonable. Therefore, a landlord was not liable for damages when he shut off water and elevator services during conversion of an apartment building to condominiums. (*Badaraco v. Suncoast Towers V Assoc.*, 676 So.2d 502 (Fla. 3 DCA 1996).)

Violations of Privacy

Once a landlord rents a unit to a tenant, the tenant usually has exclusive rights to that unit, and entry or observation of the tenant by the landlord can be a violation of the tenant's rights. One court found a landlord and his wife liable for $1,286,582 in damages because the landlord made a peephole in a closet through which he could look into the tenants' apartment.

Destruction of the Premises

If the premises are damaged by fire, hurricane, or other casualty, such event does not automatically terminate the lease.

Nonresidential

In nonresidential tenancies, the rights of the parties are usually spelled out in the lease. If they are not, Florida Statutes, Section 83.201 allows nonresidential tenants to withhold rent if the premises are *wholly untenantable,* if under the lease it is the landlord's duty to maintain the premises. The landlord must first be given notice and twenty days to complete the repairs. If the repairs are not complete, then the tenant may vacate the premises and keep the withheld rent.

Residential

Florida Statutes, Section 83.63 states that if the enjoyment of the premises is substantially impaired, then the tenant may terminate the tenancy and immediately vacate the premises. The tenant also has the option of vacating the part of the premises that is unusable and paying partial rent. The landlord does not have the right to terminate the tenancy unless such a right is spelled out in the lease.

> 📖 In a case in Dade County after Hurricane Andrew, a landlord attempted to terminate the lease to do repairs. Because of the shortage of housing after the hurricane, the court was quite upset that the landlord was trying to evict the tenants and their three children. It awarded attorney's fees to the tenant and severely criticized the landlord's attorney for bringing the case. (*Baldo v. Georgoulakis*, 1 FLW Supp. 432 (11 Cir. 1993).)

8 PROBLEMS AT THE END OF THE TENANCY

Just as there can be problems during a tenancy, problems can also occur at the end of a tenancy.

Tenant Holding Over

When the tenant *holds over* at the end of a lease, the landlord has three options. The landlord can:

1. demand double rent and possession of the property;

2. demand a specific amount of continuing rent; or,

3. sue for possession of the property plus damages including special damages for loss of the property's use.

In a nonresidential tenancy, the landlord has to demand double rent. This is not the case in a residential tenancy because of the wording of the statutes. The statutes allowing double rent are Florida Statutes, Section 83.06 (nonresidential) and Section 83.58 (residential).

A landlord can collect double rent and remove the tenant in an eviction proceeding or may bring an action for the double rent after the tenant moves.

If a landlord accepts regular rent after the lease expires, the landlord loses his or her right to double rent, and can only terminate the tenancy under the rules for tenancies with "no specific term."

No notice is required at the end of a lease, but a letter to the tenant expressing an intention to terminate or to renew is a good idea. When trouble is expected, a **LETTER TO VACATING TENANT** can be used. (see form 16, p.197.)

In Public Housing, Section 8 housing, and Section 236 housing, a landlord cannot refuse to renew a lease without good cause.

Damage to the Premises

If the landlord finds damage at the end of a tenancy, then he or she may deduct the amount of the damage from the security deposit. In a residential tenancy, the landlord forfeits that right if he or she does not send the correct notice within fifteen days of when the tenant vacates the premises. (see Chapter 3.)

If the damages exceed the amount of the security deposit, the landlord may sue the tenant. If they are under $5,000, the landlord can file the case in small claims court.

Property Abandoned by Tenant

Landlords have two options for disposing of property abandoned by the tenant. If they have a written agreement with the tenant, they are free to dispose of it as they wish. If not, they can follow the procedures in Chapter 715 of Florida Statutes.

For residential tenancies, landlords are allowed to have an agreement with the tenants that they are not responsible for storage or disposition of property left behind when a tenant leaves. Under Florida Statutes, Section 83.67(3), the agreement can be included in the lease or as a separate agreement. A separate

AGREEMENT REGARDING ABANDONED PROPERTY is included in this book. (see form 7, p.179.) The clause that must be in the lease is:

> BY SIGNING THIS RENTAL AGREEMENT THE TENANT AGREES THAT UPON SURRENDER OR ABANDONMENT, AS DEFINED BY CHAPTER 83, FLORIDA STATUTES, THE LANDLORD SHALL NOT BE LIABLE OR RESPONSIBLE FOR STORAGE OR DISPOSITION OF THE TENANT'S PERSONAL PROPERTY.

NOTE: *The statute has the clause capitalized, so it should be in the lease.*

Under Florida Statutes, Sections 715.10–715.111, the landlord may protect him- or herself from liability for disposing of personal property left behind by a tenant, or by someone else who left property in the rental unit, by following certain procedures.

Applicability The law applies to both residential and nonresidential tenancies. It is an optional procedure that a landlord can use to protect him- or herself.

Procedure In order to take advantage of the law, the landlord must follow the procedures laid out in the statute.

Notice A notice must be sent to the tenant (or to any person the landlord believes owns the property, such as a cable TV company or telephone company) carefully describing the property.

Form The form of the notice is printed in the statute. (see forms 49, 50, 51, and 52.)

Delivery It should be personally delivered to the "last known address" of the tenant or the person believed to be the owner. It may be sent to the premises that had been rented, but if the landlord knows that the mail is not being forwarded, then it should be sent to any address known to the landlord at which the tenant may receive it.

Storage Costs A reasonable storage charge may be required before release of the property. The property may be stored on the premises or in a place of safekeeping. Tenants may be required to pay all costs of storage, but owners other than tenants need only pay storage costs for their own items. No more than one person may be charged for the same costs. If the property is stored on the premises, only the fair value of the space used may be charged.

Date   A date by which the property may be claimed must be given. It must be at least ten days after notice is personally given or fifteen days after notice is mailed.

Liability   The landlord must exercise reasonable care in storing the property, but he or she is not liable for any loss unless caused by his or her deliberate act.

Release   The landlord must release the property to the tenant or person reasonably believed to be the owner upon payment of the storage charges and advertising. It must be released if claimed at any time before a landlord takes possession or holds the sale as described next.

Valued Property under $500. If the value of all abandoned property is reasonably believed to be under $500, it may be kept, sold, or destroyed by the landlord after the date given in the notice. If a landlord is not sure of the value, it is always safer to assume it is worth over $500.

Property Valued over $500. If the value of the abandoned property is over $500, it must be sold at a public sale. A landlord or tenant may bid at the sale. The sale must be held in the nearest suitable place to where the property is stored.

Notice of the time and place of the sale must be advertised in a newspaper of general circulation once a week for two weeks. The sale must not be sooner than ten days from the first ad and five days from the second ad.

If there is no newspaper of general circulation, then a notice must be posted in six conspicuous places in the neighborhood of the sale. The notice must adequately describe the property except that contents of a locked or fastened container need not be listed.

If there is a surplus of funds after storage, advertising, and sale costs are deducted, they must be turned over to the treasury of the county within thirty days. Any person claiming an interest in the funds may apply to the county treasurer for them within one year.

Municipal Liens

Florida Statutes, Section 180.135 states that no municipality may refuse utilities, water, or sewer services or assert a lien against a property for nonpayment by a former occupant. The municipality also may not force the landlord to guarantee the tenant's bills.

Not all municipalities in Florida comply with this law. Many require landlords to put the bills in their name, which in effect makes the landlord guarantee the bill for the tenant. Unfortunately, if a city refuses to follow the law, your only recourse is to file suit, which is more expensive than the utility bills would be.

9 TERMINATING A TENANCY

The tenancy may be terminated in several ways. Unless the tenancy is terminated properly, the tenant may not be evicted. If you file an eviction without properly terminating the tenancy, then the tenant may win the case and you may be ordered to pay damages to the tenant as well as the tenant's attorney's fees.

Tenancies with No Specific Term

Even when there is no written lease between the parties, the law is strict about how the tenancy may be terminated. Any variation from these procedures can delay the eviction for months. If done right, however, a tenant can be removed quickly.

Residential   Under Florida Statutes, Section 83.57, if a unit is rented without a specific term, either party may terminate the rental by giving written notice as follows:

✪   when the rent is paid yearly, the notice must be given at least sixty days prior to the end of the rental year;

✪   when the rent is paid quarterly, the notice must be given at least thirty days prior to the end of the quarter;

✪   when the rent is paid monthly, the notice must be given at least fifteen days prior to the end of the month; and,

✪   when the rent is paid weekly, the notice must be given at least seven days prior to the end of the week.

This means that if a tenant paying rent monthly, for example, does not give notice fifteen days prior to the end of the month that he or she plans to terminate, the tenant is liable for the rent for an additional month. Likewise, if a landlord wants to terminate a monthly rental, then he or she must give the tenant notice fifteen days prior to the end of the month or the tenant may stay another month.

A tenancy may not be terminated in the middle of a term. For example, if a landlord or tenant on a monthly basis gives notice on August 12th that they wish to terminate the tenancy, then they may terminate effective August 31st (not August 27th). If they give notice on August 17th, then they may terminate it effective September 30th and not sooner. (Unless both parties agree.)

Unwritten tenancies are considered *tenancies at will.* This means they can be terminated at any time by giving the proper notice. If the length of the tenancy of an unwritten lease is not agreed upon, then the term is determined by the frequency rent is paid. If the rent is paid monthly, it is a month-to-month tenancy, if the rent is paid yearly, it is a yearly tenancy, etc. (Fla. Stat., Sec. 83.01.)

When the length of a written lease is not specified, it is considered a tenancy at will and can be terminated the same as an unwritten lease, as explained in the previous paragraph. (Fla. Stat., Sec. 83.02.)

This law also applies to tenancies in which the tenant stays after a lease expires. If the tenant fails to give the notice required by Section 83.57, the tenant is liable for one month additional rent after leaving. (Fla. Stat., Sec. 83.575.)

Nonresidential   Under Florida Statutes, Section 83.03, if a unit is rented without a specific term, either party may terminate the rental by giving written notice as follows:

- ✪ when the rent is paid yearly, the notice must be given at least three months prior to the end of the year;

- ✪ when the rent is paid quarterly, the notice must be given at least forty-five days prior to the end of the quarter;

- ✪ when the rent is paid monthly, the notice must be given at least fifteen days prior to the end of the month; and,

- ✪ when the rent is paid weekly, the notice must be given at least seven days prior to the end of the week.

Local Laws The City of Miami Beach asked the Attorney General if it could require a longer period of notice to terminate a tenancy and was told it could. Therefore, you should find out if the city in which your unit is located has rules different from the above. (AGO 94-41, May 5, 1994.)

Expiration of Rental Term

In some states, a lease is presumed to automatically renew unless a tenant gives the landlord notice that he or she is leaving. In Florida, however, the law is that a lease ends at its term unless the parties agree to renew it.

A lease can require that a tenant give up to sixty days notice that he or she will leave at the end of the lease and that it can require the tenant to pay liquidated damages if he or she does not. (Fla. Stat., Sec. 83.575(1) and (2).)

However, it does not say that the lease automatically renews. It will take a few court cases to see how this statute will be interpreted. If you want a tenant to leave at the end of a lease, and do not expect that he or she will, you can use the **NOTICE OF NON-RENEWAL**. (see form 24, p.213.)

If a tenant continues to rent the premises with your permission after a lease expires, the tenant is required to give notice before leaving just as if there were no lease. If the tenant fails to give such notice, he or she must pay one month rent as damages. (Fla. Stat., Sec. 83.575(3).)

Employment Rentals

Where a dwelling unit is furnished without rent as part of employment, the rental period is determined by how often the employee's salary is paid. If no salary is paid, it is considered a month-to-month tenancy. If the employee ceases employment, the employer is entitled to rent for the unit from the day after the employment is terminated until the day the former employee vacates the premises at a rate equivalent to similar units in the area. This does not apply to resident apartment managers when there is a written contract to the contrary. (Fla. Stat., Sec. 83.46.)

Early Termination by Tenant

If the tenant leaves the premises before the end of the lease agreement, he or she may be liable for damages unless the tenant is able to legally terminate the tenancy under Florida Statutes, Section 83.56(1) or 83.63.

Destruction of the Premises

If the premises are damaged or destroyed other than by wrongful or negligent acts of the tenant, and if the premises are *substantially impaired,* the tenant may immediately vacate the premises and terminate the rental. (For more information see "Damage to the Premises" on page 103.)

Landlord's Noncompliance

If the landlord materially fails to comply with the maintenance obligations or with the terms of the lease and does not comply seven days after written notice is given by the tenant, the tenant may terminate the rental and vacate the premises. (Fla. Stat., Sec. 83.56(1).) If the tenant fails to give proper notice, then he or she is not entitled to damages. 📖

Efforts to Cure

If the landlord makes every reasonable effort to comply with his or her maintenance obligations and the noncompliance is beyond the control of the landlord, then the parties may terminate or amend the rental agreement as follows:

- ✪ if the premises are not livable, the tenant may vacate and not be liable for rent as long as it remains unlivable and

- ✪ if the premises are livable, the tenant may pay reduced rent based on the lost value of the premises.

Remedies for Breach If the tenant breaches the lease by vacating early, the landlord has three options (Fla. Stat., Sec. 83.595.):

1. the landlord may retake the premises for his or her own account, thereby terminating all further liability of the tenant;

2. the landlord may retake the premises for the account of the tenant, relet the premises, and hold the tenant liable for any difference in the rent received; or,

3. the landlord may do nothing and sue the tenant for the lost rent as it comes due.

If the landlord opts to find a new tenant, he or she must make a good faith effort and use the same efforts used previously or for other units. If the landlord has other vacant units, then he or she does not have to rent out the tenant's unit first.

Early Termination of Residential Tenancy by Landlord

A landlord may terminate a tenancy before the end of the term for three reasons:

1. nonpayment of rent;

2. breach of the lease other than nonpayment of rent; or,

3. violation of Florida statutes.

Strict Requirements The laws are very strict about terminating a tenancy and if they are not followed, the landlord may lose in court and be required to pay the tenant damages and attorney's fees. Be sure to read all of these instructions carefully and follow them exactly.

Wording of the Notice The notice should use the exact wording shown. The law states that the notice is invalid if it does not substantially comply with the wording. 📖

📖 When a landlord added the words "in cash" to the three-day notice, it was eventually held to be valid since all obligations are due in cash. However, it took three different courts and eighteen months for the landlord to prevail. (*Moskowitz v. Aslam*, 575 So.2d 1367 (Fla. 3 DCA 1991).)

📖 One Florida case has held that a notice that did not state when the three day period began or ended and did not include the landlord's address was adequate. (*Multach v. Snipes*, 15 Fla. Supp. 2d 52 (Palm Beach Co. 1986).) However, this was a local court decision and is not binding on other courts and may not be followed.

📖 In a case in which extra wording was added to the three-day notice, a court said that it was confusing to the low-income tenant and ruled the notice to be void. (*Housing Authority of Ft. Lauderdale v. Butts*, 1 FLW Supp. 529 (Broward Co. 1993).)

Delivery of the Notice

These notices may be mailed, hand-delivered, or posted on the tenant's door. (Fla. Stat., Sec. 83.56(4).) If they are mailed, then the tenant will probably be entitled to five extra days for mailing time. 📖 The notice should only be posted if the tenant is absent from the premises.

Waiver

If either the landlord accepts rent or the tenant pays rent after a known violation, that person has waived the right to terminate the rental for the period, but they may terminate it the next time rent comes due if the violation continues. (Fla. Stat., Sec. 83.56(5).)

If the tenant fails to pay the rent, the landlord may send the following three-day notice. (see form 21, p.207.)

YOU ARE HEREBY NOTIFIED THAT YOU ARE INDEBTED TO ME IN THE SUM OF $_____ FOR THE RENT AND USE OF THE PREMISES _____[address of premises, including county], FLORIDA, NOW OCCUPIED BY YOU AND THAT I DEMAND PAYMENT OF THE RENT OR POSSESSION OF THE PREMISES WITHIN THREE DAYS (EXCLUDING SATURDAY, SUNDAY, AND LEGAL HOLIDAYS) FROM THE DATE OF DELIVERY OF THIS NOTICE, TO WIT: ON OR BEFORE THE _____ DAY OF _____, 20___. _____(Landlord's name, address and phone number).

Calculating Three Days. The most common reason for a landlord to lose an eviction is because he or she wrongly executed the three-day notice. The most common mistake is getting the three day period wrong. If you make such a mistake, you can lose the case and be forced to pay the tenant's attorney's fees.

One big problem with this in the past has been that landlords did not know about Florida's obscure legal holidays such as Confederate Memorial Day (April 26th) and Jefferson Davis' Birthday (June 3rd). Now the law states, "Legal holidays for the purpose of this section shall be court-observed holidays only." This will eliminate some surprises, but it should still be noted that when a holiday falls on Sunday, Monday is considered a holiday, and some counties have their own legal holidays such as Parade Day and Gasparilla Day in Hillsborough County, and DeSoto Day in Manatee County. Also, judges may declare Rosh Hashanah, Yom Kippur, and Good Friday as court holidays. A full list of Florida legal holidays is included in Appendix C.

NOTE: *Call your court clerk to see what days are "court observed holidays" in your area before preparing your three-day notice.*

Amount Due. The second most common mistake landlords make is in the amount of rent due. The notice should only include amounts due for rent, not late charges or utility bills. If the lease clearly states that late charges are part of the *rent*, then you may get away with including them. 📖

   📖 One court has held that even if they are included in the rent, they may not be included in the notice. If the three-day notice does include other charges, then you may lose your case and be required to pay the tenant's attorney's fees. (*Metropolitan Dade County v. Dansey*, 39 Fla. Supp. 2d 216 (1990).)

   📖 One case held that an eviction suit does not have to be dismissed because of a defective three-day notice, but that the landlord can be given an opportunity to deliver a proper notice to the tenant. This well-reasoned opinion should be pointed out to any judge who is considering dismissing a suit for a defective notice. (*Levenshon Emerald Park Partners, Ltd. v. Walantus*, 3 FLW Supp. 556 (Broward Co. 1995).)

   📖 In another good case for landlords, a court ruled that if a case is dismissed for some procedural error rather than on the merits of the case, then there is no prevailing party who can be awarded attorney's fees. (*Paramount v. P.R.D. Holding*, 4 FLW Supp. 683 (Cir.Ct. Dade 1997).)

📖 When a tenant was discovered to owe back rent due to a miscalculation, a court held that the back rent could not be included in a three-day notice. (*Flagship Property Management, Inc., v. Mannings*, 46 FLW Supp.2d 136 (Co.Ct. Palm Beach, 1990).)

📖 When a landlord sued for eviction for failure to pay for repairs, eviction was denied because the landlord had not yet done the repairs. (*Gunby v. Caldwell*, 4 FLW Supp. 609 (Co.Ct. Putnam 1997).)

Address. The landlord's address on the three-day notice should not be a post office box. Otherwise, the tenant must be given an additional five days for the rent to arrive by mail. 📖

Attempts to Pay. If a tenant attempts to pay the rent before the three-day notice is up, then the landlord must accept it. 📖 If the landlord wants to evict the tenant anyway, the only way to do it is if the tenant violates another clause in the lease. If the tenant attempts to pay the rent after the tenancy has been terminated (after the three days are up), then the landlord does not have to accept it. 📖

Acceptance of Rent. If the landlord accepts rent with the knowledge that the tenant is not complying with some aspect of the lease, then the landlord waives the right to evict for that noncompliance. (Fla. Stat., Sec. 83.56(5).)

Early Notice. In a case in which a landlord routinely delivered a notice of nonpayment of rent to tenants before it was due, the notice was held to be invalid. 📖

Undated Notice. The notice should explain in detail when, how, and what violation occurred. When landlords merely cite which clause is violated, the notice has been held by some courts to be defective. 📖

If the tenant violates the terms of the lease or the maintenance obligations under Florida Statutes, Section 83.52, and if the violation is material, then the landlord can terminate the rental agreement by using the notices provided in the statutes.

Attorneys. If an attorney sends a three-day notice for a tenant, some courts have held that the federal *Fair Debt Collection Act* applies, and the attorney can be liable for thousands of dollars in damages for failure to comply with the act.

Breach of Lease

As explained in Chapter 7, the landlord must decide whether the breach of the lease is curable or incurable. If it is curable, then the landlord must use the notice in Chapter 7 to give the tenant seven days to cure the breach. To be safe, a landlord should always assume a breach is curable unless it is really bad, such as intentional damage of property or continued unreasonable disturbance.

If the violation is not curable or if the tenant repeats a violation after receiving the above notice, then the landlord may terminate the tenancy by sending the following notice to the tenant. (see form 22, p.209.)

YOU ARE ADVISED THAT YOUR LEASE IS TERMINATED EFFECTIVE IMMEDIATELY. YOU SHALL HAVE SEVEN (7) DAYS FROM THE DELIVERY OF THIS LETTER TO VACATE THE PREMISES. THIS ACTION IS TAKEN BECAUSE _____

_____

The notices should explain in detail when, how, and what violation occurred. When landlords merely cited which clause was violated, the notice has been held by some courts to be defective. 📖

Public and Subsidized Housing

For nonpayment of rent, the landlord must give the tenant fourteen-days notice rather than a three-day notice, and it must be mailed or hand delivered, not posted. (C.F.R., Title 24, Sec. 866.4(1)(2).) The notice must inform the tenant of his or her right to a grievance procedure.

It is suggested that the landlord only use a fourteen-day notice. If both a fourteen-day and three-day notice are given, deliver the three-day notice so that the deadline is the same as for the fourteen-day notice. 📖

For breach of the terms of the lease other than payment of rent, a thirty-day notice must be given, except in emergencies, and it must inform the tenant of the reasons for termination, the right to reply, and the right to a grievance procedure.

(C.F.R., Title 24, Sec. 366(4)(1).) If the tenant requests a grievance hearing, a second notice must be given, even if the tenant loses in the hearing.

Section 236 Apartments

For nonpayment of rent, tenants must be given the three-day notice and be advised that if there is a judicial proceeding, they can present a valid defense, if any. Service must be by first-class mail and hand-delivered or placed under the door. (C.F.R., Title 24, Sec. 450.4(a).)

For breach of the terms of the lease other than payment of rent, the tenant must first have been given notice that in the future such conduct would be grounds for terminating the lease. The notice of termination must state when the tenancy will be terminated, specifically why it is being terminated, and it must advise the tenant of the right to present a defense in the eviction suit. (C.F.R., Title 24, Sec. 450.)

The section of the law that states acceptance or payment of rent is a waiver of any past noncompliance does not apply to the portion of the rent that is subsidized. (Fla. Stat., Sec. 83.56 (5).) However, waiver will occur if legal action is not taken within forty-five days.

Section 8 Apartments

Under the Code of Federal Regulations, Section 882.215(c)(4), the landlord must notify the housing authority in writing at the commencement of the eviction proceedings. Also, the previous paragraph applies to Section 8 housing as well.

Early Termination of Nonresidential Tenancy by Landlord

The rules for terminating a nonresidential tenancy are much more lenient than for residential tenancies. In most cases, the procedure can be spelled out in the lease itself, since the statutes do not give detailed rules. The rules that are in the statute are as follows.

✪ A three-day notice must be given to the tenant as with residential tenancies. (Fla. Stat., Sec. 83.20 (2).)

✪ In nonresidential tenancies, the wording of the notice does not have to match the statute, and nothing states that the three days excludes Saturdays, Sundays, and legal holidays. A waiver of the right to a three-day notice in the lease may also be legal. To avoid letting the tenant make an issue out of it, it would be prudent to use the residential **THREE-DAY NOTICE** form. (see form 21, p.207.)

✪ The notice must be given to the tenant, or if the tenant is absent from the rented premises, it may be left at the rented premises.

Acceptance of Rent If the landlord accepts the full amount of past due rent, then the landlord waives his or her right to proceed with eviction. (Fla. Stat., Sec. 83.202.)

Early Termination by Armed Forces Member

Any member of the armed forces may cancel a rental agreement by giving at least thirty-days notice if:

✪ he or she is permanently stationed thirty-five miles or more from the rental unit; or

✪ he or she is prematurely or involuntarily discharged or released from active duty; and,

✪ the written notice to cancel is accompanied by a copy of the orders or written verification signed by the commanding officer. (Section 83.682.)

If a member dies during active duty, a family member may terminate the tenancy under the same terms.

The tenant must pay prorated rent to the termination date. If the rental agreement is terminated fourteen or more days before occupancy of a unit, no rent is due. In the past, law required the tenant to pay liquidated damages.

NOTE: *These rules may not be waived or modified by either landlord or tenant.*

Death of a Tenant

If a lease contains a clause binding the "heirs, successors, and assigns" of the lessee, then the lease continues after the death of the tenant unless cancelled by the lessor and the heirs. 📖 Otherwise, it is a personal contract that expires at death. 📖

Options to Cancel

Generally, when a lease allows one party to cancel it at will, the lease is not considered binding and the courts will allow either party to cancel it at will. A lease will probably be held to be valid if the option to cancel is contingent upon some event.

📖 If a lease may be cancelled by the landlord upon sale of the property, the lease is valid and the option may be exercised by the new owner. (*Manzo v. Patch Publishing Co., Inc.*, 403 So.2d 469 (Fla. 5 DCA 1981).)

📖 When a lease provided for termination only if the landlord decided to alter or demolish at least part of the premises and also returned the security deposit and gave the tenant sixty-days notice, it was enforceable. (*In re Alchar Hardware Co., Inc.*, 759 F.2d 867 (11th Cir. Fla. 1985).)

📖 A lease that did not specify whether an option to cancel upon sale of the property was to be exercised by the buyer or seller, the buyer was allowed to exercise it. (*Manzo v. Patch Publishing Co., Inc.*, 403 So.2d 469 (Fla. 5 DCA 1981).)

IO | EVICTING A TENANT

The only way a landlord may recover possession of a dwelling unit is if the tenant voluntarily surrenders it to the landlord, abandons it, or if the landlord gets a court order giving the landlord possession. Fortunately, the eviction process usually works quite quickly in Florida. In some cases, tenants' lawyers have abused the system and allowed nonpaying tenants to remain in possession for months, but most of the time the system allows delinquent tenants to be removed quickly.

Self-Help by Landlord

As explained in Chapter 8, self-help methods, such as shutting off electricity or changing locks, can result in thousands of dollars in fines. Residential landlords are specifically forbidden to use self-help methods to evict tenants, even if the lease allows it. (Fla. Stat., Sec. 83.67.) As explained in the section "Retaliatory Conduct" on page 93, if a landlord directly or indirectly terminates utilities such as water, electricity, gas, elevators, lights, garbage collection, or refrigeration, or if the landlord locks up the unit or takes off the doors, windows, roofs, walls, etc., then the landlord is liable for damages of at least three months rent plus court costs and attorney's fees.

📖 A landlord posted a three-day notice and when the tenant was absent from the premises, he entered and removed her possessions. In a lawsuit, she testified that her possessions were all heirlooms and antiques and since the landlord had disposed of them, he could not prove otherwise. She was awarded $31,000.00 in damages. (*Reynolds v. Towne Mgt. of Fla., Inc.,* 426 So.2d 1011 (Fla. 2 DCA 1983).)

The potential for even greater damages exist, especially if the landlord's self-help actions result in punitive damages being awarded as well. A jury awarded the occupant $250,000 in punitive damages in a situation in which purchasers of a tax deed to property kept changing the locks on the property, nailing the door shut, and placing "for sale" signs on the property when the occupant was away.

Surrender or Abandonment

To surrender a dwelling, a tenant must tell the landlord that they are leaving or leave the keys. It can be presumed that a tenant abandoned the dwelling if the tenant has been absent for half of the rental term (unless the rent is current or notice is given). (Fla. Stat., Sec. 83.59(3)(c).)

NOTE: *In some other cases, such as when all of a tenant's possessions are gone and the electricity has been turned off, a landlord would be safe in assuming abandonment, but in the unlikely event that it went to court, the landlord may lose.*

📖 A landlord changed the locks the day after a lease expired and the tenant had moved most of his things out and had the utilities shut off. When the tenant sued saying he left a valuable Rolex on the premises, he lost. (*Newman v. Gray,* 4 FLW Supp. 271 (11th Cir. Dade 1996).)

Settling with the Tenant

Although in ninety percent of all Florida evictions the tenants do not answer the complaint and the landlord wins quickly, some tenants can create nightmares for landlords. Clever tenants and legal aid lawyers can delay the case for months, and vindictive tenants can destroy the property with little worry of ever paying for it. Therefore, in some cases, lawyers advise their clients to offer the tenant a cash settlement to leave. For example, a tenant may be offered $200 to be out of the premises and leave it clean within a week. Of course, it hurts to give money to a tenant who already owes you money, but it could be cheaper than the court costs, vacancy time, and damages to the premises. You will have to make your own decision based upon your tenant.

Grounds for Eviction

A tenant can be evicted for violating one of the terms of the lease, for violating the Florida landlord/tenant law, or for failing to leave at the end of the lease. The most common violation of the lease is that the tenant has failed to pay the rent, but a tenant can also be evicted for violating other terms of the rental agreement, such as disturbing other tenants.

Terminating the Tenancy

It is an ancient rule of law that an eviction suit cannot be filed until the tenancy is legally terminated. There are cases from the 1500s in which evictions were dismissed because the landlord failed to properly terminate the tenancy. If you make the same mistake, do not expect the judge to overlook it. What the judges often do is order the landlord to pay the tenant's attorney's fees.

Termination for Cause

The tenancy may terminate by natural expiration or by action by the landlord. If you need to evict a tenant whose tenancy has not expired, then you should carefully read the previous chapter and follow the procedures to properly terminate the tenancy.

Termination by Expiration

If parties to a rental agreement do not agree to renew or extend the agreement, then it automatically ends at its expiration date. (This is different from some areas in which the lease is automatically renewed unless notice is given that it is not being renewed.)

Using an Attorney

The landlord/tenant statutes provide that the loser in a landlord/tenant case can be charged with the winner's attorney's fees. Because of this, it is important to do an eviction carefully. In some cases, the tenant may just be waiting for the eviction notice before leaving the premises. In such a case, the landlord may regain the premises no matter what kind of papers he or she files. However, in other cases, tenants with no money and no defenses have gotten free lawyers, who find technical defects in the case. This can cause a delay in the eviction and cause the landlord to be ordered to pay the tenant's attorney's fees. A simple error in a landlord's court papers can cost him or her the case.

A landlord facing an eviction should consider the costs and benefits of using an attorney compared to doing it without one. One possibility is to file the case without an attorney and hope the tenant moves out. If the tenant stays and fights the case, an attorney can be hired to finish the case. Some landlords who prefer to do their evictions themselves start by paying a lawyer for a half-hour or hour of his or her time to review the facts of the case and point out problems.

Whenever a tenant has an attorney, the landlord should also have one.

> 📖 In a suit by a cooperative association against a tenant for $191.33 in maintenance fees and to enforce the association rules, the tenant won the suit and was awarded $87,375 in attorney's fees. (*Royal Saxon, Inc. v. Jaye*, 13 FLW 1809 (Fla. 4 DCA 1988).)

> 📖 An argument that a legal aid organization was not entitled to attorney's fees did not win. The landlord had to pay $2,000 for twenty hours of the legal aid's time in having the case dismissed. (*Beckwith v. Kesler*, 2 FLW Supp. 82 (Broward Co. 1993).)

Under Florida Statute, Section 59.46, the winner of the case is also entitled to attorney's fees for appeals that are made to a higher court. 📖

It is, of course, important to find an attorney who both knows landlord/tenant law and charges reasonable fees. There are many subtleties of the law that can be missed by someone without experience. Some attorneys who specialize in landlord/tenant cases charge very modest fees, such as $75 or $100, to file the case and the same amount for a short hearing, unless the case gets complicated.

Others charge an hourly rate that can add up to thousands of dollars. You should check with other landlords or a local apartment association for names of good attorneys, or you might try calling the manager of a large apartment complex in the area.

If you get a security deposit at the beginning of the tenancy and start the eviction immediately upon a default, then the deposit should be nearly enough to cover the attorney's fee.

When an attorney represents a landlord in collecting rent, even for a bad check and even when following a state landlord/tenant law, some courts have held that the attorney must comply with the federal Fair Debt Collection Act. (U.S.C., Title 15, Sec. 1692.) This law requires that the debtor (the tenant) be given a specific notice and thirty days to dispute the debt. Fortunately, the Eleventh Circuit (in which Florida is located) ruled the other way. However, if in the future the court changes its ruling or the Supreme Court sides with the other courts, Florida attorneys will be required to follow this additional notice requirement. For this reason, demand letters are better sent by the landlords themselves.

Who Can Sue

An owner can represent him- or herself in court and does not need an attorney. (Fla. Stat., Sec. 454.18.) As a general rule, no one can represent another person in court except a licensed attorney. Only an attorney can represent a corporation. Not even a corporate officer can represent a corporation, except in small claims court. It is a criminal offense for a nonlawyer to represent another party in court.

In some cases, such as when a real estate agent or other agent of a landlord signed leases in his or her own name as rental agent, the agent can go to court without the owner of the property. This is because the agent is party to the contract. However, unless the agent is an attorney, the agent cannot take any action in the case other than filing the complaint. (Florida Statutes, Section 83.59.)

The Florida Supreme Court has approved simplified legal forms for the use of those who are not attorneys. These forms include several for use in landlord/tenant matters, and the legend at the bottom indicates that they can be completed with the assistance of others who are not attorneys. In the case *The Florida Bar re Advisory Opinion—Nonlawyer Preparation of and Representation of Landlord in*

Uncontested Residential Evictions, 605 So.2d 868 (Fla. 1993), the Florida Supreme Court granted the right to nonlawyer property managers to file eviction forms in cases in which only possession is sought (not damages) and the tenant does not contest the case. If the tenant contests the case, the property owner or an attorney must attend the hearing. 📖

In order to qualify to file an eviction for a landlord, a nonlawyer manager should have a written agreement with the landlord and should have the power to rent the property, to maintain the property, and to collect the rents. See the **PROPERTY MANAGEMENT AGREEMENT** in Appendix D. (see form 57, p.281.)

If the landlord happens to die prior to when an eviction is necessary, the proper party to file the suit would be the personal representative of the landlord's estate (unless the property was inherited through joint tenancy).

Court Procedures

An eviction is started by filing a *complaint* against the tenant in county court and paying the filing fee. An extra copy of the complaint must be provided for each defendant you are suing. The copies are *served* upon the tenants by the sheriff or by a private process server. A process server may cost a few dollars more than the sheriff but can often get service quicker and may be more likely to serve the papers personally, which will allow you to get a money judgment.

In an eviction action, a landlord is entitled to a *summary procedure*. (Fla. Stat., Sec. 51.011.) This procedure is designed to speed up the normal court process and allow a landlord to remove a tenant quickly. This summary procedure is not related to the *Rules of Summary Procedure* used in small claims court.

County court is not like small claims court. The procedures are different and sometimes a judge will not be sympathetic to a landlord without a lawyer. But many landlords successfully handle their own cases. To get a general idea of the eviction process, see the eviction flowcharts in Appendix C.

Forms   Because judges may be more comfortable with Supreme Court approved forms, and to allow nonlawyers to use this book, all of the approved forms have been incorporated into this book. The format of the author's original forms have also been changed to make them look more like approved forms, therefore making them more acceptable to judges. However, nonlawyers, other than landlords, are not authorized to use the court forms that do not have the legend, "Approved for use under rule 10-2.1(a) of the Rules Regulating the Florida Bar" at the bottom. Be sure to read all of the text explaining evictions and to follow each step carefully.

NOTE: *Occasionally someone will write to Sourcebooks and say that they followed this book but the judge gave the tenants extra time to move or let them speak without posting the rent into the court. Remember, most times a case will go smoothly, but judges do make mistakes. If your case gets complicated, you should invest in an experienced landlord/tenant attorney that can finish your case quickly.*

Complaint

To begin an eviction, you must prepare a **COMPLAINT** and file it with the clerk of the county court. You must attach a copy of the notice and also a copy of the lease or rental agreement if there is one. Along with the original, you must provide two copies for each defendant in the case. You should also keep a copy. (See forms 26–29 for eviction complaints.)

You cannot be granted a judgment unless you swear that your complaint is true. Usually this is done by notarizing the complaint, but for some reason the Florida Bar did not put a place for notarizing the eviction complaints. Therefore, you should attach a verification form (see form 30, p.225) to your complaint and have it notarized. This form also states that the defendants are not in the military service of the United States, because if they are, there will be a delay in granting your eviction.

The Florida Bar has a separate form of **NONMILITARY AFFIDAVIT** that is also included in this book in case some judges require it. (see form 38, p.243.) An eviction cannot proceed against a person who has provided a written notice that he or she is on active military service. (Fla. Stat., Sec. 250.5202.)

NOTE: *If your tenant is in the military service, you should consult an attorney.*

Attaching Lease. If there is a lease and a signed copy is not attached, the **COMPLAINT** may be dismissed, but the landlord should be allowed to amend the **COMPLAINT** to add a copy. 📖

Attaching three-day notice. If the three-day notice is not attached or is faulty, some courts have dismissed the case (and awarded attorney's fees to the tenant) but some recent cases have allowed the landlord to amend the **COMPLAINT**. 📖

Lost Lease. If the lease has been lost or destroyed or if the tenant has the only copy, then the landlord can still sue, but these facts must be spelled out in the **COMPLAINT** along with a statement of the terms of the lease. 📖

Venue

In some counties, such as Dade, there are several county court districts, and a landlord/tenant case is supposed to be filed in the district where the property is located. However, if you file in the wrong district and no one objects, the eviction will still be valid. 📖 Filing the eviction in a court far from the rental property might make it less likely that the tenant will fight the eviction. If the tenant does object to the court, then the case should be quickly transferred to the correct district.

Seeking Damages

More information about obtaining a money judgment against the tenant is contained later in this chapter. However, you should read that section before filing your eviction since some of the forms in the eviction will be different.

Public Housing

In Section 8 housing, under the Code of Federal Regulations, Section 882.215(c)(4), the local housing authority must be notified in writing before the tenant can be served with the eviction. 📖

Service of Process

Once the **COMPLAINT** has been filed, the copies must be served on the tenants along with a summons. A summons is a legal document that tells the tenant that he or she must reply to your **COMPLAINT** or have a judgment entered against him or her. In an eviction, a tenant has five days to answer. If you are also asking for back rent, the tenant has twenty days to respond to that portion of the **COMPLAINT**. In some counties the **SUMMONS** is prepared by the clerk of the court but in others the landlord must prepare it. The forms approved by the Florida Supreme Court include two **SUMMONS** forms, one for possession and one for damages. (see forms 31 and 32.) If your clerk's office has its own **SUMMONS** available, use that instead of the forms in this book.

Service of process can be done by either the sheriff or a process server. In some areas where the sheriff will be unable to handle the service for several days, a private process server can offer the advantage of quick service. A process server can be found by checking with the clerk or looking in the phone book under "Process Servers" or "Detective Agencies." The sheriff's fee for serving process is $25.

The **SUMMONS** and **COMPLAINT** must be handed to the tenant or to a resident of the unit who is over 15 years of age. If after two attempts at least six hours apart the tenant has not been served, the papers may be served by posting them on the premises. If the tenant is served by posting, then a copy must also be mailed to the tenant by the clerk. If you anticipate service by posting, then extra copies and stamped envelopes with return addresses should be given to the clerk at the time the suit is filed. If you wish to obtain a money judgment, then the tenant must be personally served with the summons. Some landlords feel it is more important to get the tenant out quickly than to get a worthless judgment, so they instruct the sheriff or process server to post the summons.

- A five-day summons is sufficient for a suit for both possession and money damages. When a court said that both a five- and a twenty-day summons had to be served, it was reversed by the appeals court. (*Stein v. Hubbs*, 439 So.2d 1005 (Fla. 5 DCA 1983).)

- If the tenant does not read English, then the summons may not be valid if it is not in his or her language. Although there is no translation of the eviction summons provided by the court rules, at least one court held an eviction invalid when the landlord and tenant corresponded in Spanish and the lease was in Spanish. (*Estevez v. Olarte*, 47 Fla. Supp. 2d 86 (Co.Ct. Dade 1991).)

- The summons cannot be served on a Sunday unless the landlord is afraid that the tenant is planning to escape from the state and files an affidavit so stating. (Fla. Stat., Sec. 48.20.) (*Beckwith v. Kesler*, 1 FLW Supp. 494 (Broward Co. 1993).)

- In one case, a public housing authority obtained a tenant's signature on a stipulation that agreed to a default without needing service of process. The court found this was contrary to federal law. (*Housing Authority of the City of Ft. Lauderdale v. Vinson*, 6 FLW Supp. 299 (17th Cir. App. Div. 1999).) Such a waiver would probably be held illegal even in nonpublic housing.

- If a tenant was not personally served, the court cannot enter a money judgment for the costs of the case. (*Springbrook Commons, Ltd. v. Brown*, 761 So.2d 1192 (Fla. 4 DCA 2000).)

Wait Five Days   After the papers have been served upon the tenants, they have five days (excluding Saturdays, Sundays, and legal holidays) in which to file an answer or else to vacate the premises. Most tenants leave at this point.

Default   If the tenants have not vacated the premises and have not filed any answer with the court within the five days, you must file a **MOTION FOR CLERK'S DEFAULT** (see form 33, p.233) and then ask the judge in the case to sign a **FINAL JUDGMENT**. (see form 39, p.245.)

A few years ago the clerks in some counties required the landlord to wait more than five days before entering the default in case an answer was mailed. However, Florida Statutes, Section 51.011 makes it clear that the tenant must have the answer filed within five days.

Hearing   If the tenants have filed any answer, even a post card stating something nonsensical, you must have a hearing before the judge. If the tenant has a lawyer, you should also get one because a small mistake by you could cost you the case and you will have to pay the tenant's attorney's fees, possibly thousands of dollars.

NOTE: *You may feel that you cannot afford hundreds of dollars in attorney's fees, but an occasional bad tenant is a risk of investing in real property. The cost should be factored into your return. Next time, screen your tenant better or get a bigger deposit.*

If the tenant filed an answer, then you should check with the clerk or the judge's secretary to set a hearing. Mention that this is a *summary proceeding* landlord/tenant case and that you need ten or fifteen minutes. You should be able to get a hearing within a week or ten days. If they want to schedule it a month or two away, state that you want a quick hearing under Florida Statutes, Section 51.011. When their calendars are crowded, some judges say a thirty-day wait for a hearing is reasonable. More sympathetic judges will squeeze you in for ten minutes early in the morning. If nothing is available, ask if the case might be transferred to a judge who has more time. If that does not help, check with an attorney.

If you are evicting for nonpayment of rent and the tenant has not deposited the rent into the registry of the court, you should file a **MOTION TO STRIKE** and a **NOTICE OF HEARING** (see form 42, p.251 and form 41, p.249), and send copies by regular mail to the tenants.

Some judges require that a trial be set at the same time, and in different counties they use either a **MOTION TO SET CAUSE FOR TRIAL** or a **PLAINTIFF'S NOTICE FOR TRIAL**. (see form 45, p.257 or form 46, p.259.) If you use the **MOTION TO SET CAUSE FOR TRIAL**, copies of the Motion for Trial (with only the top filled in by you) must be sent to the tenants by regular mail, and extra copies for each tenant and the landlord must be given to the judge along with stamped, addressed envelopes. If you use the **PLAINTIFF'S NOTICE FOR TRIAL**, send a copy to the tenant, keep a copy, and file the original with the court. If this sounds complicated, ask the judge's assistant exactly what is required of you.

If you are evicting for breach of the lease or if the tenant deposits the rent into the registry of the court, then you will need to go right to the trial instead of using the **MOTION TO STRIKE**. Use the **MOTION TO SET CAUSE FOR TRIAL** (form 45), or a **PLAINTIFF'S NOTICE FOR TRIAL** (form 46) as explained in the previous paragraph.

If no one shows up at the hearing except you, then you should present to the judge your **MOTION FOR DEFAULT FINAL JUDGMENT** and **FINAL JUDGMENT** (see form 35, p.237 and form 39, p.245) along with extra copies for yourself and all tenants and stamped envelopes addressed to the tenants.

If the tenants show up, they should not be able to present any defenses unless they have deposited rent with the clerk of the court. (Fla. Stat., Sec. 83.60(2).) Even if they want to talk about building code violations, they should not be allowed to bring up the subject, unless they gave written notice to the landlord that they would withhold rent unless the premises were repaired within seven days. (Fla. Stat., Sec. 83.60(1).)

The judge should enter a default. Section 83.56(5) states: *The court may not set a date for mediation or trial unless the provisions of Section 83.60(2) have been met, but shall enter a default judgment for removal of the tenant with a writ of possession to issue immediately if the tenant fails to comply with Section 83.60(2).* You should be granted a **FINAL JUDGMENT** at this hearing if you did everything right. If not, you should consult an attorney who can move your case to judgment quickly.

If the tenant wishes to dispute the amount of rent claimed in the **COMPLAINT**, he or she must file a *Motion to Determine the Amount of Rent to be Paid into the Registry* within five days of receiving the summons (excluding Saturdays, Sundays, and legal holidays). This action by the tenant can delay the eviction. However, the tenant must also attach to the motion some documentary evidence that the **COMPLAINT** is in error. (Fla. Stat., Sec. 83.60(2).)

In the past, tenants were allowed to file a *Motion to Dismiss* without paying the rent into the court to contest the sufficiency of the three-day notice. Today this should not be allowed. 📖 However, if the tenant's Motion to Dismiss is allowed, you will probably have to refile your case. However, in a recent case, a landlord was allowed to deliver a proper notice without refiling (and paying another filing fee). 📖

> 📖 In another case, the court ruled that if the case is dismissed because of a procedural error rather than on the merits of the case, the tenant is not entitled to attorney's fees. (*Paramount v. P.R.D. Holding*, 4 FLW Supp. 683 (Cir. Ct. Dade 1997).)

> 📖 If it is denied, the judge may grant your judgment or may schedule another hearing a few days later. An explanation of this situation can be found in the case *Cook v. Arrowhead Mobile Home Community*, 50 Fla. Supp. 2d 26 (3rd Cir. Columbia 1991).

If the tenant shows up with an attorney and you were not told previously, you should ask the judge for a continuance to get your own attorney. If you make a mistake and lose, you may have to pay the tenant's attorney's fees.

If the tenant pays the rent into the registry of the court, then a trial will be held. In a trial, you would need to go through each paragraph of your complaint and prove it was true. This would be done by sworn testimony by you or a witness. You would also need to present evidence to the court such as an original lease and a copy of the three-day notice that you served on the tenant. After you present your side, the tenant is able to rebut your case with testimony and evidence such as cancelled checks. The judge may make a ruling immediately after a trial or may take the case *under advisement* and mail out a judgment a few days later.

Depositions and Subpoenas

It is possible to take depositions of the parties and to subpoena their records. This means they are called before a court reporter, asked questions under oath, and required to show their records. The answers are then used in court to contradict what the party might say to the judge. (Legal aides sometimes use this to complicate the case for landlords.)

☐ When a landlord failed to show up for a deposition, he was ordered to pay $228.50 in attorney's fees and go to jail for three days unless he appeared at the next scheduled deposition. (*Jacobs v. Mobely*, 9 FLW Supp. 403 (Brevard Co. 2002).)

Mediation

Failure to show up at mediation can result in having the case dismissed and being ordered to pay the tenant's attorney's fees. In some areas, mediation services are recommended or required before trial. At a mediation, the parties are encouraged to resolve their differences. This may mean a planned date of departure for the tenant or perhaps allowing the tenant to stay in the premises with a timetable for paying the back rent. In some cases damage to the premises or animosity between the parties may make it impossible to continue the tenancy. If a settlement is reached, then it should be in the form of a *stipulation* that is filed with the court. If you merely dismiss your case as part of the settlement, then you will have to start all over from scratch if the tenant again defaults.

Stipulation

Whether or not mediation is used, the parties may be able to resolve the matter without going through a hearing. This will allow the landlord to recover some back rent and avoid the hassle of cleaning and rerenting the unit. If you wish to settle with the tenant and come to an agreement in which the rent will be paid over time, then you can enter into a stipulation to delay the case. You should never accept any rent from the tenant once the case is filed without signing a stipulation. Some counties have their own forms, but a **STIPULATION** form is included in this book in case your county does not provide one. (see form 44, p.255.)

Basically, the **STIPULATION** is an agreement that the tenant will pay the back rent in installments and keep current in the rent and that the landlord will not proceed in the case. If the tenant fails to pay as agreed, the landlord can go to the judge without a hearing and get a **WRIT OF POSSESSION** upon presentation of a sworn, notarized statement that the tenant has defaulted on the **STIPULATION**. Be sure that any **STIPULATION** you sign says exactly when and how much rent the tenant must pay and that you are entitled to a default judgment in the event of default. A poorly worded **STIPULATION** can cause the landlord to lose the eviction. ☐

Writ of Possession

Once your **FINAL JUDGMENT** has been signed by the judge, if the tenant has still not vacated the premises, you must take a **WRIT OF POSSESSION** and one extra copy of it to the clerk and pay the sheriff's fee for the eviction. (see form 47, p.261.) Recent laws provide that the landlord has the choice of changing the locks on the premises and asserting his or her lien on the tenant's possessions or moving the tenant's possessions out to the street. (Fla. Stat., Sec. 83.625 and

Sec. 713.691.) The landlord is not liable for what happens to the tenant's possessions if put out on the street. (Fla. Stat., Sec. 83.625.) 📖

Regaining Possession

Different counties have different procedures for removing a tenant's possessions. Check with your local sheriff. In some cases, the sheriff stands by while the landlord moves the property out. In such a case, the landlord would in effect be acting as a deputy sheriff and would be protected by law from the tenant. (Fla. Stat., Sec. 843.01–.02.) The law now allows the sheriff to charge an hourly fee for such service. With some tenants and some property, it is not worth the trouble of attempting to claim a landlord's lien on the personal property left in the premises. The first $1000 in value is exempt from the lien and some tenants may break into the premises to retrieve their possessions. In many cases, it is just better to put the property on the street and hope you never hear from the tenant again.

The landlord can remove the tenant's possessions at the time the sheriff executes the **Writ of Possession** or at any time thereafter. (Fla. Stat., Sec. 83.62.) If the personal property left on the premises appears to have been abandoned, then it should be treated as explained in Chapter 8.

Money Damages and Back Rent

Procedures for collecting money damages and back rent from a tenant are explained in the next chapter.

Tenant's Possible Defenses

A tenant who is behind in rent usually has one objective—to stay in the property rent-free as long as possible. Tenants and the lawyers provided to them at no charge by legal aid clinics sometimes come up with creative, though ridiculous, defenses. Below is case law, with some cases dating back several years, showing how long these arguments have been blocked. Remember, the tenant should not be able to bring up any defenses unless he or she has paid the rent alleged to be due into the registry of the court.

If a tenant or the tenant's attorney attempts to delay an eviction by using an argument without factual or legal basis, Section 57.105 allows the court to award attorney's fees and sanctions and can require the tenant's attorney to pay. (See Appendix B for the full statute.)

Constitutionality A tenant claims it is unconstitutional to have a quick eviction procedure and to require the tenant to pay the rent into the court before he or she is allowed to present any defenses. The U.S. Supreme Court says that such procedures can be constitutional. 📖

> 📖 In 1988, a Florida appellate court held Florida's law to be constitutional. (*Karstetter v. Graham Companies*, 521 So.2d 298 (Fla. 3 DCA 1988).)

Security Deposit A tenant says that he or she is not in default because the landlord has a security deposit that covers the default. That is wrong. A security deposit is for a specific purpose at the end of the tenancy and does *not* cover current rent. 📖

Amount Incorrect A tenant disputes the amount of rent due. This is not a defense because if any rent is due, then the landlord is entitled to eviction. However, if the amount stated in the three-day notice is wrong, the case may be dismissed. 📖

Title A tenant claims that the landlord has not proved he or she has good title to the property. But a tenant who has entered into a rental agreement with a landlord is *estopped* (prevented) from denying that the landlord has good title. 📖

Fictitious Name A tenant says that the landlord is using a fictitious name that has not been registered with the county. If the landlord actually is using an unregistered name, the case is abated until he or she complies with the statute. However, in order to use this defense, the tenant must raise the issue no later than in the written answer to the complaint. 📖

Corporation is Dissolved Under Florida corporate law, a court action may not be maintained by a corporation that is not in good standing with the Florida Department of State. If your corporation has been dissolved for nonpayment of fees, it can be reinstated by paying previous year's fees and a penalty. There are companies in Tallahassee that will hand carry your payment to the Division of Corporations and send you a certificate of good standing immediately.

Corporation Not Represented by Attorney If the landlord is a corporation, it is required to be represented by an attorney. If not, the suit may be dismissed. While not all courts have agreed, the court in one case ruled that the pleadings could be made valid by amending them to add an attorney's signature. This would avoid filing a new case. 📖

Waiver by Refusal

A tenant says that because the landlord refused the rent after the three days were up that it is a waiver of the rent. Wrong again. While the landlord does have to give the tenant three days to pay all past due rent, he or she does not have to accept rent after the three-day grace period expires. 📖

Waiver by Acceptance of Rent

Usually, if a landlord accepts rent after serving a notice or filing suit, then he or she waives the right to continue and must serve a new notice or file a new suit. (Fla. Stat., Sec. 83.56(5).)

📖 When the tenant placed a check through the landlord's mail slot and the landlord immediately returned it by certified mail, this was not acceptance of rent by the landlord or a waiver. (*Gene B. Glick Co., Inc. v. Oliver,* 36 Fla. Supp. 2d 208 (Co.Ct. Brevard Co. 1989).)

📖 When the evidence indicated that the landlords did not know of an assignment of the lease when they accepted rent, such acceptance did not constitute a waiver of their rights. (*El Prado Restaurant, Inc. v. Weaver,* 268 So.2d 382 (Fla. 3 DCA 1972).)

📖 When a landlord accepted rent after giving tenants notice to vacate, a court found there was no waiver because the landlord only accepted past due rent and refused current rent. (*Russo v. Manfredo,* 35 Fla. Supp. 2d 23 (Cir.Ct. Citrus Co. 1989).)

📖 When a landlord accepted late payments without protest and never at any time notified the tenant that it was in default, this was a waiver of the landlord's right to claim a default on the part of the tenant even though the lease contained an *anti-waiver* clause. (*Protean Investors Inc. v. Travel, Etc., Inc.,* 499 So.2d 49 (Fla. 3 DCA 1986).)

Reg. Z

A tenant says that the landlord has not complied with *Reg. Z,* in the Code of Federal Regulations, which is a truth-in-lending requirement, but this federal regulation does not apply to the rental of property. (C.F.R., Title 12, Sec. 226.1(c)(1).)

Unconscionability of Rent

A tenant claims that rent is unconscionable, but this is a legal conclusion and a tenant must state facts that would prove to the court that the rent is unconscionable. 📖

Insufficient Complaint   A tenant says that the landlord's complaint is not drawn properly and does not state a cause of action. The complaints included in this book include all elements necessary. Forms 26, 27, and 28 are Florida Supreme Court approved forms, and form 29 is a modified version of them.

Maintenance of Premises   A tenant says that the landlord has not complied with Florida Statutes, Section 83.51(1), and that the tenant is withholding rent. This defense may not be raised unless seven days have elapsed between when written notice was sent to the landlord and when the tenant withheld the rent. (Fla. Stat., Sec. 83.60(1).)

> 📖   In a case in which the tenant did not raise the issue of the condition of the premises until after he had received the three-day notice, the tenant was not allowed to use this defense. (*Lakeway Management Co. of Fla., Inc. v. Stolowilsky,* 13 FLW 1576 (1988).)

The notice may be given by the tenant to the landlord, the landlord's representative, a resident manager, or anyone who collects rent for the landlord. (Fla. Stat., Sec. 83.60(1).)

The violation must be a material violation of the building code. Minor problems should not be allowed as defenses for withholding rent.

Also, the tenant must attach a copy of the seven-day notice to his or her answer, and the tenant must attach a copy of the code that the landlord has allegedly violated and request the court to take judicial notice of it. If the tenant does not do all these things, then he or she should not be able to use this defense.

There is a good argument that this statute is unconstitutional. The statute does not set certain standards, but lets any and all housing authorities throughout the state set the standards. This may be an unconstitutional delegation of legislative authority under Article II, Section 3 of the Florida constitution. 📖

Equitable Defenses   There is a general rule that only circuit court can hear *equitable matters.* Tenants sometimes try to raise *equitable defenses* in an eviction case in order to delay it by transferring it to circuit court. But courts have ruled that in a landlord/tenant dispute, the county court has exclusive jurisdiction and may consider all defenses. 📖

Retaliatory Conduct   A tenant says that he or she is being evicted in retaliation for some lawful action and that this is illegal under Florida Statutes, Section 83.64. This defense does not apply if the landlord is evicting the tenant for good cause—such as nonpayment of rent, violation of the lease or reasonable rules, or violation of the landlord/tenant law.

Discovery

A tenant wants more time in order to take *discovery*, which means to ask questions of the landlord and any witnesses under oath before a court reporter. This should not delay the case. The discovery should be done quickly in order to comply with Florida Statutes, Section 51.011, which applies to an eviction suit under Florida Statutes, Section 83.59.

Jury Trial

If a tenant makes a request for a jury trial, then he or she should be required to first post the past rent and any rent that comes due during the pendency of the suit. If there is a jury presently impaneled, then it should go to that jury, and if not, one should be immediately summoned. The tenant must pay the costs of the jury. If the tenant requests a jury, the landlord should file a *Preliminary Motion to Summon a Jury and Determine Fees.* This can be found in a civil procedure form book in the courthouse law library.

Attorney Busy or Unprepared

The tenant's attorney may say that he or she just got on the case and needs time to prepare or has a busy schedule and is not available for trial for a month or so. This should not delay the case. The landlord has a right to a quick procedure under Florida Statutes, Section 51.01. If the tenant's attorney is unavailable, he or she should not have taken the case. If the tenant has a lawyer, the landlord should have one too.

Attorney's Fees for Dismissal

When a tenant moves out of the property, the landlord sometimes dismisses his or her case. In some cases, the tenants have then claimed that they should have their attorney's fees paid because they were the *prevailing party* in the case. But, if the landlord dismisses his or her case as moot, this does not make the tenant the prevailing party. 📖

If a landlord is handling his or her own eviction, then the landlord should not dismiss the case after the tenant moves out. He or she should proceed to judgment at least for the court costs and to be officially granted possession. If the landlord is represented by an attorney, then he or she will have to weigh the costs.

Grievance Procedure

In federally subsidized housing, the regulations require that tenants be given a *grievance procedure* in some evictions. However, when the tenant is a threat to the health and safety of other tenants or employees, the Code of Federal Regulations, Title 24, Chapter 9, Section 966.51(a) states such a hearing is not required. 📖

Right to Possession One court dismissed a suit because the landlord did not "prove he had a right to possession." The appellate court reversed, stating that he did not need to prove so. 📖

Bad Faith A mere claim of *bad faith* was not enough to state a cause of action under the mobile home section of the Landlord-Tenant Act as to entitle the state attorney to seek an injunction. 📖

Tenant's Possible Countersuits

Another way tenants try to delay things is by filing a countersuit. This should not delay the eviction.

Exceeding Jurisdiction Since county court can only hear cases of amounts under $15,000, tenants sometimes try to claim over $15,000 in damages against the landlords. This way they hope to transfer the case to circuit court where it will drag out for a long time.

- ✪ In most cases, a claim of over $15,000 is clearly ridiculous and obviously intended as a delaying tactic. In such cases a **MOTION TO STRIKE** (see form 42, p.251) should be filed along with the **MOTION FOR DEFAULT**. (see form 43, p.253.) 📖

- ✪ If the tenant does submit a legitimate claim for over $15,000, then he or she must also pay the additional filing fee for transfer of the case. (Rule 1.170(j), Florida Rules of Civil Procedure.)

- ✪ One way to speed things along is to request that the circuit court designate the county court judge as an acting circuit judge for the purpose of hearing your action. 📖

Negligence A landlord's failure to maintain the premises may be a breach of contract, but alone it is not actionable negligence. 📖

Malicious Prosecution A *malicious prosecution* action cannot be brought in the same case being complained. It is a separate suit that can be brought if the landlord loses the original suit. 📖

Punitive Damages There is no such thing as *punitive damages* in a case regarding a contract. 📖 In order for a party to be entitled to punitive damages, there must be a tort committed by the landlord and there must be proof of "fraud, actual malice, deliberate violence, or oppression or such gross negligence as to indicate wanton disregard for the rights of others." 📖 Even when a landlord wrongfully overcharged tenants and lied to a federal agency, he could not be charged with punitive damages because it was merely a breach of contract. 📖

Moving Expenses
Tenants are not entitled to moving expenses after a lawful eviction. 📖

Harassment
There is no such thing as an *action for harassment* in Florida. 📖

Class Action
Since the claims of each tenant will in most cases be different, they probably cannot counterclaim as a *class action suit* on behalf of all tenants in the building. 📖

Civil Theft
Tenants have claimed that failing to return a security deposit and removing belongings were *civil theft*, which would entitle them to triple damages. However, courts have held that the tenant must prove that the landlord had criminal intent, and this is difficult. 📖

Withdrawal of Money from the Court

If the tenant actually has paid any rent money into the registry of the court, it will in most cases be awarded to the landlord at some point in the case. This is done by filing a **MOTION TO DISBURSE FUNDS FROM THE COURT REGISTRY** (see form 48, p.263) and having the judge sign an **ORDER DISBURSING FUNDS FROM THE COURT REGISTRY**. (see form 49, p.265.) If the landlord is in danger of losing the premises or has some other hardship, he or she can do this during the pendency of the case by setting a special hearing for this purpose. (This would only be necessary if the tenant has been successful in delaying the case with a motion or appeal.)

Abandonment after Dismissal

In some cases, the tenant will fight the eviction, have it dismissed on a technicality, and then move out. In such a situation, if you have been given the right to refile the case to correct the error, you should do so. 📖

Tenant's Appeal

A tenant has thirty days in which to file a notice of appeal, but since the **WRIT OF POSSESSION** gives the tenant twenty-four hours to vacate the property, the tenant will have to act immediately if he or she wants to stop the eviction. The eviction should not be halted by filing a notice of appeal. If the tenant files a notice of appeal, then the landlord should immediately file a Motion to Set a Supersedeas Bond. (Rule 9.310, Florida Rules of Appellate Procedure.) The amount of the bond will have to be decided by a judge and should be done at a hearing with both parties present. 📖

A tenant can file an appeal after vacating the premises as long as it is within the thirty days. If the tenant wins the appeal, it is possible that they will be allowed to move back into the premises, so it is not a good idea for the landlord to enter into a long-term lease with a new tenant if there is a chance the tenant will win on appeal.

If the tenant files a frivolous appeal, the landlord may be able to collect damages. Florida Statutes, Section 57.105 was recently strengthened to allow attorney's fees and sanctions to be awarded for frivolous claims. (see Appendix B.)

Tenant's Bankruptcy

If a tenant files bankruptcy, all legal actions must stop immediately. This provision is automatic from the moment the bankruptcy petition is filed. (United States Code (U.S.C.), Title 11, Section 362.) If you take any action in court, seize the tenant's property, try to impose a landlord's lien, or use the security deposit for unpaid rent, then you can be held in contempt of federal court. It is not necessary that you receive formal notice. Verbal notice is sufficient. If you do not believe the tenant, then you should call the bankruptcy court to confirm the filing.

The stay lasts until the debtor is discharged, the case is dismissed, or until the property is abandoned or voluntarily surrendered.

Relief from Stay

The landlord may ask for the right to continue with the eviction by filing a *Motion for Relief from Stay* and paying the filing fee. Within thirty days of filing the Motion for Relief from Stay a hearing is held and it may be held by telephone. The motion is governed by Bankruptcy Rule 9014 and the requirements of how the tenant must be served are contained in Rule 7004. However, for such a hearing, the services of an attorney are usually necessary.

Post-Filing Rent

The bankruptcy stay only applies to amounts owed to the landlord at the time of filing the bankruptcy. Therefore, the landlord can sue the tenant for eviction and rent owed for any time period after the filing unless the bankruptcy trustee assumes the lease. The landlord can proceed during the bankruptcy without asking for relief from the automatic stay under three conditions:

- the landlord can only sue for rent due after the filing;

- the landlord cannot sue until the trustee rejects the lease (if the trustee does not accept the lease within sixty days of the Order for Relief, then Section 365(d)(1) provides that it is deemed rejected); or,

- the landlord must sue under the terms of the lease and may not treat the trustee's rejection as a breach.

In Chapter 10 reorganization bankruptcy, the landlord should be paid the rent as it comes due.

Filing after Judgment

If the tenant filed bankruptcy after a judgment of eviction has been entered, there should be no problem lifting the automatic stay since the tenant has no interest in the property.

If your tenant files bankruptcy and you decide it is worth hiring a lawyer, you should locate an attorney who is experienced in bankruptcy work. Prior to the meeting with the attorney, you should gather as much information as possible (type of bankruptcy filed, assets, liabilities, case number, etc.).

Landlord's Appeal

If the landlord loses, then he or she has the right to appeal the judgment. Appeals from county court are usually made to the local circuit court, but the county court judge can certify a question to the district court of appeal. (Rule 9.160, Florida Rules of Appellate Procedure.) If the circuit court makes an error in an appellate ruling, it can be appealed to the District Court of Appeals. Appealing a county court judgment to circuit court may take a matter of weeks or months, but appealing a case to the district court may take a year or longer. 📖

Grounds

Our legal system allows one chance to bring a case to court. If you did not prepare for your trial, or thought you would not need a witness, you do not have the right to try again. However, in certain limited circumstances you may be able to have your case reviewed.

- ✪ If the judge made a mistake in interpreting the law that applies to your case, then that is grounds for reversal.

- ✪ If new evidence is discovered after the trial that could not have been discovered before the trial, then a new trial might be granted, but this is not very common.

- ✪ If one party lied at trial and that party was believed by the judge or jury, there is usually not much that can be done.

- ✪ There are certain other grounds for rehearing such as misconduct of an attorney or errors during the trial, but these matters are beyond the scope of this book. (For more detailed information in this area of the law see *Trawick's Florida Practice and Procedure*, available at most law libraries.)

Motion for Rehearing

The first way to appeal a decision is to ask the judge to listen to the case again. If important new evidence has been discovered or an important court case was overlooked by the judge, then this may work, but if the judge was clearly on the side of the tenant, it may be a waste of time. If the case was a jury trial, the motion used is a *Motion for New Trial*, not a *Motion for Rehearing*. A Motion for Rehearing must be filed within five days of entry of judgment. A Motion for New Trial must be filed within five days of the verdict. When the Motion is filed with the court, a copy is sent to the other party (or their attorney) and a hearing is scheduled before the judge, with notice of the hearing also sent to the other side.

When a landlord lost a case and was ordered to pay attorney's fees, he asked for a rehearing. After losing the rehearing, the landlord was ordered to pay an additional $750 in attorney's fees for the rehearing. The judge was reversed for two reasons, first that a rehearing cannot be called frivolous just because it restates issues since it is normal for rehearing to restate issues and second, that attorney's fees should not be awarded for arguing about attorney's fees. (*Miami Beach Equity Investors Ltd. Ptn. v. Granoff,* 4 FLW Supp. 755 (11th Cir. 1997).)

Notice of Appeal   If the judge made an error in interpreting the law, or ignored the law (it does happen), then you can appeal to a higher court. This is done by filing two copies of a *Notice of Appeal* within thirty days of the rendition of the judgment and paying the filing fee for the appeal. (If the tenant is the one to file the appeal, the landlord can cross-appeal within ten days.)

✪   Within fifty days of the filing of the Notice of Appeal, the clerk of the circuit court should prepare the record.

✪   Within seventy days of the filing of Notice, the parties should file their *appellate briefs.*

✪   Within 110 days of the filing of the Notice, the clerk should transmit the record to the circuit court.

✪   More detailed information on how to proceed with an appeal can be found in the *Florida Rules of Appellate Procedure.*

Satisfaction of Judgment

If, after a judgment has been entered against the tenant, the tenant pays the amount due, it is the landlord's responsibility to file a **SATISFACTION OF JUDGMENT**. (see form 56, p.279.)

II MONEY DAMAGES AND BACK RENT

Trying to collect on a judgment against a former tenant is usually not worth the time and expense. Most landlords are just glad to regain possession of the property. Tenants who do not pay rent usually do not own property that can be seized, and it is very difficult to garnish wages in Florida. However, occasionally former tenants come into money, and some landlords have been surprised many years later when called by a title insurance company wanting to pay off their judgment. Therefore, it is usually worthwhile to put a claim for back rent into an eviction complaint.

Making a Claim

To make a claim against a tenant for back rent, you can include a *Count II* in your **COMPLAINT FOR EVICTION AND DAMAGES** (see form 26, p.217) asking for the rent owed. However, if you do so, the complaint must be filed by the owner or an attorney, not a nonattorney agent.

Residential   In a residential eviction, if you have not included a demand for rent, the court should still award rent in the case but only if the tenant was personally served or properly served with certified or registered mail. This is because Florida

Statutes, Section 83.625 states that the court "shall direct...the entry of a money judgment."

> At least one county court has ruled that if a Count II for rent is not included in the complaint, it must at least make a demand for rent or the court cannot grant it. (*Pollard v. Alpert,* 48 Fla. Supp. 2d 127 (Palm Beach Co. 1991).) However, this is not what the statute says, and other courts are not following this case.

If you forgot to ask for rent, did not get personal service, or if the tenant moved out without the need for an eviction preceding, you can file a separate suit for the rent owed. If the amount is less than $5000, then the suit can be filed in small claims court.

Nonresidential

In a nonresidential tenancy, a demand must be made for rent in the eviction complaint or it cannot be awarded. However, you can sue for it separately in small claims court.

Amount

In county court, the limit on claims is $15,000. When the tenant has breached the lease, the landlord is entitled to several types of monetary damages. However, the landlord should review his or her options on default before deciding which type of claim to make against the tenant.

Pro-rated Rent

Under Florida Statutes, Section 83.46(1), rent is uniformly pro-rated over the month. Therefore, if a landlord took possession of the dwelling unit for his or her own benefit, then the tenant would be liable for rent only until he or she vacates the premises.

Future Rent

Under Florida Statutes, Section 83.595(1)(c), the landlord can sue the tenant for future rent if he or she takes possession for the benefit of the tenant.

Interest

A landlord is entitled to interest on the rent from the day it is due until the date of the judgment.

Double Rent   Under Florida Statutes, Section 83.58, if the tenant holds over at the end of the rental period, the landlord is entitled to double rent for the period during which the tenant refuses to surrender the dwelling unit.

✪   The landlord is not entitled to double rent when the tenant is evicted, only when he or she holds over at the expiration of the lease. 📖

✪   There can be double rent when a tenant holds over after a periodic tenancy even if there was no lease. 📖

Damage to the Premises   The landlord may sue the tenant for damage to the premises, but this does not include *normal wear and tear*.

Other Losses   A landlord may make a claim against the tenant for other losses related to the damage or breach.

📖   When a landlord lost rent while he was repairing the premises, he was allowed to claim this amount against the tenant. (*Waters v. Visage*, 20 Fla. Supp. 2d 93 (Co.Ct. Orange Co. 1986).)

Hearings

When asking for a money judgment in an eviction action, it is usually necessary to have two hearings. This is because the judgment for possession can be granted after five days, but a money judgment may not be granted until twenty days after the complaint was served.

Usually after the first hearing, the landlord is granted a **FINAL JUDGMENT— EVICTION** (form 39), and after the second hearing the landlord is granted a **FINAL JUDGMENT—DAMAGES** (form 40).

If the tenants move out prior to holding the first hearing, then it can be skipped. But, if it was already scheduled, be sure to check with the judge's office to see if it can be rescheduled after the twenty day period has ended. Also, if the first hearing is cancelled because the tenants move out, the **FINAL JUDGMENT—EVICTION** should also state that the landlord is entitled to possession to be sure the tenant does not make trouble later.

Defenses

Although the law states that failure to deposit rent into the registry of the court shall be an absolute waiver of all defenses, that only applies to the eviction portion of the case. The tenant is still able to assert any defenses he or she has to the money damages portion of the case. 📖

Liens

There are three types of landlord liens that can apply to tenant's property—statutory liens, judgments, and nonresidential statutory liens.

Statutory Liens   Under Florida Statutes, Section 713.691, a landlord is given a lien on the property of the tenant that has been brought onto the premises. (see Appendix B.)

✪   The statute states that a head of household can claim $1000 in exempt property; however, the Florida constitution gives that right to every natural person and not just heads of households. In any event, a landlord who does not want to risk getting into an extended court case with a tenant who has unlimited free legal aid would be advised to avoid using the lien. 📖

✪   One way the landlord's lien might be useful would be when following the procedures for abandoned property. The landlord's lien could be asserted against any surplus proceeds.

Judgments   If a court issues a money judgment against the tenant, it can be a lien against property of the tenant. First, by filing a certified copy of the judgment in the official records of any county you can make the judgment a lien on any real estate owned by the tenant. This lien is good for seven years but can be refilled twice for a total of up to twenty years. (You can obtain a certified copy of the judgment from the recording office where you file the judgment.)

Second, by filing a judgment lien certificate with the secretary of state you can make it a lien on personal property owned by the tenant anywhere in the state of Florida. This lien is good for five years and can be renewed for a second five years. Information on how to do this is available on the secretary of state's website:

www.sunbiz.org/corpweb/inquiry/jlien_info.html

Nonresidential Statutory Liens

A landlord has a lien for rent against property of the tenant. (Fla. Stat., Sec. 83.08-83.10.) The only property of the tenant which is exempt is wearing apparel, bedclothes, and beds. Since this law only applies to nonresidential tenancies, this may not seem to make sense, but the reason is that when the law was written, it applied to all tenancies. When the new residential law was passed, it was changed to apply to nonresidential tenancies, but this exemption was not removed.

Some other things about nonresidential statutory liens you should knows include the following.

- ✪ The lien can also be for loans made to the tenant.

- ✪ The landlord's lien is superior to all other liens on agricultural products raised on the land.

- ✪ The lien on property brought to the premise is superior to liens given after the date the property is placed on the land.

- ✪ The lien does not start on the tenant's other property until the county sheriff has made a *levy* on the property. This means that the sheriff either seizes the property or posts a notice on them that they are under the sheriff's control.

- ✪ A liquor license is not considered tangible property on which a landlord can have a lien. 📖

- ✪ The landlord's lien is superior to other "unperfected" liens. For example, if a store takes goods on consignment and the owners of the consigned goods do not perfect their liens on the goods by filing a UCC financing statement, then the landlord's lien is ahead of the rights of the owners of the goods. 📖

NOTE: *Before attempting to enforce a landlord's lien, be sure to consult an attorney. The law is complicated. For a horror story in which a court said a landlord could be liable for civil theft, see Seymore v. Adams, 638 So.2d 1044 (Fla. 1 DCA 1994).*

Distress for Rent and Replevin

In nonresidential tenancies there is a procedure for posting a bond and having the sheriff levy upon the tenant's property and forbid him or her to move it from the premises. (Fla. Stat., Sec. 83.12-.13.) It is called *distress for rent*. It is complicated and should be handled by an attorney. (Forms for this procedure are published by the Florida Bar in their continuing education legal forms workbook.)

In nonresidential tenancies, there is also a procedure called *replevin*, by which the property of the tenant may be sold to pay the rent owed to the landlord. (Fla. Stat., Sec. 83.13–.19.) The sale must be advertised and the landlord has the right to bid for the tenant's property.

NOTE: *A replevin action is complicated and should be handled by an attorney.*

12 SELF-SERVICE STORAGE SPACE

Sections 83.801 through 83.809 of the Landlord-Tenant Act apply to any real property designed and used for renting individual storage space to tenants who have access for storing and removing personal property.

If an owner issues a warehouse receipt or other receipt for property in storage, then the relationship of the parties is governed by Chapter 677 rather than these sections. Agreements entered into before July 1, 1982 are not covered by this law unless they were renewed or extended after July 1, 1982.

Withholding Access

After rent is five days overdue, the owner of a self-storage facility may withhold access to the property located in the unit without giving notice. (Fla. Stat., Sec. 83.8055.)

Liens

The owner of a self-storage facility has a lien for rent, labor, or other charges on the property in the unit. It does not matter whose property it is, the lien attaches to any property in the unit on the date it is brought to the facility. (Fla. Stat., Sec. 83.805–806.)

First, notice must be sent by registered mail to the last-known address of the tenant and posted in a conspicuous place at the facility. The notice must include:

- ✪ an itemized statement of the owner's claim, showing the sum due at the time of the notice and the date when the sum became due;

- ✪ the same description, or a reasonably similar description, of the personal property as provided in the rental agreement;

- ✪ a demand for payment within a specified time, not less than fourteen days after delivery of the notice;

- ✪ a conspicuous statement that, unless the claim is paid within the time stated in the notice, the personal property will be advertised for sale or other disposition, and will be sold or otherwise disposed of at a specified time and place; and,

- ✪ the name, street address, and telephone number of the owner whom the tenant may contact to respond to the notice.

After the fourteen days have passed, an advertisement for the sale or other disposition (which could mean to throw away) must be published once a week for two consecutive weeks in a newspaper of general circulation in the area. The property of several tenants may be listed in one ad if one sale will be held. The ad must include:

- ✪ a brief and general description of what is believed to constitute the personal property contained in the storage unit;

- ✪ the address of the self-service storage facility and the name of the tenant; and,

✪ the time, place, and manner of the sale or other disposition. The sale or other disposition shall take place not sooner than fifteen days after the first publication.

The final disposition must conform to the terms in the ad and must be in a *commercially reasonable manner*, which means the property may be sold in one lot, or individually if that is more reasonable, and the owner may buy at the sale.

Any time before the sale, the tenant may redeem the property by paying the money due plus the expenses in preparing for the sale.

The rights of purchasers at the sale and of the landlord to the proceeds are complicated by the complex laws of lien priority. For larger, expensive items of personal property, such as vehicles and machinery, a search for liens should be made through the Department of Motor Vehicles, the County Recorder's office, or the Secretary of State UCC division. Prior liens of this type would remain on the property. However, in most cases, the property is inexpensive personal items that would not have liens against it, and no future claims can be expected.

If there are excess funds after the sale, a notice must be sent to the tenant's last known address (even if the last notice came back unclaimed) and to any known lienholders. Either the tenant or a secured lienholder may claim the excess proceeds from the landlord within two years of the sale. If they are not claimed within this time, the landlord may keep them.

13 | MOBILE HOME PARKS

Several years ago, cases came to light in which owners of mobile home parks had taken terrible advantage of the mobile home owners who rented spaces in the parks. Because of the costs of moving and many other factors, the residents were at the mercy of the park owners. Some of the abuses were quite outrageous, and they inspired the Florida Legislature to pass laws protecting the residents.

Because of these situations, the explanation of the park owners' rights is beyond the scope of this book. Any park owner in a confrontation with the residents should carefully read the law that is contained in the Florida Statutes, Chapter 723, and should seek the counsel of an experienced attorney.

Parts of the law have already been declared unconstitutional. Perhaps other parts will also fall. The biggest weakness should be the fact that the legislature has confiscated property rights and given them to the residents without compensating the owners.

A brief summary of the major parts of the law is as follows.

- ✪ The law applies to parks of ten or more lots (but you cannot reduce the number of lots to avoid the law).

✪   Parks are regulated by the Division of Florida Land Sales, Condominiums, and Mobile Homes of the Department of Business Regulation.

✪   Fines for violations may be up to $5,000.

✪   Lot owners must pay an annual fee for each lot in their park.

✪   Parks with twenty-six or more lots must file a prospectus with the division, which contains certain language as described in Section 723.012.

✪   All advertising materials must be filed with the Division of Florida Land Sales, Condominiums, and Mobile Homes of the Department of Business Regulation.

✪   Publishing misleading information is prohibited.

✪   All dealings must be in good faith.

✪   Park owners must comply with all building, housing, and health codes.

✪   Park owners have no right of access to the mobile homes, except in emergencies.

✪   Rental agreements must comply with Sections 723.031 and .032.

✪   Rents must be reasonable.

✪   Rent increases are controlled by Section 723.037.

✪   Mediation is required in disputes.

✪   Tenants may not be required to purchase equipment from the park owner.

✪   Park owners may not charge extra for utilities.

✪   Sales of mobile homes may not be restricted.

✪   Evictions must follow the rules of Section 723.061, which requires a five-day notice for late rent.

✪   Tenants have a right to buy the park prior to its sale to someone else.

✪   Tenants have a right to buy any recreation facilities prior to their sale to someone else.

✪   Tenants must be notified of an application to change zoning.

Appendix A:
Table of Authorities—
Case Citations

The following appendix includes case citations to areas covered in the book. You will find the topic heading along with a page reference to its location. Under the topic heading will be a case or cases to support this area of landlord/tenant law.

Purcell v. Williams, 511 So.2d 1080 (Fla. 1 DCA 1980).

Buyer's Advantage Finance Co., Inc. v. Morse, 4 Florida Law Weekly Supplement (FLW Supp.) 475 (Co.Ct. Santa Rosa 1997).

Ferraro v. Parker, 229 So.2d 621 (Fla. 2 DCA 1969).

Saoud v. Skorski, 3 FLW Supp. 35 (Manatee Co. 1994).

Dehnel v. Paradise R.V. Resort, 588 So.2d 668 (1991).

Schoenbach v. VMS Realty, Inc., 503 So.2d 382 (Fla. 3 DCA 1987).

Haynes v. Lloyd, 533 So.2d 944 (Fla. 5 DCA 1988).

Veterans Gas Co. v. Gibbs, 538 So.2d 1325 (Fla. 1 DCA 1989).

Fitzgerald v. Cestari, SC, No. 75,538, Nov. 8, 1990.

Iber v. R.P.A. International Corp., 585 So.2d 367 (Fla 3 DCA 1991).

McDonald v. Wingard, 309 So.2d 192 (Fla. 1 DCA 1975).

Firth v. Marhoeffer, 406 So.2d 521 (Fla. 4 DCA 1981).

Vasquez v. Lopez, 509 So.2d 1241 (Fla. 4 DCA 1987).

Giaculli v. Bright, 584 So.2d 187 (Fla. 5 DCA 1991).

John's Pass Seafood Co. v. Weber, 369 So.2d 616 (Fla. 2 DCA 1969).

Lambert v. Doe, 453 So.2d 844 (Fla. 1 DCA 1984).

Paterson v. Deeb, 472 So.2d 1210 (Fla. 1 DCA 1985).

Holley v. Mt. Zion Terrace Apartments, Inc., 382 So.2d 98 (Fla. 3 DCA 1980).

Gonpere Corp. v. Rebull, 440 So.2d 1307 (Fla. 3 DCA 1983).

Perez v. Zazo, 498 So.2d 463 (Fla. 3 DCA 1986).

Green Cos. v. DiVincenzo, 432 So.2d 86 (Fla. 3 DCA 1983).

Bad Faith **95**

State v. De Anza Corp., 416 So.2d 1173 (1982).

Exceeding Jurisdictions **95**

Pearce v. Parsons, 414 So.2d 296 (Fla. 2 DCA 1982).

A-One Coin Laundry v. Waterside Towers, 561 So.2d 590 (Fla. 3 DCA 1990).

Negligence **95**

K.D. Lewis Ent. Corp., Inc. v. Smith, 445 So.2d 1032 (Fla. 5 DCA 1984).

Malicious Prosecution **95**

Blue v. Weinstein, 381 So.2d 308 (Fla. 3 DCA 1980).

Punitive Damages **95**

Club Eden Roc, Inc. v. Fortune Cookie Restaurant, Inc., 490 So.2d 210 (Fla. 3 DCA 1986).

K.D. Lewis Ent. Corp., Inc., v. Smith, 445 So.2d 1032 (Fla. 5 DCA 1984).

Guthartz v. Lewis, 408 So.2d 600 (Fla. 3 DCA 1981).

Moving Expenses **96**

Bruce v. Stork's Nest, Inc., 477 So.2d 51 (Fla. 2 DCA 1985).

Harassment **96**

Kamhi v. Waterview Towers Condominium Association, Inc., 793 So.2d 1033 (Fla. 4 DCA 2001).

Class Action **96**

K.D. Lewis Ent. Corp., Inc. v. Smith, 445 So.2d 1032 (Fla. 5 DCA 1984).

Civil Theft. *96*

Globe Communications Corp. v. 2112 Congress Assoc. Ltd., 538 So.2d 949 (Fla. 4 DCA 1989).

Pelletier v. Cutler, 543 So.2d 406 (Fla. 4 DCA 1989).

Abandonment after Dismissal. *97*

Beckwith v. Kesler, 2 FLW Supp. 82 (Broward Co. 1993).

Levenshon Emerald Park Partners, Ltd. v. Walantus, 3 FLW Supp. 556 (Broward Co. 1995).

Tenant's Appeal. *97*

Palm Beach Hts. Dv. & Sales Corp. v. Decillis, 385 So.2d 1170 (Fla. 3 DCA 1980).

Jenkins Trucking, Inc. v. Emmons, 207 So.2d 280 (Fla. 3 DCA 1968).

Filing after Judgment. *98*

In re Cowboys, Inc., 24 B.R. (S.D. Fla. 1982).

Landlord's Appeals. *99*

Dooley v. Culver, 392 So.2d 575 (Fla. 4 DCA 1980).

Motion for Rehearing. *99*

Miami Beach Equity Investors Ltd. Ptn. v. Granoff, 4 FLW Supp. 755 (11th Cir. 1997).

Residential. *101*

Pollard v. Alpert, 48 Fla. Supp. 2d 127 (Palm Beach Co. 1991).

APPENDIX B:
FLORIDA STATUTES

This appendix includes the following statutes that apply to landlord/tenant relationships:

- ✪ Section 51.011 Summary procedure

- ✪ Section 57.105 Attorney's fee; sanctions for raising unsupported claims or defenses

- ✪ Chapter 83 Landlord and Tenant

- ✪ Section 212.03 Transient rentals tax; rate, procedure, enforcement, exemptions

- ✪ Section 212.031 Tax on rental or license fee for use of real property

- ✪ Section 713.691 Landlord's lien for rent; exemptions

- ✪ Section 715.07 Storage of abandoned property

- ✪ Sections 715.10–715.111 Disposition of Personal Property Landlord and Tenant Act

51.011 Summary procedure.—The procedure in this section applies only to those actions specified by statute or rule. Rules of procedure apply to this section except when this section or the statute or rule prescribing this section provides a different procedure. If there is a difference between the time period prescribed in a rule and in this section, this section governs.

(1) PLEADINGS.—Plaintiff's initial pleading shall contain the matters required by the statute or rule prescribing this section or, if none is so required, shall state a cause of action. All defenses of law or fact shall be contained in defendant's answer which shall be filed within 5 days after service of process. If the answer incorporates a counterclaim, plaintiff shall include all defenses of law or fact in his or her answer to the counterclaim and shall serve it within 5 days after service of the counterclaim. No other pleadings are permitted. All defensive motions, including motions to quash, shall be heard by the court prior to trial.

(2) DISCOVERY.—Depositions on oral examination may be taken by any party at any time. Other discovery and admissions may be had only on order of court setting the time for compliance. No discovery postpones the time for trial except for good cause shown or by stipulation of the parties.

(3) JURY.—If a jury trial is authorized by law, any party may demand it in any pleading or by a separate paper served not later than 5 days after the action comes to issue. When a jury is in attendance at the close of pleading or the time of demand for jury trial, the action may be tried immediately; otherwise, the court shall order a special venire to be summoned immediately. If a special venire be summoned, the party demanding the jury shall deposit sufficient money with the clerk to pay the jury fees which shall be taxed as costs if he or she prevails.

(4) NEW TRIAL.—Motion for new trial shall be filed and served within 5 days after verdict, if a jury trial was had, or after entry of judgment, if trial was by the court. A reserved motion for directed verdict shall be renewed within the period for moving for a new trial.

(5) APPEAL.—Notice of appeal shall be filed and served within 30 days from the rendition of the judgment appealed from.

57.105 Attorney's fee; sanctions for raising unsupported claims or defenses; service of motions; damages for delay of litigation.—

(1) Upon the court's initiative or motion of any party, the court shall award a reasonable attorney's fee to be paid to the prevailing party in equal amounts by the losing party and the losing party's attorney on any claim or defense at any time during a civil proceeding or action in which the court finds that the losing party or the losing party's attorney knew or should have known that a claim or defense when initially presented to the court or at any time before trial:

(a) Was not supported by the material facts necessary to establish the claim or defense; or

(b) Would not be supported by the application of then-existing law to those material facts.

However, the losing party's attorney is not personally responsible if he or she has acted in good faith, based on the representations of his or her client as to the existence of those material facts. If the court awards attorney's fees to a claimant pursuant to this subsection, the court shall also award prejudgment interest.

(2) Paragraph (1)(b) does not apply if the court determines that the claim or defense was initially presented to the court as a good faith argument for the extension, modification, or reversal of existing law or the establishment of new law, as it applied to the material facts, with a reasonable expectation of success.

(3) At any time in any civil proceeding or action in which the moving party proves by a preponderance of the evidence that any action taken by the opposing party, including, but not limited to, the filing of any pleading or part thereof, the assertion of or response to any discovery demand, the assertion of any claim or defense, or the response to any request by any other party, was taken primarily for the purpose of unreasonable delay, the court shall award damages to the moving party for its reasonable expenses incurred in obtaining the order, which may include attorney's fees, and other loss resulting from the improper delay.

(4) A motion by a party seeking sanctions under this section must be served but may not be filed with or presented to the court unless, within 21 days after service of the motion, the challenged paper, claim, defense, contention, allegation, or denial is not withdrawn or appropriately corrected.

(5) In administrative proceedings under chapter 120, an administrative law judge shall award a reasonable attorney's fee and damages to be paid to the prevailing party in equal amounts by the losing party and a losing party's attorney or qualified representative in the same manner and upon the same basis as provided in subsections (1)-(4). Such award shall be a final order subject to judicial review pursuant to s. 120.68. If the losing party is an agency as defined in s. 120.52(1), the award to the prevailing party shall be against and paid by the agency. A voluntary dismissal by a nonprevailing party does not divest the administrative law judge of jurisdiction to make the award described in this subsection.

(6) The provisions of this section are supplemental to other sanctions or remedies available under law or under court rules.

(7) If a contract contains a provision allowing attorney's fees to a party when he or she is required to take any action to enforce the contract, the court may also allow reasonable attorney's fees to the other party when that party prevails in any action, whether as plaintiff or defendant, with respect to the contract. This subsection applies to any contract entered into on or after October 1, 1988.

CHAPTER 83

LANDLORD AND TENANT

PART I

NONRESIDENTIAL TENANCIES (ss. 83.001-83.251)

PART II

RESIDENTIAL TENANCIES (ss. 83.40-83.682)

PART III

SELF-SERVICE STORAGE SPACE (ss. 83.801-83.809)

PART I

NONRESIDENTIAL TENANCIES

83.001 Application.

83.01 Unwritten lease tenancy at will; duration.

83.02 Certain written leases tenancies at will; duration.

83.03 Termination of tenancy at will; length of notice.

83.04 Holding over after term, tenancy at sufferance, etc.

83.05 Right of possession upon default in rent; determination of right of possession in action or surrender or abandonment of premises.

83.06 Right to demand double rent upon refusal to deliver possession.

83.07 Action for use and occupation.

83.08 Landlord's lien for rent.

83.09 Exemptions from liens for rent.

83.10 Landlord's lien for advances.

83.11 Distress for rent; complaint.

83.12 Distress writ.

83.13 Levy of writ.

83.135 Dissolution of writ.

83.14 Replevy of distrained property.

83.15 Claims by third persons.

83.18 Distress for rent; trial; verdict; judgment.

83.19 Sale of property distrained.

83.20 Causes for removal of tenants.

83.201 Notice to landlord of failure to maintain or repair, rendering premises wholly untenantable; right to withhold rent.

83.202 Waiver of right to proceed with eviction claim.

83.21 Removal of tenant.

83.22 Removal of tenant; service.

83.231 Removal of tenant; judgment.

83.232 Rent paid into registry of court.

83.241 Removal of tenant; process.

83.251 Removal of tenant; costs.

83.001 Application.—This part applies to nonresidential tenancies and all tenancies not governed by part II of this chapter.

83.01 Unwritten lease tenancy at will; duration.—Any lease of lands and tenements, or either, made shall be deemed and held to be a tenancy at will unless it shall be in writing signed by the lessor. Such tenancy shall be from year to year, or quarter to quarter, or month to month, or week to week, to be determined by the periods at which the rent is payable. If the rent is payable weekly, then the tenancy shall be from week to week; if payable monthly, then from month to month; if payable quarterly, then from quarter to quarter; if payable yearly, then from year to year.

83.02 Certain written leases tenancies at will; duration.—Where any tenancy has been created by an instrument in writing from year to year, or quarter to quarter, or month to month, or week to week, to be determined by the periods at which the rent is payable, and the term of which tenancy is unlimited, the tenancy shall be a tenancy at will. If the rent is payable weekly, then the tenancy shall be from week to week; if payable monthly, then the tenancy shall

be from month to month; if payable quarterly, then from quarter to quarter; if payable yearly, then from year to year.

83.03 Termination of tenancy at will; length of notice.—A tenancy at will may be terminated by either party giving notice as follows:

(1) Where the tenancy is from year to year, by giving not less than 3 months' notice prior to the end of any annual period;

(2) Where the tenancy is from quarter to quarter, by giving not less than 45 days' notice prior to the end of any quarter;

(3) Where the tenancy is from month to month, by giving not less than 15 days' notice prior to the end of any monthly period; and

(4) Where the tenancy is from week to week, by giving not less than 7 days' notice prior to the end of any weekly period.

83.04 Holding over after term, tenancy at sufferance, etc.—When any tenancy created by an instrument in writing, the term of which is limited, has expired and the tenant holds over in the possession of said premises without renewing the lease by some further instrument in writing then such holding over shall be construed to be a tenancy at sufferance. The mere payment or acceptance of rent shall not be construed to be a renewal of the term, but if the holding over be continued with the written consent of the lessor then the tenancy shall become a tenancy at will under the provisions of this law.

83.05 Right of possession upon default in rent; determination of right of possession in action or surrender or abandonment of premises.—

(1) If any person leasing or renting any land or premises other than a dwelling unit fails to pay the rent at the time it becomes due, the lessor has the right to obtain possession of the premises as provided by law.

(2) The landlord shall recover possession of rented premises only:

(a) In an action for possession under s. 83.20, or other civil action in which the issue of right of possession is determined;

(b) When the tenant has surrendered possession of the rented premises to the landlord; or

(c) When the tenant has abandoned the rented premises.

(3) In the absence of actual knowledge of abandonment, it shall be presumed for purposes of paragraph (2)(c) that the tenant has abandoned the rented premises if:

(a) The landlord reasonably believes that the tenant has been absent from the rented premises for a period of 30 consecutive days;

(b) The rent is not current; and

(c) A notice pursuant to s. 83.20(2) has been served and 10 days have elapsed since service of such notice.

However, this presumption does not apply if the rent is current or the tenant has notified the landlord in writing of an intended absence.

83.06 Right to demand double rent upon refusal to deliver possession.—

(1) When any tenant refuses to give up possession of the premises at the end of the tenant's lease, the landlord, the landlord's agent, attorney, or legal representatives, may demand of such ten-

ant double the monthly rent, and may recover the same at the expiration of every month, or in the same proportion for a longer or shorter time by distress, in the manner pointed out hereinafter.

(2) All contracts for rent, verbal or in writing, shall bear interest from the time the rent becomes due, any law, usage or custom to the contrary notwithstanding.

83.07 Action for use and occupation.—Any landlord, the landlord's heirs, executors, administrators or assigns may recover reasonable damages for any house, lands, tenements, or hereditaments held or occupied by any person by the landlord's permission in an action on the case for the use and occupation of the lands, tenements, or hereditaments when they are not held, occupied by or under agreement or demise by deed; and if on trial of any action, any demise or agreement (not being by deed) whereby a certain rent was reserved is given in evidence, the plaintiff shall not be dismissed but may make use thereof as an evidence of the quantum of damages to be recovered.

83.08 Landlord's lien for rent.—Every person to whom rent may be due, the person's heirs, executors, administrators or assigns, shall have a lien for such rent upon the property found upon or off the premises leased or rented, and in the possession of any person, as follows:

(1) Upon agricultural products raised on the land leased or rented for the current year. This lien shall be superior to all other liens, though of older date.

(2) Upon all other property of the lessee or his or her sublessee or assigns, usually kept on the premises. This lien shall be superior to any lien acquired subsequent to the bringing of the property on the premises leased.

(3) Upon all other property of the defendant. This lien shall date from the levy of the distress warrant hereinafter provided.

83.09 Exemptions from liens for rent.—No property of any tenant or lessee shall be exempt from distress and sale for rent, except beds, bedclothes and wearing apparel.

83.10 Landlord's lien for advances.—Landlords shall have a lien on the crop grown on rented land for advances made in money or other things of value, whether made directly by them or at their instance and requested by another person, or for which they have assumed a legal responsibility, at or before the time at which such advances were made, for the sustenance or well-being of the tenant or the tenant's family, or for preparing the ground for cultivation, or for cultivating, gathering, saving, handling, or preparing the crop for market. They shall have a lien also upon each and every article advanced, and upon all property purchased with money advanced, or obtained, by barter or exchange for any articles advanced, for the aggregate value or price of all the property or articles so advanced. The liens upon the crop shall be of equal dignity with liens for rent, and upon the articles advanced shall be paramount to all other liens.

83.11 Distress for rent; complaint.—Any person to whom any rent or money for advances is due or the person's agent or attorney may file an action in the court in the county where the land lies having jurisdiction of the amount claimed, and the court shall have jurisdiction to order the relief provided in this part. The complaint shall be verified and shall allege the name and relationship of the defendant to the plaintiff, how the obligation for rent arose, the amount or quality and value of the rent due for such land, or

the advances, and whether payable in money, an agricultural product, or any other thing of value.

83.12 Distress writ.—A distress writ shall be issued by a judge of the court which has jurisdiction of the amount claimed. The writ shall enjoin the defendant from damaging, disposing of, secreting, or removing any property liable to distress from the rented real property after the time of service of the writ until the sheriff levies on the property, the writ is vacated, or the court otherwise orders. A violation of the command of the writ may be punished as a contempt of court. If the defendant does not move for dissolution of the writ as provided in s. 83.135, the sheriff shall, pursuant to a further order of the court, levy on the property liable to distress forthwith after the time for answering the complaint has expired. Before the writ issues, the plaintiff or the plaintiff's agent or attorney shall file a bond with surety to be approved by the clerk payable to defendant in at least double the sum demanded or, if property, in double the value of the property sought to be levied on, conditioned to pay all costs and damages which defendant sustains in consequence of plaintiff's improperly suing out the distress.

83.13 Levy of writ.—The sheriff shall execute the writ by service on defendant and, upon the order of the court, by levy on property distrainable for rent or advances, if found in the sheriff's jurisdiction. If the property is in another jurisdiction, the party who had the writ issued shall deliver the writ to the sheriff in the other jurisdiction; and that sheriff shall execute the writ, upon order of the court, by levying on the property and delivering it to the sheriff of the county in which the action is pending, to be disposed of according to law, unless he or she is ordered by the court from which the writ emanated to hold the property and dispose of it in his or her jurisdiction according to law. If the plaintiff shows by a sworn statement that the defendant cannot be found within the state, the levy on the property suffices as service on the defendant.

83.135 Dissolution of writ.—The defendant may move for dissolution of a distress writ at any time. The court shall hear the motion not later than the day on which the sheriff is authorized under the writ to levy on property liable under distress. If the plaintiff proves a prima facie case, or if the defendant defaults, the court shall order the sheriff to proceed with the levy.

83.14 Replevy of distrained property.—The property distrained may be restored to the defendant at any time on the defendant's giving bond with surety to the sheriff levying the writ. The bond shall be approved by such sheriff; made payable to plaintiff in double the value of the property levied on, with the value to be fixed by the sheriff; and conditioned for the forthcoming of the property restored to abide the final order of the court. It may be also restored to defendant on defendant's giving bond with surety to be approved by the sheriff making the levy conditioned to pay the plaintiff the amount or value of the rental or advances which may be adjudicated to be payable to plaintiff. Judgment may be entered against the surety on such bonds in the manner and with like effect as provided in s. 76.31.

83.15 Claims by third persons.—Any third person claiming any property so distrained may interpose and prosecute his or her claim for it in the same manner as is provided in similar cases of claim to property levied on under execution.

83.18 Distress for rent; trial; verdict; judgment.—If the verdict or the finding of the court is for plaintiff, judgment shall be rendered against defendant for the amount or value of the rental or advances, including interest and costs, and against the surety on defendant's bond as provided for in s. 83.14, if the property has been restored to defendant, and execution shall issue. If the verdict or the finding of the court is for defendant, the action shall be dismissed and defendant shall have judgment and execution against plaintiff for costs.

83.19 Sale of property distrained.—

(1) If the judgment is for plaintiff and the property in whole or in part has not been replevied, it, or the part not restored to the defendant, shall be sold and the proceeds applied on the payment of the execution. If the rental or any part of it is due in agricultural products and the property distrained, or any part of it, is of a similar kind to that claimed in the complaint, the property up to a quantity to be adjudged of by the officer holding the execution (not exceeding that claimed), may be delivered to the plaintiff as a payment on the plaintiff's execution at his or her request.

(2) When any property levied on is sold, it shall be advertised two times, the first advertisement being at least 10 days before the sale. All property so levied on shall be sold at the location advertised in the notice of sheriff's sale.

(3) Before the sale if defendant appeals and obtains supersedeas and pays all costs accrued up to the time that the supersedeas becomes operative, the property shall be restored to defendant and there shall be no sale.

(4) In case any property is sold to satisfy any rent payable in cotton or other agricultural product or thing, the officer shall settle with the plaintiff at the value of the rental at the time it became due.

83.20 Causes for removal of tenants.—Any tenant or lessee at will or sufferance, or for part of the year, or for one or more years, of any houses, lands or tenements, and the assigns, under tenants or legal representatives of such tenant or lessee, may be removed from the premises in the manner hereinafter provided in the following cases:

(1) Where such person holds over and continues in the possession of the demised premises, or any part thereof, after the expiration of the person's time, without the permission of the person's landlord.

(2) Where such person holds over without permission as aforesaid, after any default in the payment of rent pursuant to the agreement under which the premises are held, and 3 days' notice in writing requiring the payment of the rent or the possession of the premises has been served by the person entitled to the rent on the person owing the same. The service of the notice shall be by delivery of a true copy thereof, or, if the tenant is absent from the rented premises, by leaving a copy thereof at such place.

(3) Where such person holds over without permission after failing to cure a material breach of the lease or oral agreement, other than nonpayment of rent, and when 15 days' written notice requiring the cure of such breach or the possession of the premises has been served on the tenant. This subsection applies only when the lease is silent on the matter or when the tenancy is an oral one at will. The notice may give a longer time period for cure of the breach or surrender of the premises. In the absence of a lease provision prescribing the method for serving notices, service must be by mail, hand delivery, or, if the tenant is absent from the rental premises or the address designated by the lease, by posting.

83.201 Notice to landlord of failure to maintain or repair, rendering premises wholly untenantable; right to withhold rent.—When the lease is silent on the procedure to be followed to effect repair or maintenance and the payment of rent relating thereto, yet affirmatively and expressly places the obligation for same upon the landlord, and the landlord has failed or refused to do so, rendering the leased premises wholly untenantable, the tenant may withhold rent after notice to the landlord. The tenant shall serve the landlord, in the manner prescribed by s. 83.20(3), with a written notice declaring the premises to be wholly untenantable, giving the landlord at least 20 days to make the specifically described repair or maintenance, and stating that the tenant will withhold the rent for the next rental period and thereafter until the repair or maintenance has been performed. The lease may provide for a longer period of time for repair or maintenance. Once the landlord has completed the repair or maintenance, the tenant shall pay the landlord the amounts of rent withheld. If the landlord does not complete the repair or maintenance in the allotted time, the parties may extend the time by written agreement or the tenant may abandon the premises, retain the amounts of rent withheld, terminate the lease, and avoid any liability for future rent or charges under the lease. This section is cumulative to other existing remedies, and this section does not prevent any tenant from exercising his or her other remedies.

83.202 Waiver of right to proceed with eviction claim.—The landlord's acceptance of the full amount of rent past due, with knowledge of the tenant's breach of the lease by nonpayment, shall be considered a waiver of the landlord's right to proceed with an eviction claim for nonpayment of that rent. Acceptance of the rent includes conduct by the landlord concerning any tender of the rent by the tenant which is inconsistent with reasonably prompt return of the payment to the tenant.

83.21 Removal of tenant.—The landlord, the landlord's attorney or agent, applying for the removal of any tenant, shall file a complaint stating the facts which authorize the removal of the tenant, and describing the premises in the proper court of the county where the premises are situated and is entitled to the summary procedure provided in s. 51.011.

83.22 Removal of tenant; service.—

(1) After at least two attempts to obtain service as provided by law, if the defendant cannot be found in the county in which the action is pending and either the defendant has no usual place of abode in the county or there is no person 15 years of age or older residing at the defendant's usual place of abode in the county, the sheriff shall serve the summons by attaching it to some part of the premises involved in the proceeding. The minimum time delay between the two attempts to obtain service shall be 6 hours.

(2) If a landlord causes, or anticipates causing, a defendant to be served with a summons and complaint solely by attaching them to some conspicuous part of the premises involved in the proceeding, the landlord shall provide the clerk of the court with two additional copies of the complaint and two prestamped envelopes addressed to the defendant. One envelope shall be addressed to such address or location as has been designated by the tenant for receipt of notice in a written lease or other agreement or, if none has been designated, to the residence of the tenant, if known. The second envelope shall be addressed to the last known business address of the tenant. The clerk of the court shall immediately mail

the copies of the summons and complaint by first-class mail, note the fact of mailing in the docket, and file a certificate in the court file of the fact and date of mailing. Service shall be effective on the date of posting or mailing, whichever occurs later; and at least 5 days from the date of service must have elapsed before a judgment for final removal of the defendant may be entered.

83.231 Removal of tenant; judgment.—If the issues are found for plaintiff, judgment shall be entered that plaintiff recover possession of the premises. If the plaintiff expressly and specifically sought money damages in the complaint, in addition to awarding possession of the premises to the plaintiff, the court shall also direct, in an amount which is within its jurisdictional limitations, the entry of a money judgment in favor of the plaintiff and against the defendant for the amount of money found due, owing, and unpaid by the defendant, with costs. However, no money judgment shall be entered unless service of process has been effected by personal service or, where authorized by law, by certified or registered mail, return receipt, or in any other manner prescribed by law or the rules of the court, and no money judgment may be entered except in compliance with the Florida Rules of Civil Procedure. Where otherwise authorized by law, the plaintiff in the judgment for possession and money damages may also be awarded attorney's fees and costs. If the issues are found for defendant, judgment shall be entered dismissing the action.

Note.—Former s. 83.34.

83.232 Rent paid into registry of court.—

(1) In an action by the landlord which includes a claim for possession of real property, the tenant shall pay into the court registry the amount alleged in the complaint as unpaid, or if such amount is contested, such amount as is determined by the court, and any rent accruing during the pendency of the action, when due, unless the tenant has interposed the defense of payment or satisfaction of the rent in the amount the complaint alleges as unpaid. Unless the tenant disputes the amount of accrued rent, the tenant must pay the amount alleged in the complaint into the court registry on or before the date on which his or her answer to the claim for possession is due. If the tenant contests the amount of accrued rent, the tenant must pay the amount determined by the court into the court registry on the day that the court makes its determination. The court may, however, extend these time periods to allow for later payment, upon good cause shown. Even though the defense of payment or satisfaction has been asserted, the court, in its discretion, may order the tenant to pay into the court registry the rent that accrues during the pendency of the action, the time of accrual being as set forth in the lease. If the landlord is in actual danger of loss of the premises or other hardship resulting from the loss of rental income from the premises, the landlord may apply to the court for disbursement of all or part of the funds so held in the court registry.

(2) If the tenant contests the amount of money to be placed into the court registry, any hearing regarding such dispute shall be limited to only the factual or legal issues concerning:

(a) Whether the tenant has been properly credited by the landlord with any and all rental payments made; and

(b) What properly constitutes rent under the provisions of the lease.

(3) The court, on its own motion, shall notify the tenant of the requirement that rent be paid into the court registry by order, which shall be issued immediately upon filing of the tenant's initial pleading, motion, or other paper.

(4) The filing of a counterclaim for money damages does not relieve the tenant from depositing rent due into the registry of the court.

(5) Failure of the tenant to pay the rent into the court registry pursuant to court order shall be deemed an absolute waiver of the tenant's defenses. In such case, the landlord is entitled to an immediate default for possession without further notice or hearing thereon.

83.241 Removal of tenant; process.—After entry of judgment in favor of plaintiff the clerk shall issue a writ to the sheriff describing the premises and commanding the sheriff to put plaintiff in possession.

Note.—Former s. 83.35.

83.251 Removal of tenant; costs.—The prevailing party shall have judgment for costs and execution shall issue therefor.

Note.—Former s. 83.37.

PART II

RESIDENTIAL TENANCIES

83.40 Short title.

83.41 Application.

83.42 Exclusions from application of part.

83.43 Definitions.

83.44 Obligation of good faith.

83.45 Unconscionable rental agreement or provision.

83.46 Rent; duration of tenancies.

83.47 Prohibited provisions in rental agreements.

83.48 Attorney's fees.

83.49 Deposit money or advance rent; duty of landlord and tenant.

83.50 Disclosure.

83.51 Landlord's obligation to maintain premises.

83.52 Tenant's obligation to maintain dwelling unit.

83.53 Landlord's access to dwelling unit.

83.535 Flotation bedding system; restrictions on use.

83.54 Enforcement of rights and duties; civil action.

83.55 Right of action for damages.

83.56 Termination of rental agreement.

83.57 Termination of tenancy without specific term.

83.575 Termination of tenancy with specific duration.

83.58 Remedies; tenant holding over.

83.59 Right of action for possession.

83.595 Choice of remedies upon breach by tenant.

83.60 Defenses to action for rent or possession; procedure.

83.61 Disbursement of funds in registry of court; prompt final hearing.

83.62 Restoration of possession to landlord.

83.625 Power to award possession and enter money judgment.

83.63 Casualty damage.

83.64 Retaliatory conduct.

83.67 Prohibited practices.

83.681 Orders to enjoin violations of this part.

83.682 Termination of rental agreement by a servicemember.

83.40 Short title.—This part shall be known as the "Florida Residential Landlord and Tenant Act."

83.41 Application.—This part applies to the rental of a dwelling unit.

83.42 Exclusions from application of part.—This part does not apply to:

(1) Residency or detention in a facility, whether public or private, when residence or detention is incidental to the provision of medical, geriatric, educational, counseling, religious, or similar services.

(2) Occupancy under a contract of sale of a dwelling unit or the property of which it is a part.

(3) Transient occupancy in a hotel, condominium, motel, roominghouse, or similar public lodging, or transient occupancy in a mobile home park.

(4) Occupancy by a holder of a proprietary lease in a cooperative apartment.

(5) Occupancy by an owner of a condominium unit.

83.43 Definitions.—As used in this part, the following words and terms shall have the following meanings unless some other meaning is plainly indicated:

(1) "Building, housing, and health codes" means any law, ordinance, or governmental regulation concerning health, safety, sanitation or fitness for habitation, or the construction, maintenance, operation, occupancy, use, or appearance, of any dwelling unit.

(2) "Dwelling unit" means:

(a) A structure or part of a structure that is rented for use as a home, residence, or sleeping place by one person or by two or more persons who maintain a common household.

(b) A mobile home rented by a tenant.

(c) A structure or part of a structure that is furnished, with or without rent, as an incident of employment for use as a home, residence, or sleeping place by one or more persons.

(3) "Landlord" means the owner or lessor of a dwelling unit.

(4) "Tenant" means any person entitled to occupy a dwelling unit under a rental agreement.

(5) "Premises" means a dwelling unit and the structure of which it is a part and a mobile home lot and the appurtenant facilities and grounds, areas, facilities, and property held out for the use of tenants generally.

(6) "Rent" means the periodic payments due the landlord from the tenant for occupancy under a rental agreement and any other pay-ments due the landlord from the tenant as may be designated as rent in a written rental agreement.

(7) "Rental agreement" means any written agreement, or oral agreement if for less duration than 1 year, providing for use and occupancy of premises.

(8) "Good faith" means honesty in fact in the conduct or transaction concerned.

(9) "Advance rent" means moneys paid to the landlord to be applied to future rent payment periods, but does not include rent paid in advance for a current rent payment period.

(10) "Transient occupancy" means occupancy when it is the intention of the parties that the occupancy will be temporary.

(11) "Deposit money" means any money held by the landlord on behalf of the tenant, including, but not limited to, damage deposits, security deposits, advance rent deposit, pet deposit, or any contractual deposit agreed to between landlord and tenant either in writing or orally.

(12) "Security deposits" means any moneys held by the landlord as security for the performance of the rental agreement, including, but not limited to, monetary damage to the landlord caused by the tenant's breach of lease prior to the expiration thereof.

(13) "Legal holiday" means holidays observed by the clerk of the court.

(14) "Servicemember" shall have the same meaning as provided in s. 250.01.

(15) "Active duty" shall have the same meaning as provided in s. 250.01.

(16) "State active duty" shall have the same meaning as provided in s. 250.01.

83.44 Obligation of good faith.—Every rental agreement or duty within this part imposes an obligation of good faith in its performance or enforcement.

83.45 Unconscionable rental agreement or provision.—

(1) If the court as a matter of law finds a rental agreement or any provision of a rental agreement to have been unconscionable at the time it was made, the court may refuse to enforce the rental agreement, enforce the remainder of the rental agreement without the unconscionable provision, or so limit the application of any unconscionable provision as to avoid any unconscionable result.

(2) When it is claimed or appears to the court that the rental agreement or any provision thereof may be unconscionable, the parties shall be afforded a reasonable opportunity to present evidence as to meaning, relationship of the parties, purpose, and effect to aid the court in making the determination.

83.46 Rent; duration of tenancies.—

(1) Unless otherwise agreed, rent is payable without demand or notice; periodic rent is payable at the beginning of each rent payment period; and rent is uniformly apportionable from day to day.

(2) If the rental agreement contains no provision as to duration of the tenancy, the duration is determined by the periods for which the rent is payable. If the rent is payable weekly, then the tenancy is from week to week; if payable monthly, tenancy is from month to month; if payable quarterly, tenancy is from quarter to quarter; if payable yearly, tenancy is from year to year.

(3) If the dwelling unit is furnished without rent as an incident of employment and there is no agreement as to the duration of the tenancy, the duration is determined by the periods for which wages are payable. If wages are payable weekly or more frequently, then the tenancy is from week to week; and if wages are payable monthly or no wages are payable, then the tenancy is from month to month. In the event that the employee ceases employment, the employer shall be entitled to rent for the period from the day after the employee ceases employment until the day that the dwelling unit is vacated at a rate equivalent to the rate charged for similarly situated residences in the area. This subsection shall not apply to an employee or a resident manager of an apartment house or an apartment complex when there is a written agreement to the contrary.

83.47 Prohibited provisions in rental agreements.—

(1) A provision in a rental agreement is void and unenforceable to the extent that it:

(a) Purports to waive or preclude the rights, remedies, or requirements set forth in this part.

(b) Purports to limit or preclude any liability of the landlord to the tenant or of the tenant to the landlord, arising under law.

(2) If such a void and unenforceable provision is included in a rental agreement entered into, extended, or renewed after the effective date of this part and either party suffers actual damages as a result of the inclusion, the aggrieved party may recover those damages sustained after the effective date of this part.

83.48 Attorney's fees.—In any civil action brought to enforce the provisions of the rental agreement or this part, the party in whose favor a judgment or decree has been rendered may recover reasonable court costs, including attorney's fees, from the nonprevailing party.

83.49 Deposit money or advance rent; duty of landlord and tenant.—

(1) Whenever money is deposited or advanced by a tenant on a rental agreement as security for performance of the rental agreement or as advance rent for other than the next immediate rental period, the landlord or the landlord's agent shall either:

(a) Hold the total amount of such money in a separate non-interest-bearing account in a Florida banking institution for the benefit of the tenant or tenants. The landlord shall not commingle such moneys with any other funds of the landlord or hypothecate, pledge, or in any other way make use of such moneys until such moneys are actually due the landlord;

(b) Hold the total amount of such money in a separate interest-bearing account in a Florida banking institution for the benefit of the tenant or tenants, in which case the tenant shall receive and collect interest in an amount of at least 75 percent of the annualized average interest rate payable on such account or interest at the rate of 5 percent per year, simple interest, whichever the landlord elects. The landlord shall not commingle such moneys with any other funds of the landlord or hypothecate, pledge, or in any other way make use of such moneys until such moneys are actually due the landlord; or

(c) Post a surety bond, executed by the landlord as principal and a surety company authorized and licensed to do business in the state as surety, with the clerk of the circuit court in the county in which the dwelling unit is located in the total amount of the security deposits and advance rent he or she holds on behalf of the tenants or $50,000, whichever is less. The bond shall be conditioned upon the faithful compliance of the landlord with the provisions of this section and shall run to the Governor for the benefit of any tenant injured by the landlord's violation of the provisions of this section. In addition to posting the surety bond, the landlord shall pay to the tenant interest at the rate of 5 percent per year, simple interest. A landlord, or the landlord's agent, engaged in the renting of dwelling units in five or more counties, who holds deposit moneys or advance rent and who is otherwise subject to the provisions of this section, may, in lieu of posting a surety bond in each county, elect to post a surety bond in the form and manner provided in this paragraph with the office of the Secretary of State. The bond shall be in the total amount of the security deposit or advance rent held on behalf of tenants or in the amount of $250,000, whichever is less. The bond shall be conditioned upon the faithful compliance of the landlord with the provisions of this section and shall run to the Governor for the benefit of any tenant injured by the landlord's violation of this section. In addition to posting a surety bond, the landlord shall pay to the tenant interest on the security deposit or advance rent held on behalf of that tenant at the rate of 5 percent per year simple interest.

(2) The landlord shall, within 30 days of receipt of advance rent or a security deposit, notify the tenant in writing of the manner in which the landlord is holding the advance rent or security deposit and the rate of interest, if any, which the tenant is to receive and the time of interest payments to the tenant. Such written notice shall:

(a) Be given in person or by mail to the tenant.

(b) State the name and address of the depository where the advance rent or security deposit is being held, whether the advance rent or security deposit is being held in a separate account for the benefit of the tenant or is commingled with other funds of the landlord, and, if commingled, whether such funds are deposited in an interest-bearing account in a Florida banking institution.

(c) Include a copy of the provisions of subsection (3).

Subsequent to providing such notice, if the landlord changes the manner or location in which he or she is holding the advance rent or security deposit, he or she shall notify the tenant within 30 days of the change according to the provisions herein set forth. This subsection does not apply to any landlord who rents fewer than five individual dwelling units. Failure to provide this notice shall not be a defense to the payment of rent when due.

(3)(a) Upon the vacating of the premises for termination of the lease, if the landlord does not intend to impose a claim on the security deposit, the landlord shall have 15 days to return the security deposit together with interest if otherwise required, or the landlord shall have 30 days to give the tenant written notice by certified mail to the tenant's last known mailing address of his or her intention to impose a claim on the deposit and the reason for imposing the claim. The notice shall contain a statement in substantially the following form:

This is a notice of my intention to impose a claim for damages in the amount of _____ upon your security deposit, due to _____.

It is sent to you as required by s. 83.49(3), Florida Statutes. You are hereby notified that you must object in writing to this deduction from your security deposit within 15 days from the time you receive this notice or I will be authorized to deduct my claim from your security deposit. Your objection must be sent to (landlord's address) .

If the landlord fails to give the required notice within the 30-day period, he or she forfeits the right to impose a claim upon the security deposit.

(b) Unless the tenant objects to the imposition of the landlord's claim or the amount thereof within 15 days after receipt of the landlord's notice of intention to impose a claim, the landlord may then deduct the amount of his or her claim and shall remit the balance of the deposit to the tenant within 30 days after the date of the notice of intention to impose a claim for damages.

(c) If either party institutes an action in a court of competent jurisdiction to adjudicate the party's right to the security deposit, the prevailing party is entitled to receive his or her court costs plus a reasonable fee for his or her attorney. The court shall advance the cause on the calendar.

(d) Compliance with this section by an individual or business entity authorized to conduct business in this state, including Florida-licensed real estate brokers and sales associates, shall constitute compliance with all other relevant Florida Statutes pertaining to security deposits held pursuant to a rental agreement or other landlord-tenant relationship. Enforcement personnel shall look solely to this section to determine compliance. This section prevails over any conflicting provisions in chapter 475 and in other sections of the Florida Statutes, and shall operate to permit licensed real estate brokers to disburse security deposits and deposit money without having to comply with the notice and settlement procedures contained in s. 475.25(1)(d).

(4) The provisions of this section do not apply to transient rentals by hotels or motels as defined in chapter 509; nor do they apply in those instances in which the amount of rent or deposit, or both, is regulated by law or by rules or regulations of a public body, including public housing authorities and federally administered or regulated housing programs including s. 202, s. 221(d)(3) and (4), s. 236, or s. 8 of the National Housing Act, as amended, other than for rent stabilization. With the exception of subsections (3), (5), and (6), this section is not applicable to housing authorities or public housing agencies created pursuant to chapter 421 or other statutes.

(5) Except when otherwise provided by the terms of a written lease, any tenant who vacates or abandons the premises prior to the expiration of the term specified in the written lease, or any tenant who vacates or abandons premises which are the subject of a tenancy from week to week, month to month, quarter to quarter, or year to year, shall give at least 7 days' written notice by certified mail or personal delivery to the landlord prior to vacating or abandoning the premises which notice shall include the address where the tenant may be reached. Failure to give such notice shall relieve the landlord of the notice requirement of paragraph (3)(a) but shall not waive any right the tenant may have to the security deposit or any part of it.

(6) For the purposes of this part, a renewal of an existing rental agreement shall be considered a new rental agreement, and any security deposit carried forward shall be considered a new security deposit.

(7) Upon the sale or transfer of title of the rental property from one owner to another, or upon a change in the designated rental agent, any and all security deposits or advance rents being held for the benefit of the tenants shall be transferred to the new owner or agent, together with any earned interest and with an accurate accounting showing the amounts to be credited to each tenant account. Upon the transfer of such funds and records as stated herein, and upon transmittal of a written receipt therefor, the transferor shall be free from the obligation imposed in subsection (1) to hold such moneys on behalf of the tenant. However, nothing herein shall excuse the landlord or agent for a violation of the provisions of this section while in possession of such deposits.

(8) Any person licensed under the provisions of s. 509.241, unless excluded by the provisions of this part, who fails to comply with the provisions of this part shall be subject to a fine or to the suspension or revocation of his or her license by the Division of Hotels and Restaurants of the Department of Business and Professional Regulation in the manner provided in s. 509.261.

(9) In those cases in which interest is required to be paid to the tenant, the landlord shall pay directly to the tenant, or credit against the current month's rent, the interest due to the tenant at least once annually. However, no interest shall be due a tenant who wrongfully terminates his or her tenancy prior to the end of the rental term.

Note.—Former s. 83.261.

83.50 Disclosure.—

(1) The landlord, or a person authorized to enter into a rental agreement on the landlord's behalf, shall disclose in writing to the tenant, at or before the commencement of the tenancy, the name and address of the landlord or a person authorized to receive notices and demands in the landlord's behalf. The person so authorized to receive notices and demands retains authority until the tenant is notified otherwise. All notices of such names and addresses or changes thereto shall be delivered to the tenant's residence or, if specified in writing by the tenant, to any other address.

(2) The landlord or the landlord's authorized representative, upon completion of construction of a building exceeding three stories in height and containing dwelling units, shall disclose to the tenants initially moving into the building the availability or lack of availability of fire protection.

83.51 Landlord's obligation to maintain premises.—

(1) The landlord at all times during the tenancy shall:

(a) Comply with the requirements of applicable building, housing, and health codes; or

(b) Where there are no applicable building, housing, or health codes, maintain the roofs, windows, screens, doors, floors, steps, porches, exterior walls, foundations, and all other structural components in good repair and capable of resisting normal forces and loads and the plumbing in reasonable working condition. However, the landlord shall not be required to maintain a mobile home or other structure owned by the tenant.

The landlord's obligations under this subsection may be altered or modified in writing with respect to a single-family home or duplex.

(2)(a) Unless otherwise agreed in writing, in addition to the requirements of subsection (1), the landlord of a dwelling unit other than a single-family home or duplex shall, at all times during the tenancy, make reasonable provisions for:

1. The extermination of rats, mice, roaches, ants, wood-destroying organisms, and bedbugs. When vacation of the premises is required for such extermination, the landlord shall not be liable for damages but shall abate the rent. The tenant shall be required to temporarily vacate the premises for a period of time not to exceed 4 days, on 7 days' written notice, if necessary, for extermination pursuant to this subparagraph.

2. Locks and keys.

3. The clean and safe condition of common areas.

4. Garbage removal and outside receptacles therefor.

5. Functioning facilities for heat during winter, running water, and hot water.

(b) Unless otherwise agreed in writing, at the commencement of the tenancy of a single-family home or duplex, the landlord shall install working smoke detection devices. As used in this paragraph, the term "smoke detection device" means an electrical or battery-operated device which detects visible or invisible particles of combustion and which is listed by Underwriters Laboratories, Inc., Factory Mutual Laboratories, Inc., or any other nationally recognized testing laboratory using nationally accepted testing standards.

(c) Nothing in this part authorizes the tenant to raise a noncompliance by the landlord with this subsection as a defense to an action for possession under s. 83.59.

(d) This subsection shall not apply to a mobile home owned by a tenant.

(e) Nothing contained in this subsection prohibits the landlord from providing in the rental agreement that the tenant is obligated to pay costs or charges for garbage removal, water, fuel, or utilities.

(3) If the duty imposed by subsection (1) is the same or greater than any duty imposed by subsection (2), the landlord's duty is determined by subsection (1).

(4) The landlord is not responsible to the tenant under this section for conditions created or caused by the negligent or wrongful act or omission of the tenant, a member of the tenant's family, or other person on the premises with the tenant's consent.

83.52 Tenant's obligation to maintain dwelling unit.—The tenant at all times during the tenancy shall:

(1) Comply with all obligations imposed upon tenants by applicable provisions of building, housing, and health codes.

(2) Keep that part of the premises which he or she occupies and uses clean and sanitary.

(3) Remove from the tenant's dwelling unit all garbage in a clean and sanitary manner.

(4) Keep all plumbing fixtures in the dwelling unit or used by the tenant clean and sanitary and in repair.

(5) Use and operate in a reasonable manner all electrical, plumbing, sanitary, heating, ventilating, air-conditioning and other facilities and appliances, including elevators.

(6) Not destroy, deface, damage, impair, or remove any part of the premises or property therein belonging to the landlord nor permit any person to do so.

(7) Conduct himself or herself, and require other persons on the premises with his or her consent to conduct themselves, in a manner that does not unreasonably disturb the tenant's neighbors or constitute a breach of the peace.

83.53 Landlord's access to dwelling unit.—

(1) The tenant shall not unreasonably withhold consent to the landlord to enter the dwelling unit from time to time in order to inspect the premises; make necessary or agreed repairs, decorations, alterations, or improvements; supply agreed services; or exhibit the dwelling unit to prospective or actual purchasers, mortgagees, tenants, workers, or contractors.

(2) The landlord may enter the dwelling unit at any time for the protection or preservation of the premises. The landlord may enter the dwelling unit upon reasonable notice to the tenant and at a reasonable time for the purpose of repair of the premises. "Reasonable notice" for the purpose of repair is notice given at least 12 hours prior to the entry, and reasonable time for the purpose of repair shall be between the hours of 7:30 a.m. and 8:00 p.m. The landlord may enter the dwelling unit when necessary for the further purposes set forth in subsection (1) under any of the following circumstances:

(a) With the consent of the tenant;

(b) In case of emergency;

(c) When the tenant unreasonably withholds consent; or

(d) If the tenant is absent from the premises for a period of time equal to one-half the time for periodic rental payments. If the rent is current and the tenant notifies the landlord of an intended absence, then the landlord may enter only with the consent of the tenant or for the protection or preservation of the premises.

(3) The landlord shall not abuse the right of access nor use it to harass the tenant.

83.535 Flotation bedding system; restrictions on use.—No landlord may prohibit a tenant from using a flotation bedding system in a dwelling unit, provided the flotation bedding system does not violate applicable building codes. The tenant shall be required to carry in the tenant's name flotation insurance as is standard in the industry in an amount deemed reasonable to protect the tenant and owner against personal injury and property damage to the dwelling units. In any case, the policy shall carry a loss payable clause to the owner of the building.

83.54 Enforcement of rights and duties; civil action.—Any right or duty declared in this part is enforceable by civil action.

83.55 Right of action for damages.—If either the landlord or the tenant fails to comply with the requirements of the rental agreement or this part, the aggrieved party may recover the damages caused by the noncompliance.

83.56 Termination of rental agreement.—

(1) If the landlord materially fails to comply with s. 83.51(1) or material provisions of the rental agreement within 7 days after

delivery of written notice by the tenant specifying the noncompliance and indicating the intention of the tenant to terminate the rental agreement by reason thereof, the tenant may terminate the rental agreement. If the failure to comply with s. 83.51(1) or material provisions of the rental agreement is due to causes beyond the control of the landlord and the landlord has made and continues to make every reasonable effort to correct the failure to comply, the rental agreement may be terminated or altered by the parties, as follows:

(a) If the landlord's failure to comply renders the dwelling unit untenantable and the tenant vacates, the tenant shall not be liable for rent during the period the dwelling unit remains uninhabitable.

(b) If the landlord's failure to comply does not render the dwelling unit untenantable and the tenant remains in occupancy, the rent for the period of noncompliance shall be reduced by an amount in proportion to the loss of rental value caused by the noncompliance.

(2) If the tenant materially fails to comply with s. 83.52 or material provisions of the rental agreement, other than a failure to pay rent, or reasonable rules or regulations, the landlord may:

(a) If such noncompliance is of a nature that the tenant should not be given an opportunity to cure it or if the noncompliance constitutes a subsequent or continuing noncompliance within 12 months of a written warning by the landlord of a similar violation, deliver a written notice to the tenant specifying the noncompliance and the landlord's intent to terminate the rental agreement by reason thereof. Examples of noncompliance which are of a nature that the tenant should not be given an opportunity to cure include, but are not limited to, destruction, damage, or misuse of the landlord's or other tenants' property by intentional act or a subsequent or continued unreasonable disturbance. In such event, the landlord may terminate the rental agreement, and the tenant shall have 7 days from the date that the notice is delivered to vacate the premises. The notice shall be adequate if it is in substantially the following form:

You are advised that your lease is terminated effective immediately. You shall have 7 days from the delivery of this letter to vacate the premises. This action is taken because (cite the noncompliance).

(b) If such noncompliance is of a nature that the tenant should be given an opportunity to cure it, deliver a written notice to the tenant specifying the noncompliance, including a notice that, if the noncompliance is not corrected within 7 days from the date the written notice is delivered, the landlord shall terminate the rental agreement by reason thereof. Examples of such noncompliance include, but are not limited to, activities in contravention of the lease or this act such as having or permitting unauthorized pets, guests, or vehicles; parking in an unauthorized manner or permitting such parking; or failing to keep the premises clean and sanitary. The notice shall be adequate if it is in substantially the following form:

You are hereby notified that (cite the noncompliance). Demand is hereby made that you remedy the noncompliance within 7 days of receipt of this notice or your lease shall be deemed terminated and you shall vacate the premises upon such termination. If this same conduct or conduct of a similar nature is repeated within 12 months, your tenancy is subject to termination without your being given an opportunity to cure the noncompliance.

(3) If the tenant fails to pay rent when due and the default continues for 3 days, excluding Saturday, Sunday, and legal holidays, after delivery of written demand by the landlord for payment of the rent or possession of the premises, the landlord may terminate the rental agreement. Legal holidays for the purpose of this section shall be court-observed holidays only. The 3-day notice shall contain a statement in substantially the following form:

You are hereby notified that you are indebted to me in the sum of _____ dollars for the rent and use of the premises (address of leased premises, including county) , Florida, now occupied by you and that I demand payment of the rent or possession of the premises within 3 days (excluding Saturday, Sunday, and legal holidays) from the date of delivery of this notice, to wit: on or before the _____ day of _____, (year) .

(landlord's name, address and phone number)

(4) The delivery of the written notices required by subsections (1), (2), and (3) shall be by mailing or delivery of a true copy thereof or, if the tenant is absent from the premises, by leaving a copy thereof at the residence.

(5) If the landlord accepts rent with actual knowledge of a noncompliance by the tenant or accepts performance by the tenant of any other provision of the rental agreement that is at variance with its provisions, or if the tenant pays rent with actual knowledge of a noncompliance by the landlord or accepts performance by the landlord of any other provision of the rental agreement that is at variance with its provisions, the landlord or tenant waives his or her right to terminate the rental agreement or to bring a civil action for that noncompliance, but not for any subsequent or continuing noncompliance. Any tenant who wishes to defend against an action by the landlord for possession of the unit for noncompliance of the rental agreement or of relevant statutes shall comply with the provisions in s. 83.60(2). The court may not set a date for mediation or trial unless the provisions of s. 83.60(2) have been met, but shall enter a default judgment for removal of the tenant with a writ of possession to issue immediately if the tenant fails to comply with s. 83.60(2). This subsection does not apply to that portion of rent subsidies received from a local, state, or national government or an agency of local, state, or national government; however, waiver will occur if an action has not been instituted within 45 days of the noncompliance.

(6) If the rental agreement is terminated, the landlord shall comply with s. 83.49(3).

83.57 Termination of tenancy without specific term.—A tenancy without a specific duration, as defined in s. 83.46(2) or (3), may be terminated by either party giving written notice in the manner provided in s. 83.56(4), as follows:

(1) When the tenancy is from year to year, by giving not less than 60 days' notice prior to the end of any annual period;

(2) When the tenancy is from quarter to quarter, by giving not less than 30 days' notice prior to the end of any quarterly period;

(3) When the tenancy is from month to month, by giving not less than 15 days' notice prior to the end of any monthly period; and

(4) When the tenancy is from week to week, by giving not less than 7 days' notice prior to the end of any weekly period.

83.575 Termination of tenancy with specific duration.—

(1) A rental agreement with a specific duration may contain a provision requiring the tenant to notify the landlord before vacating the premises at the end of the rental agreement; however, a rental agreement may not require more than 60 days' notice before vacating the premises.

(2) A rental agreement with a specific duration may provide that if a tenant fails to give the required notice before vacating the premises at the end of the rental agreement, the tenant may be liable for liquidated damages as specified in the rental agreement if the landlord provides written notice to the tenant specifying the tenant's obligations under the notification provision contained in the lease and the date the rental agreement is terminated. The landlord must provide such written notice to the tenant within 15 days before the start of the notification period contained in the lease. The written notice shall list all fees, penalties, and other charges applicable to the tenant under this subsection.

(3) If the tenant remains on the premises with the permission of the landlord after the rental agreement has terminated and fails to give notice required under s. 83.57(3), the tenant is liable to the landlord for an additional 1 month's rent.

83.58 Remedies; tenant holding over.—If the tenant holds over and continues in possession of the dwelling unit or any part thereof after the expiration of the rental agreement without the permission of the landlord, the landlord may recover possession of the dwelling unit in the manner provided for in s. 83.59 [F.S. 1973]. The landlord may also recover double the amount of rent due on the dwelling unit, or any part thereof, for the period during which the tenant refuses to surrender possession.

83.59 Right of action for possession.—

(1) If the rental agreement is terminated and the tenant does not vacate the premises, the landlord may recover possession of the dwelling unit as provided in this section.

(2) A landlord, the landlord's attorney, or the landlord's agent, applying for the removal of a tenant shall file in the county court of the county where the premises are situated a complaint describing the dwelling unit and stating the facts that authorize its recovery. A landlord's agent is not permitted to take any action other than the initial filing of the complaint, unless the landlord's agent is an attorney. The landlord is entitled to the summary procedure provided in s. 51.011 [F.S. 1971], and the court shall advance the cause on the calendar.

(3) The landlord shall not recover possession of a dwelling unit except:

(a) In an action for possession under subsection (2) or other civil action in which the issue of right of possession is determined;

(b) When the tenant has surrendered possession of the dwelling unit to the landlord; or

(c) When the tenant has abandoned the dwelling unit. In the absence of actual knowledge of abandonment, it shall be presumed that the tenant has abandoned the dwelling unit if he or she is absent from the premises for a period of time equal to one-half the time for periodic rental payments. However, this presumption shall not apply if the rent is current or the tenant has notified the landlord, in writing, of an intended absence.

(4) The prevailing party is entitled to have judgment for costs and execution therefor.

83.595 Choice of remedies upon breach by tenant.—

(1) If the tenant breaches the lease for the dwelling unit and the landlord has obtained a writ of possession, or the tenant has surrendered possession of the dwelling unit to the landlord, or the tenant has abandoned the dwelling unit, the landlord may:

(a) Treat the lease as terminated and retake possession for his or her own account, thereby terminating any further liability of the tenant; or

(b) Retake possession of the dwelling unit for the account of the tenant, holding the tenant liable for the difference between rental stipulated to be paid under the lease agreement and what, in good faith, the landlord is able to recover from a reletting; or

(c) Stand by and do nothing, holding the lessee liable for the rent as it comes due.

(2) If the landlord retakes possession of the dwelling unit for the account of the tenant, the landlord has a duty to exercise good faith in attempting to relet the premises, and any rentals received by the landlord as a result of the reletting shall be deducted from the balance of rent due from the tenant. For purposes of this section, "good faith in attempting to relet the premises" means that the landlord shall use at least the same efforts to relet the premises as were used in the initial rental or at least the same efforts as the landlord uses in attempting to lease other similar rental units but does not require the landlord to give a preference in leasing the premises over other vacant dwelling units that the landlord owns or has the responsibility to rent.

83.60 Defenses to action for rent or possession; procedure.—

(1) In an action by the landlord for possession of a dwelling unit based upon nonpayment of rent or in an action by the landlord under s. 83.55 seeking to recover unpaid rent, the tenant may defend upon the ground of a material noncompliance with s. 83.51(1) [F.S. 1973], or may raise any other defense, whether legal or equitable, that he or she may have, including the defense of retaliatory conduct in accordance with s. 83.64. The defense of a material noncompliance with s. 83.51(1) [F.S. 1973] may be raised by the tenant if 7 days have elapsed after the delivery of written notice by the tenant to the landlord, specifying the noncompliance and indicating the intention of the tenant not to pay rent by reason thereof. Such notice by the tenant may be given to the landlord, the landlord's representative as designated pursuant to s. 83.50(1), a resident manager, or the person or entity who collects the rent on behalf of the landlord. A material noncompliance with s. 83.51(1) [F.S. 1973] by the landlord is a complete defense to an action for possession based upon nonpayment of rent, and, upon hearing, the court or the jury, as the case may be, shall determine the amount, if any, by which the rent is to be reduced to reflect the diminution in value of the dwelling unit during the period of noncompliance with s. 83.51(1) [F.S. 1973]. After consideration of all other relevant issues, the court shall enter appropriate judgment.

(2) In an action by the landlord for possession of a dwelling unit, if the tenant interposes any defense other than payment, the tenant shall pay into the registry of the court the accrued rent as

alleged in the complaint or as determined by the court and the rent which accrues during the pendency of the proceeding, when due. The clerk shall notify the tenant of such requirement in the summons. Failure of the tenant to pay the rent into the registry of the court or to file a motion to determine the amount of rent to be paid into the registry within 5 days, excluding Saturdays, Sundays, and legal holidays, after the date of service of process constitutes an absolute waiver of the tenant's defenses other than payment, and the landlord is entitled to an immediate default judgment for removal of the tenant with a writ of possession to issue without further notice or hearing thereon. In the event a motion to determine rent is filed, documentation in support of the allegation that the rent as alleged in the complaint is in error is required. Public housing tenants or tenants receiving rent subsidies shall be required to deposit only that portion of the full rent for which the tenant is responsible pursuant to federal, state, or local program in which they are participating.

83.61 Disbursement of funds in registry of court; prompt final hearing.—When the tenant has deposited funds into the registry of the court in accordance with the provisions of s. 83.60(2) and the landlord is in actual danger of loss of the premises or other personal hardship resulting from the loss of rental income from the premises, the landlord may apply to the court for disbursement of all or part of the funds or for prompt final hearing. The court shall advance the cause on the calendar. The court, after preliminary hearing, may award all or any portion of the funds on deposit to the landlord or may proceed immediately to a final resolution of the cause.

83.62 Restoration of possession to landlord.—

(1) In an action for possession, after entry of judgment in favor of the landlord, the clerk shall issue a writ to the sheriff describing the premises and commanding the sheriff to put the landlord in possession after 24 hours' notice conspicuously posted on the premises.

(2) At the time the sheriff executes the writ of possession or at any time thereafter, the landlord or the landlord's agent may remove any personal property found on the premises to or near the property line. Subsequent to executing the writ of possession, the landlord may request the sheriff to stand by to keep the peace while the landlord changes the locks and removes the personal property from the premises. When such a request is made, the sheriff may charge a reasonable hourly rate, and the person requesting the sheriff to stand by to keep the peace shall be responsible for paying the reasonable hourly rate set by the sheriff. Neither the sheriff nor the landlord or the landlord's agent shall be liable to the tenant or any other party for the loss, destruction, or damage to the property after it has been removed.

83.625 Power to award possession and enter money judgment.— In an action by the landlord for possession of a dwelling unit based upon nonpayment of rent, if the court finds the rent is due, owing, and unpaid and by reason thereof the landlord is entitled to possession of the premises, the court, in addition to awarding possession of the premises to the landlord, shall direct, in an amount which is within its jurisdictional limitations, the entry of a money judgment with costs in favor of the landlord and against the tenant for the amount of money found due, owing, and unpaid by the tenant to the landlord. However, no money judgment shall be entered unless service of process has been effected by per-

sonal service or, where authorized by law, by certified or registered mail, return receipt, or in any other manner prescribed by law or the rules of the court; and no money judgment may be entered except in compliance with the Florida Rules of Civil Procedure. The prevailing party in the action may also be awarded attorney's fees and costs.

83.63 Casualty damage.—If the premises are damaged or destroyed other than by the wrongful or negligent acts of the tenant so that the enjoyment of the premises is substantially impaired, the tenant may terminate the rental agreement and immediately vacate the premises. The tenant may vacate the part of the premises rendered unusable by the casualty, in which case the tenant's liability for rent shall be reduced by the fair rental value of that part of the premises damaged or destroyed. If the rental agreement is terminated, the landlord shall comply with s. 83.49(3) [F.S. 1973].

83.64 Retaliatory conduct.—

(1) It is unlawful for a landlord to discriminatorily increase a tenant's rent or decrease services to a tenant, or to bring or threaten to bring an action for possession or other civil action, primarily because the landlord is retaliating against the tenant. In order for the tenant to raise the defense of retaliatory conduct, the tenant must have acted in good faith. Examples of conduct for which the landlord may not retaliate include, but are not limited to, situations where:

(a) The tenant has complained to a governmental agency charged with responsibility for enforcement of a building, housing, or health code of a suspected violation applicable to the premises;

(b) The tenant has organized, encouraged, or participated in a tenants' organization;

(c) The tenant has complained to the landlord pursuant to s. 83.56(1); or

(d) The tenant is a servicemember who has terminated a rental agreement pursuant to s. 83.682.

(2) Evidence of retaliatory conduct may be raised by the tenant as a defense in any action brought against him or her for possession.

(3) In any event, this section does not apply if the landlord proves that the eviction is for good cause. Examples of good cause include, but are not limited to, good faith actions for nonpayment of rent, violation of the rental agreement or of reasonable rules, or violation of the terms of this chapter.

(4) "Discrimination" under this section means that a tenant is being treated differently as to the rent charged, the services rendered, or the action being taken by the landlord, which shall be a prerequisite to a finding of retaliatory conduct.

83.67 Prohibited practices.—

(1) A landlord of any dwelling unit governed by this part shall not cause, directly or indirectly, the termination or interruption of any utility service furnished the tenant, including, but not limited to, water, heat, light, electricity, gas, elevator, garbage collection, or refrigeration, whether or not the utility service is under the control of, or payment is made by, the landlord.

(2) A landlord of any dwelling unit governed by this part shall not prevent the tenant from gaining reasonable access to the dwelling

unit by any means, including, but not limited to, changing the locks or using any bootlock or similar device.

(3) A landlord of any dwelling unit governed by this part shall not discriminate against a servicemember in offering a dwelling unit for rent or in any of the terms of the rental agreement.

(4) A landlord shall not prohibit a tenant from displaying one portable, removable, cloth or plastic United States flag, not larger than 4 and 1/2 feet by 6 feet, in a respectful manner in or on the dwelling unit regardless of any provision in the rental agreement dealing with flags or decorations. The United States flag shall be displayed in accordance with s. 83.52(6). The landlord is not liable for damages caused by a United States flag displayed by a tenant. Any United States flag may not infringe upon the space rented by any other tenant.

(5) A landlord of any dwelling unit governed by this part shall not remove the outside doors, locks, roof, walls, or windows of the unit except for purposes of maintenance, repair, or replacement; and the landlord shall not remove the tenant's personal property from the dwelling unit unless such action is taken after surrender, abandonment, or a lawful eviction. If provided in the rental agreement or a written agreement separate from the rental agreement, upon surrender or abandonment by the tenant, the landlord is not required to comply with s. 715.104 and is not liable or responsible for storage or disposition of the tenant's personal property; if provided in the rental agreement, there must be printed or clearly stamped on such rental agreement a legend in substantially the following form:

BY SIGNING THIS RENTAL AGREEMENT, THE TENANT AGREES THAT UPON SURRENDER OR ABANDONMENT, AS DEFINED BY CHAPTER 83, FLORIDA STATUTES, THE LANDLORD SHALL NOT BE LIABLE OR RESPONSIBLE FOR STORAGE OR DISPOSITION OF THE TENANT'S PERSONAL PROPERTY.

For the purposes of this section, abandonment shall be as set forth in s. 83.59(3)(c).

(6) A landlord who violates any provision of this section shall be liable to the tenant for actual and consequential damages or 3 months' rent, whichever is greater, and costs, including attorney's fees. Subsequent or repeated violations that are not contemporaneous with the initial violation shall be subject to separate awards of damages.

(7) A violation of this section constitutes irreparable harm for the purposes of injunctive relief.

(8) The remedies provided by this section are not exclusive and do not preclude the tenant from pursuing any other remedy at law or equity that the tenant may have. The remedies provided by this section shall also apply to a servicemember who is a prospective tenant who has been discriminated against under subsection (3).

83.681 Orders to enjoin violations of this part.—

(1) A landlord who gives notice to a tenant of the landlord's intent to terminate the tenant's lease pursuant to s. 83.56(2)(a), due to the tenant's intentional destruction, damage, or misuse of the landlord's property may petition the county or circuit court for an injunction prohibiting the tenant from continuing to violate any of the provisions of that part.

(2) The court shall grant the relief requested pursuant to subsection (1) in conformity with the principles that govern the granting of injunctive relief from threatened loss or damage in other civil cases.

(3) Evidence of a tenant's intentional destruction, damage, or misuse of the landlord's property in an amount greater than twice the value of money deposited with the landlord pursuant to s. 83.49 or $300, whichever is greater, shall constitute irreparable harm for the purposes of injunctive relief.

83.682 Termination of rental agreement by a servicemember.—

(1) Any servicemember may terminate his or her rental agreement by providing the landlord with a written notice of termination to be effective on the date stated in the notice that is at least 30 days after the landlord's receipt of the notice if any of the following criteria are met:

(a) The servicemember is required, pursuant to a permanent change of station orders, to move 35 miles or more from the location of the rental premises;

(b) The servicemember is prematurely or involuntarily discharged or released from active duty or state active duty;

(c) The servicemember is released from active duty or state active duty after having leased the rental premises while on active duty or state active duty status and the rental premises is 35 miles or more from the servicemember's home of record prior to entering active duty or state active duty;

(d) After entering into a rental agreement, the servicemember receives military orders requiring him or her to move into government quarters or the servicemember becomes eligible to live in and opts to move into government quarters;

(e) The servicemember receives temporary duty orders, temporary change of station orders, or state active duty orders to an area 35 miles or more from the location of the rental premises, provided such orders are for a period exceeding 60 days; or

(f) The servicemember has leased the property, but prior to taking possession of the rental premises, receives a change of orders to an area that is 35 miles or more from the location of the rental premises.

(2) The notice to the landlord must be accompanied by either a copy of the official military orders or a written verification signed by the servicemember's commanding officer.

(3) In the event a servicemember dies during active duty, an adult member of his or her immediate family may terminate the servicemember's rental agreement by providing the landlord with a written notice of termination to be effective on the date stated in the notice that is at least 30 days after the landlord's receipt of the notice. The notice to the landlord must be accompanied by either a copy of the official military orders showing the servicemember was on active duty or a written verification signed by the servicemember's commanding officer and a copy of the servicemember's death certificate.

(4) Upon termination of a rental agreement under this section, the tenant is liable for the rent due under the rental agreement prorated to the effective date of the termination payable at such time as would have otherwise been required by the terms of the rental agreement. The tenant is not liable for any other rent or damages due to the early termination of the tenancy as provided for in this

section. Notwithstanding any provision of this section to the contrary, if a tenant terminates the rental agreement pursuant to this section 14 or more days prior to occupancy, no damages or penalties of any kind will be assessable.

(5) The provisions of this section may not be waived or modified by the agreement of the parties under any circumstances.

PART III

SELF-SERVICE STORAGE SPACE

83.801 Short title.

83.803 Definitions.

83.805 Lien.

83.8055 Withholding access to personal property upon nonpayment of rent.

83.806 Enforcement of lien.

83.808 Contractual liens.

83.809 Application of act.

83.801 Short title.—Sections 83.801-83.809 shall be known and may be cited as the "Self-storage Facility Act."

83.803 Definitions.—As used in ss. 83.801-83.809:

(1) "Self-service storage facility" means any real property designed and used for the purpose of renting or leasing individual storage space to tenants who are to have access to such space for the purpose of storing and removing personal property. No individual storage space may be used for residential purposes. A self-service storage facility is not a "warehouse" as that term is used in chapter 677. If an owner issues any warehouse receipt, bill of lading, or other document of title for the personal property stored, the owner and the tenant shall be subject to the provisions of chapter 677, and the provisions of this act shall not apply.

(2) "Self-contained storage unit" means any unit not less than 600 cubic feet in size, including, but not limited to, a trailer, box, or other shipping container, which is leased by a tenant primarily for use as storage space whether the unit is located at a facility owned or operated by the owner or at another location designated by the tenant.

(3) "Owner" means the owner, operator, lessor, or sublessor of a self-service storage facility or self-contained storage unit or his or her agent or any other person authorized by him or her to manage the facility or to receive rent from a tenant under a rental agreement.

(4) "Tenant" means a person or the person's sublessee, successor, or assign entitled to the use of storage space at a self-service storage facility or in a self-contained unit, under a rental agreement, to the exclusion of others.

(5) "Rental agreement" means any agreement or lease which establishes or modifies terms, conditions, rules, or any other provisions concerning the use and occupancy of a self-service storage facility or use of a self-contained storage unit.

(6) "Last known address" means that address provided by the tenant in the latest rental agreement or the address provided by the tenant by hand delivery or certified mail in a subsequent written notice of a change of address.

83.805 Lien.—The owner of a self-service storage facility or self-contained storage unit and the owner's heirs, executors, administrators, successors, and assigns have a lien upon all personal property, whether or not owned by the tenant, located at a self-service storage facility or in a self-contained storage unit for rent, labor charges, or other charges, present or future, in relation to the personal property and for expenses necessary for its preservation or expenses reasonably incurred in its sale or other disposition pursuant to ss. 83.801-83.809. The lien provided for in this section attaches as of the date that the personal property is brought to the self-service storage facility or as of the date the tenant takes possession of the self-contained storage unit, and the priority of this lien shall be the same as provided in s. 83.08; however, in the event of default, the owner must give notice to persons who hold perfected security interests under the Uniform Commercial Code in which the tenant is named as the debtor.

83.8055 Withholding access to personal property upon nonpayment of rent.—Upon the failure of a tenant to pay the rent when it becomes due, the owner may, without notice, after 5 days from the date the rent is due, deny the tenant access to the personal property located in the self-service storage facility or self-contained storage unit. In denying the tenant access to personal property contained in the self-contained storage unit, the owner may proceed without judicial process, if this can be done without breach of the peace, or may proceed by action.

83.806 Enforcement of lien.—An owner's lien as provided in s. 83.805 may be satisfied as follows:

(1) The tenant shall be notified by written notice delivered in person or by certified mail to the tenant's last known address and conspicuously posted at the self-service storage facility or on the self-contained storage unit.

(2) The notice shall include:

(a) An itemized statement of the owner's claim, showing the sum due at the time of the notice and the date when the sum became due.

(b) The same description, or a reasonably similar description, of the personal property as provided in the rental agreement.

(c) A demand for payment within a specified time not less than 14 days after delivery of the notice.

(d) A conspicuous statement that, unless the claim is paid within the time stated in the notice, the personal property will be advertised for sale or other disposition and will be sold or otherwise disposed of at a specified time and place.

(e) The name, street address, and telephone number of the owner whom the tenant may contact to respond to the notice.

(3) Any notice given pursuant to this section shall be presumed delivered when it is deposited with the United States Postal Service, registered, and properly addressed with postage prepaid.

(4) After the expiration of the time given in the notice, an advertisement of the sale or other disposition shall be published once a week for 2 consecutive weeks in a newspaper of general circulation in the area where the self-service storage facility or self-contained storage unit is located. Inasmuch as any sale may involve property of more than one tenant, a single advertisement may be used to dispose of property at any one sale.

(a) The advertisement shall include:

1. A brief and general description of what is believed to constitute the personal property contained in the storage unit, as provided in paragraph (2)(b).

2. The address of the self-service storage facility or the address where the self-contained storage unit is located and the name of the tenant.

3. The time, place, and manner of the sale or other disposition. The sale or other disposition shall take place not sooner than 15 days after the first publication.

(b) If there is no newspaper of general circulation in the area where the self-service storage facility or self-contained storage unit is located, the advertisement shall be posted at least 10 days before the date of the sale or other disposition in not fewer than three conspicuous places in the neighborhood where the self-service storage facility or self-contained storage unit is located.

(5) Any sale or other disposition of the personal property shall conform to the terms of the notification as provided for in this section and shall be conducted in a commercially reasonable manner, as that term is used in s. 679.610.

(6) Before any sale or other disposition of personal property pursuant to this section, the tenant may pay the amount necessary to satisfy the lien and the reasonable expenses incurred under this section and thereby redeem the personal property. Upon receipt of such payment, the owner shall return the property to the tenant and thereafter shall have no liability to any person with respect to such personal property. If the tenant fails to redeem the personal property or satisfy the lien, including reasonable expenses, he or she will be deemed to have unjustifiably abandoned the self-service storage facility or self-contained storage unit, and the owner may resume possession of the premises for himself or herself.

(7) A purchaser in good faith of the personal property sold to satisfy a lien provided for in s. 83.805 takes the property free of any claims, except those interests provided for in s. 83.808, despite noncompliance by the owner with the requirements of this section.

(8) In the event of a sale under this section, the owner may satisfy his or her lien from the proceeds of the sale, provided the owner's lien has priority over all other liens in the personal property. The lien rights of secured lienholders are automatically transferred to the remaining proceeds of the sale. The balance, if any, shall be held by the owner for delivery on demand to the tenant. A notice of any balance shall be delivered by the owner to the tenant in person or by certified mail to the last known address of the tenant. If the tenant does not claim the balance of the proceeds within 2 years of the date of sale, the proceeds shall be deemed abandoned, and the owner shall have no further obligation with regard to the payment of the balance. In the event that the owner's lien does not have priority over all other liens, the sale proceeds shall be held for the benefit of the holders of those liens having priority. A notice of the amount of the sale proceeds shall be delivered by the owner to the tenant or secured lienholders in person or by certified mail to their last known addresses. If the tenant or the secured lienholders do not claim the sale proceeds within 2 years of the date of sale, the proceeds shall be deemed abandoned, and the owner shall have no further obligation with regard to the payment of the proceeds.

83.808 Contractual liens.—Nothing in ss. 83.801-83.809 shall be construed as in any manner impairing or affecting the right of parties to create liens by special contract or agreement nor shall it in any manner impair or affect any other lien arising at common law, in equity, or by any statute of this state or any other lien not provided for in s. 83.805.

83.809 Application of act.—

(1) Nothing in this act shall be construed as in any manner impairing or affecting the right of parties to create additional rights, duties, and obligations in and by virtue of a rental agreement. The provisions of ss. 83.801-83.809 shall be in addition to all other rights allowed by law in a creditor-debtor or landlord-tenant relationship.

(2) Chapter 82-151, Laws of Florida, shall apply to all rental agreements entered into, extended, or renewed after July 1, 1982.

212.03 Transient rentals tax; rate, procedure, enforcement, exemptions.—

(1) It is hereby declared to be the legislative intent that every person is exercising a taxable privilege who engages in the business of renting, leasing, letting, or granting a license to use any living quarters or sleeping or housekeeping accommodations in, from, or a part of, or in connection with any hotel, apartment house, roominghouse, or tourist or trailer camp. However, any person who rents, leases, lets, or grants a license to others to use, occupy, or enter upon any living quarters or sleeping or housekeeping accommodations in apartment houses, roominghouses, tourist camps, or trailer camps, and who exclusively enters into a bona fide written agreement for continuous residence for longer than 6 months in duration at such property is not exercising a taxable privilege. For the exercise of such taxable privilege, a tax is hereby levied in an amount equal to 6 percent of and on the total rental charged for such living quarters or sleeping or housekeeping accommodations by the person charging or collecting the rental. Such tax shall apply to hotels, apartment houses, roominghouses, or tourist or trailer camps whether or not there is in connection with any of the same any dining rooms, cafes, or other places where meals or lunches are sold or served to guests.

(2) The tax provided for herein shall be in addition to the total amount of the rental, shall be charged by the lessor or person receiving the rent in and by said rental arrangement to the lessee or person paying the rental, and shall be due and payable at the time of the receipt of such rental payment by the lessor or person, as defined in this chapter, who receives said rental or payment. The owner, lessor, or person receiving the rent shall remit the tax to the department at the times and in the manner hereinafter provided for dealers to remit taxes under this chapter. The same duties imposed by this chapter upon dealers in tangible personal property respecting the collection and remission of the tax; the making of returns; the keeping of books, records, and accounts; and the compliance with the rules and regulations of the department in the administration of this chapter shall apply to and be binding upon all persons who manage or operate hotels, apartment houses, roominghouses, tourist and trailer camps, and the rental of condominium units, and to all persons who collect or receive such rents on behalf of such owner or lessor taxable under this chapter.

(3) When rentals are received by way of property, goods, wares, merchandise, services, or other things of value, the tax shall be at the rate of 6 percent of the value of the property, goods, wares, merchandise, services, or other things of value.

(4) The tax levied by this section shall not apply to, be imposed upon, or collected from any person who shall have entered into a bona fide written lease for longer than 6 months in duration for continuous residence at any one hotel, apartment house, roominghouse, tourist or trailer camp, or condominium, or to any person who shall reside continuously longer than 6 months at any one hotel, apartment house, roominghouse, tourist or trailer camp, or condominium and shall have paid the tax levied by this section for 6 months of residence in any one hotel, roominghouse, apartment house, tourist or trailer camp, or condominium. Notwithstanding other provisions of this chapter, no tax shall be imposed upon rooms provided guests when there is no consideration involved between the guest and the public lodging establishment. Further, any person who, on the effective date of this act, has resided continuously for 6 months at any one hotel, apartment house, roominghouse, tourist or trailer camp, or condominium, or, if less than 6 months, has paid the tax imposed herein until he or she shall have resided continuously for 6 months, shall thereafter be exempt, so long as such person shall continuously reside at such location. The Department of Revenue shall have the power to reform the rental contract for the purposes of this chapter if the rental payments are collected in other than equal daily, weekly, or monthly amounts so as to reflect the actual consideration to be paid in the future for the right of occupancy during the first 6 months.

(5) The tax imposed by this section shall constitute a lien on the property of the lessee or rentee of any sleeping accommodations in the same manner as and shall be collectible as are liens authorized and imposed by ss. 713.68 and 713.69.

(6) It is the legislative intent that every person is engaging in a taxable privilege who leases or rents parking or storage spaces for motor vehicles in parking lots or garages, who leases or rents docking or storage spaces for boats in boat docks or marinas, or who leases or rents tie-down or storage space for aircraft at airports. For the exercise of this privilege, a tax is hereby levied at the rate of 6 percent on the total rental charged.

(7)(a) Full-time students enrolled in an institution offering postsecondary education and military personnel currently on active duty who reside in the facilities described in subsection (1) shall be exempt from the tax imposed by this section. The department shall be empowered to determine what shall be deemed acceptable proof of full-time enrollment. The exemption contained in this subsection shall apply irrespective of any other provisions of this section. The tax levied by this section shall not apply to or be imposed upon or collected on the basis of rentals to any person who resides in any building or group of buildings intended primarily for lease or rent to persons as their permanent or principal place of residence.

(b) It is the intent of the Legislature that this subsection provide tax relief for persons who rent living accommodations rather than own their homes, while still providing a tax on the rental of lodging facilities that primarily serve transient guests.

(c) The rental of facilities, as defined in s. 212.02(10)(f), which are intended primarily for rental as a principal or permanent place of residence is exempt from the tax imposed by this chapter. The rental of such facilities that primarily serve transient guests is not exempt by this subsection. In the application of this law, or in making any determination against the exemption, the department shall consider the facility as primarily serving transient guests unless the facility owner makes a verified declaration on a form prescribed by the department that more than half of the total rental units available are occupied by tenants who have a continuous residence in excess of 3 months. The owner of a facility declared to be exempt by this paragraph must make a determination of the taxable status of the facility at the end of the owner's accounting year using any consecutive 3-month period at least one month of which is in the accounting year. The owner must use a selected consecutive 3-month period during each annual redetermination. In the event that an exempt facility no longer qualifies for exemption by this paragraph, the owner must notify the department on a form prescribed by the department by the 20th day of the first month of the owner's next succeeding accounting year that the facility no longer qualifies for such exemption. The tax levied by this section shall apply to the rental of facilities that no longer qualify for exemption under this paragraph beginning the first day of the owner's next succeeding accounting year. The provisions of this paragraph do not apply to mobile home lots regulated under chapter 723.

(d) The rental of living accommodations in migrant labor camps is not taxable under this section. "Migrant labor camps" are defined as one or more buildings or structures, tents, trailers, or vehicles, or any portion thereof, together with the land appertaining thereto, established, operated, or used as living quarters for seasonal, temporary, or migrant workers.

212.031 Tax on rental or license fee for use of real property.—

(1)1(a) It is declared to be the legislative intent that every person is exercising a taxable privilege who engages in the business of renting, leasing, letting, or granting a license for the use of any real property unless such property is:

1. Assessed as agricultural property under s. 193.461.

2. Used exclusively as dwelling units.

3. Property subject to tax on parking, docking, or storage spaces under s. 212.03(6).

4. Recreational property or the common elements of a condominium when subject to a lease between the developer or owner thereof and the condominium association in its own right or as agent for the owners of individual condominium units or the owners of individual condominium units. However, only the lease payments on such property shall be exempt from the tax imposed by this chapter, and any other use made by the owner or the condominium association shall be fully taxable under this chapter.

5. A public or private street or right-of-way and poles, conduits, fixtures, and similar improvements located on such streets or rights-of-way, occupied or used by a utility or provider of communications services, as defined by s. 202.11, for utility or communications or television purposes. For purposes of this subparagraph, the term "utility" means any person providing utility services as defined in s. 203.012. This exception also applies to property, wherever located, on which the following are placed: towers, antennas, cables, accessory structures, or equipment, not

including switching equipment, used in the provision of mobile communications services as defined in s. 202.11. For purposes of this chapter, towers used in the provision of mobile communications services, as defined in s. 202.11, are considered to be fixtures.

6. A public street or road which is used for transportation purposes.

7. Property used at an airport exclusively for the purpose of aircraft landing or aircraft taxiing or property used by an airline for the purpose of loading or unloading passengers or property onto or from aircraft or for fueling aircraft.

8.a. Property used at a port authority, as defined in s. 315.02(2), exclusively for the purpose of oceangoing vessels or tugs docking, or such vessels mooring on property used by a port authority for the purpose of loading or unloading passengers or cargo onto or from such a vessel, or property used at a port authority for fueling such vessels, or to the extent that the amount paid for the use of any property at the port is based on the charge for the amount of tonnage actually imported or exported through the port by a tenant.

b. The amount charged for the use of any property at the port in excess of the amount charged for tonnage actually imported or exported shall remain subject to tax except as provided in sub-subparagraph a.

9. Property used as an integral part of the performance of qualified production services. As used in this subparagraph, the term "qualified production services" means any activity or service performed directly in connection with the production of a qualified motion picture, as defined in s. 212.06(1)(b), and includes:

a. Photography, sound and recording, casting, location managing and scouting, shooting, creation of special and optical effects, animation, adaptation (language, media, electronic, or otherwise), technological modifications, computer graphics, set and stage support (such as electricians, lighting designers and operators, greensmen, prop managers and assistants, and grips), wardrobe (design, preparation, and management), hair and makeup (design, production, and application), performing (such as acting, dancing, and playing), designing and executing stunts, coaching, consulting, writing, scoring, composing, choreographing, script supervising, directing, producing, transmitting dailies, dubbing, mixing, editing, cutting, looping, printing, processing, duplicating, storing, and distributing;

b. The design, planning, engineering, construction, alteration, repair, and maintenance of real or personal property including stages, sets, props, models, paintings, and facilities principally required for the performance of those services listed in sub-sub-paragraph a.; and

c. Property management services directly related to property used in connection with the services described in sub-subparagraphs a. and b.

This exemption will inure to the taxpayer upon presentation of the certificate of exemption issued to the taxpayer under the provisions of s. 288.1258.

10. Leased, subleased, licensed, or rented to a person providing food and drink concessionaire services within the premises of a convention hall, exhibition hall, auditorium, stadium, theater, arena, civic center, performing arts center, publicly owned recre-

ational facility, or any business operated under a permit issued pursuant to chapter 550. A person providing retail concessionaire services involving the sale of food and drink or other tangible personal property within the premises of an airport shall be subject to tax on the rental of real property used for that purpose, but shall not be subject to the tax on any license to use the property. For purposes of this subparagraph, the term "sale" shall not include the leasing of tangible personal property.

11. Property occupied pursuant to an instrument calling for payments which the department has declared, in a Technical Assistance Advisement issued on or before March 15, 1993, to be nontaxable pursuant to rule 12A-1.070(19)(c), Florida Administrative Code; provided that this subparagraph shall only apply to property occupied by the same person before and after the execution of the subject instrument and only to those payments made pursuant to such instrument, exclusive of renewals and extensions thereof occurring after March 15, 1993.

12. Rented, leased, subleased, or licensed to a concessionaire by a convention hall, exhibition hall, auditorium, stadium, theater, arena, civic center, performing arts center, or publicly owned recreational facility, during an event at the facility, to be used by the concessionaire to sell souvenirs, novelties, or other event-related products. This subparagraph applies only to that portion of the rental, lease, or license payment which is based on a percentage of sales and not based on a fixed price.

13. Property used or occupied predominantly for space flight business purposes. As used in this subparagraph, "space flight business" means the manufacturing, processing, or assembly of a space facility, space propulsion system, space vehicle, satellite, or station of any kind possessing the capacity for space flight, as defined by s. 212.02(23), or components thereof, and also means the following activities supporting space flight: vehicle launch activities, flight operations, ground control or ground support, and all administrative activities directly related thereto. Property shall be deemed to be used or occupied predominantly for space flight business purposes if more than 50 percent of the property, or improvements thereon, is used for one or more space flight business purposes. Possession by a landlord, lessor, or licensor of a signed written statement from the tenant, lessee, or licensee claiming the exemption shall relieve the landlord, lessor, or licensor from the responsibility of collecting the tax, and the department shall look solely to the tenant, lessee, or licensee for recovery of such tax if it determines that the exemption was not applicable.

(b) When a lease involves multiple use of real property wherein a part of the real property is subject to the tax herein, and a part of the property would be excluded from the tax under subparagraph (a)1., subparagraph (a)2., subparagraph (a)3., or subparagraph (a)5., the department shall determine, from the lease or license and such other information as may be available, that portion of the total rental charge which is exempt from the tax imposed by this section. The portion of the premises leased or rented by a for-profit entity providing a residential facility for the aged will be exempt on the basis of a pro rata portion calculated by combining the square footage of the areas used for residential units by the aged and for the care of such residents and dividing the resultant sum by the total square footage of the rented premises. For purposes of this section, the term "residential facility for the aged" means a facility that is licensed or certified in whole or in part under chapter 400 or chapter 651; or that provides residences to the elderly and is financed by a mortgage or loan made or insured by the United States Department of Housing and Urban Development under s. 202, s. 202 with a s. 8 subsidy, s. 221(d)(3) or (4), s. 232, or s. 236 of the National Housing Act; or other such similar facility that provides residences primarily for the elderly.

(c) For the exercise of such privilege, a tax is levied in an amount equal to 6 percent of and on the total rent or license fee charged for such real property by the person charging or collecting the rental or license fee. The total rent or license fee charged for such real property shall include payments for the granting of a privilege to use or occupy real property for any purpose and shall include base rent, percentage rents, or similar charges. Such charges shall be included in the total rent or license fee subject to tax under this section whether or not they can be attributed to the ability of the lessor's or licensor's property as used or operated to attract customers. Payments for intrinsically valuable personal property such as franchises, trademarks, service marks, logos, or patents are not subject to tax under this section. In the case of a contractual arrangement that provides for both payments taxable as total rent or license fee and payments not subject to tax, the tax shall be based on a reasonable allocation of such payments and shall not apply to that portion which is for the nontaxable payments.

(d) When the rental or license fee of any such real property is paid by way of property, goods, wares, merchandise, services, or other thing of value, the tax shall be at the rate of 6 percent of the value of the property, goods, wares, merchandise, services, or other thing of value.

(2)(a) The tenant or person actually occupying, using, or entitled to the use of any property from which the rental or license fee is subject to taxation under this section shall pay the tax to his or her immediate landlord or other person granting the right to such tenant or person to occupy or use such real property.

(b) It is the further intent of this Legislature that only one tax be collected on the rental or license fee payable for the occupancy or use of any such property, that the tax so collected shall not be pyramided by a progression of transactions, and that the amount of the tax due the state shall not be decreased by any such progression of transactions.

*(3) The tax imposed by this section shall be in addition to the total amount of the rental or license fee, shall be charged by the lessor or person receiving the rent or payment in and by a rental or license fee arrangement with the lessee or person paying the rental or license fee, and shall be due and payable at the time of the receipt of such rental or license fee payment by the lessor or other person who receives the rental or payment. Notwithstanding any other provision of this chapter, the tax imposed by this section on the rental, lease, or license for the use of a convention hall, exhibition hall, auditorium, stadium, theater, arena, civic center, performing arts center, or publicly owned recreational facility to hold an event of not more than 7 consecutive days' duration shall be collected at the time of the payment for that rental, lease, or license but is not due and payable to the department until the first day of the month following the last day that the event for which the payment is made is actually held, and becomes delinquent on the 21st day of that month. The owner, lessor, or person receiving the rent or license fee shall remit the tax to the department at the times

and in the manner hereinafter provided for dealers to remit taxes under this chapter. The same duties imposed by this chapter upon dealers in tangible personal property respecting the collection and remission of the tax; the making of returns; the keeping of books, records, and accounts; and the compliance with the rules and regulations of the department in the administration of this chapter shall apply to and be binding upon all persons who manage any leases or operate real property, hotels, apartment houses, roominghouses, or tourist and trailer camps and all persons who collect or receive rents or license fees taxable under this chapter on behalf of owners or lessors.

(4) The tax imposed by this section shall constitute a lien on the property of the lessee or licensee of any real estate in the same manner as, and shall be collectible as are, liens authorized and imposed by ss. 713.68 and 713.69.

(5) When space is subleased to a convention or industry trade show in a convention hall, exhibition hall, or auditorium, whether publicly or privately owned, the sponsor who holds the prime lease is subject to tax on the prime lease and the sublease is exempt.

(6) The lease or rental of land or a hall or other facilities by a fair association subject to the provisions of chapter 616 to a show promoter or prime operator of a carnival or midway attraction is exempt from the tax imposed by this section; however, the sublease of land or a hall or other facilities by the show promoter or prime operator is not exempt from the provisions of this section.

(7) Utility charges subject to sales tax which are paid by a tenant to the lessor and which are part of a payment for the privilege or right to use or occupy real property are exempt from tax if the lessor has paid sales tax on the purchase of such utilities and the charges billed by the lessor to the tenant are separately stated and at the same or a lower price than those paid by the lessor.

(8) Charges by lessors to a lessee to cancel or terminate a lease agreement are presumed taxable if the lessor records such charges as rental income in its books and records. This presumption can be overcome by the provision of sufficient documentation by either the lessor or the lessee that such charges were other than for the rental of real property.

(9) The rental, lease, sublease, or license for the use of a skybox, luxury box, or other box seats for use during a high school or college football game is exempt from the tax imposed by this section when the charge for such rental, lease, sublease, or license is imposed by a nonprofit sponsoring organization which is qualified as nonprofit pursuant to s. 501(c)(3) of the Internal Revenue Code.

**(10) Separately stated charges imposed by a convention hall, exhibition hall, auditorium, stadium, theater, arena, civic center, performing arts center, or publicly owned recreational facility upon a lessee or licensee for food, drink, or services required or available in connection with a lease or license to use real property, including charges for laborers, stagehands, ticket takers, event staff, security personnel, cleaning staff, and other event-related personnel, advertising, and credit card processing, are exempt from the tax imposed by this section.

*Note.—Section 3, ch. 2000-345, as amended by s. 55, ch. 2002-218, and s. 27, ch. 2001-140, amended paragraph (1)(a) and s. 3, ch. 2000-345, as amended by s. 55, ch. 2002-218, amended subsection (3), effective July 1, 2006. Section 55, ch. 2002-218, failed to incorporate the amendments to s. 212.031(1)(a) by s. 2, ch. 2000-182, s. 1, ch. 2000-183, s. 53, ch. 2000-260, and s. 27, ch. 2001-140. Paragraph (1)(a), as amended by s. 3, ch. 2000-345, as amended by s. 55, ch. 2002-218, and as amended by s. 2, ch. 2000-182, s. 1, ch. 2000-183, s. 53, ch. 2000-260, and s. 27, ch. 2001-140, and subsection (3), as amended by s. 3, ch. 2000-345, as amended by s. 55, ch. 2002-218, effective July 1, 2006, will read:

(1)(a) It is declared to be the legislative intent that every person is exercising a taxable privilege who engages in the business of renting, leasing, letting, or granting a license for the use of any real property unless such property is:

1. Assessed as agricultural property under s. 193.461.

2. Used exclusively as dwelling units.

3. Property subject to tax on parking, docking, or storage spaces under s. 212.03(6).

4. Recreational property or the common elements of a condominium when subject to a lease between the developer or owner thereof and the condominium association in its own right or as agent for the owners of individual condominium units or the owners of individual condominium units. However, only the lease payments on such property shall be exempt from the tax imposed by this chapter, and any other use made by the owner or the condominium association shall be fully taxable under this chapter.

5. A public or private street or right-of-way and poles, conduits, fixtures, and similar improvements located on such streets or rights-of-way, occupied or used by a utility or provider of communications services, as defined by s. 202.11, for utility or communications or television purposes. For purposes of this subparagraph, the term "utility" means any person providing utility services as defined in s. 203.012. This exception also applies to property, wherever located, on which the following are placed: towers, antennas, cables, accessory structures, or equipment, not including switching equipment, used in the provision of mobile communications services as defined in s. 202.11. For purposes of this chapter, towers used in the provision of mobile communications services, as defined in s. 202.11, are considered to be fixtures.

6. A public street or road which is used for transportation purposes.

7. Property used at an airport exclusively for the purpose of aircraft landing or aircraft taxiing or property used by an airline for the purpose of loading or unloading passengers or property onto or from aircraft or for fueling aircraft.

8.a. Property used at a port authority, as defined in s. 315.02(2), exclusively for the purpose of oceangoing vessels or tugs docking, or such vessels mooring on property used by a port authority for the purpose of loading or unloading passengers or cargo onto or from such a vessel, or property used at a port authority for fueling such vessels, or to the extent that the amount paid for the use of any property at the port is based on the charge for the amount of tonnage actually imported or exported through the port by a tenant.

b. The amount charged for the use of any property at the port in excess of the amount charged for tonnage actually imported or exported shall remain subject to tax except as provided in sub-subparagraph a.

9. Property used as an integral part of the performance of qualified production services. As used in this subparagraph, the term "qualified production services" means any activity or service performed directly in connection with the production of a qualified motion picture, as defined in s. 212.06(1)(b), and includes:

a. Photography, sound and recording, casting, location managing and scouting, shooting, creation of special and optical effects, animation, adaptation (language, media, electronic, or otherwise), technological modifications, computer graphics, set and stage support (such as electricians, lighting designers and operators, greensmen, prop managers and assistants, and grips), wardrobe (design, preparation, and management), hair and makeup (design, production, and application), performing (such as acting, dancing, and playing), designing and executing stunts, coaching, consulting, writing, scoring, composing, choreographing, script supervising, directing, producing, transmitting dailies, dubbing, mixing, editing, cutting, looping, printing, processing, duplicating, storing, and distributing;

b. The design, planning, engineering, construction, alteration, repair, and maintenance of real or personal property including stages, sets, props, models, paintings, and facilities principally required for the performance of those services listed in sub-subparagraph a.; and

c. Property management services directly related to property used in connection with the services described in sub-subparagraphs a. and b.

This exemption will inure to the taxpayer upon presentation of the certificate of exemption issued to the taxpayer under the provisions of s. 288.1258.

10. Leased, subleased, licensed, or rented to a person providing food and drink concessionaire services within the premises of a convention hall, exhibition hall, auditorium, stadium, theater, arena, civic center, performing arts center, publicly owned recreational facility, or any business operated under a permit issued pursuant to chapter 550. A person providing retail concessionaire services involving the sale of food and drink or other tangible personal property within the premises of an airport shall be subject to tax on the rental of real property used for that purpose, but shall not be subject to the tax on any license to use the property. For purposes of this subparagraph, the term "sale" shall not include the leasing of tangible personal property.

11. Property occupied pursuant to an instrument calling for payments which the department has declared, in a Technical Assistance Advisement issued on or before March 15, 1993, to be nontaxable pursuant to rule 12A-1.070(19)(c), Florida Administrative Code; provided that this subparagraph shall only apply to property occupied by the same person before and after the execution of the subject instrument and only to those payments made pursuant to such instrument, exclusive of renewals and extensions thereof occurring after March 15, 1993.

12. Property used or occupied predominantly for space flight business purposes. As used in this subparagraph, "space flight business" means the manufacturing, processing, or assembly of a space facility, space propulsion system, space vehicle, satellite, or station of any kind possessing the capacity for space flight, as

defined by s. 212.02(23), or components thereof, and also means the following activities supporting space flight: vehicle launch activities, flight operations, ground control or ground support, and all administrative activities directly related thereto. Property shall be deemed to be used or occupied predominantly for space flight business purposes if more than 50 percent of the property, or improvements thereon, is used for one or more space flight business purposes. Possession by a landlord, lessor, or licensor of a signed written statement from the tenant, lessee, or licensee claiming the exemption shall relieve the landlord, lessor, or licensor from the responsibility of collecting the tax, and the department shall look solely to the tenant, lessee, or licensee for recovery of such tax if it determines that the exemption was not applicable.

* * * * *

(3) The tax imposed by this section shall be in addition to the total amount of the rental or license fee, shall be charged by the lessor or person receiving the rent or payment in and by a rental or license fee arrangement with the lessee or person paying the rental or license fee, and shall be due and payable at the time of the receipt of such rental or license fee payment by the lessor or other person who receives the rental or payment. The owner, lessor, or person receiving the rent or license fee shall remit the tax to the department at the times and in the manner hereinafter provided for dealers to remit taxes under this chapter. The same duties imposed by this chapter upon dealers in tangible personal property respecting the collection and remission of the tax; the making of returns; the keeping of books, records, and accounts; and the compliance with the rules and regulations of the department in the administration of this chapter shall apply to and be binding upon all persons who manage any leases or operate real property, hotels, apartment houses, roominghouses, or tourist and trailer camps and all persons who collect or receive rents or license fees taxable under this chapter on behalf of owners or lessors.

**Note.—Repealed July 1, 2006, by s. 3, ch. 2000-345, as amended by s. 55, ch. 2002-218.

713.691 Landlord's lien for rent; exemptions.—

(1) With regard to a residential tenancy, the landlord has a lien on all personal property of the tenant located on the premises for accrued rent due to the landlord under the rental agreement. This lien shall be in addition to any other liens upon such property which the landlord may acquire by law and may be modified or waived, in whole or in part, by the provisions of a written rental agreement. The landlord's lien for rent shall attach to the tenant's personal property at the time the sheriff gives the landlord possession of the premises, but it is not required that the tenant's property be removed in order to give the landlord possession of the premises.

(2) When the tenant is the head of a family, personal property owned by her or him in the value of $1,000 is exempt from the lien provided by this section. This subsection does not authorize an exemption any greater than that which may be available to the tenant in s. 4, Art. X of the State Constitution.

(3) The remedy of distress for rent is abolished with regard to residential tenancies.

715.07 Vehicles parked on private property; towing.—

(1) As used in this section, the term:

(a) "Vehicle" means any mobile item which normally uses wheels, whether motorized or not.

(b) "Vessel" means every description of watercraft, barge, and air boat used or capable of being used as a means of transportation on water, other than a seaplane or a "documented vessel" as defined in s. 327.02(8).

(2) The owner or lessee of real property, or any person authorized by the owner or lessee, which person may be the designated representative of the condominium association if the real property is a condominium, may cause any vehicle or vessel parked on such property without her or his permission to be removed by a person regularly engaged in the business of towing vehicles or vessels, without liability for the costs of removal, transportation, or storage or damages caused by such removal, transportation, or storage, under any of the following circumstances:

(a) The towing or removal of any vehicle or vessel from private property without the consent of the registered owner or other legally authorized person in control of that vehicle or vessel is subject to strict compliance with the following conditions and restrictions:

1. a. Any towed or removed vehicle must be stored at a site within a 10-mile radius of the point of removal in any county of 500,000 population or more, and within a 15-mile radius of the point of removal in any county of less than 500,000 population. That site must be open for the purpose of redemption of vehicles on any day that the person or firm towing such vehicle or vessel is open for towing purposes, from 8:00 a.m. to 6:00 p.m., and, when closed, shall have prominently posted a sign indicating a telephone number where the operator of the site can be reached at all times. Upon receipt of a telephoned request to open the site to redeem a vehicle or vessel, the operator shall return to the site within 1 hour or she or he will be in violation of this section.

b. If no towing business providing such service is located within the area of towing limitations set forth in sub-subparagraph a., the following limitations apply: any towed or removed vehicle or vessel must be stored at a site within a 20-mile radius of the point of removal in any county of 500,000 population or more, and within a 30-mile radius of the point of removal in any county of less than 500,000 population.

2. The person or firm towing or removing the vehicle or vessel shall, within 30 minutes after completion of such towing or removal, notify the municipal police department or, in an unincorporated area, the sheriff of such towing or removal, the storage site, the time the vehicle or vessel was towed or removed, and the make, model, color, and license plate number of the vehicle or description and registration number of the vessel and shall obtain the name of the person at that department to whom such information was reported and note that name on the trip record.

3. A person in the process of towing or removing a vehicle or vessel from the premises or parking lot in which the vehicle or vessel is not lawfully parked must stop when a person seeks the return of the vehicle or vessel. The vehicle or vessel must be returned upon the payment of a reasonable service fee of not more than one-half of the posted rate for the towing or removal service as provided in subparagraph 6. The vehicle or vessel may be

towed or removed if, after a reasonable opportunity, the owner or legally authorized person in control of the vehicle or vessel is unable to pay the service fee. If the vehicle or vessel is redeemed, a detailed signed receipt must be given to the person redeeming the vehicle or vessel.

4. A person may not pay or accept money or other valuable consideration for the privilege of towing or removing vehicles or vessels from a particular location.

5. Except for property appurtenant to and obviously a part of a single-family residence, and except for instances when notice is personally given to the owner or other legally authorized person in control of the vehicle or vessel that the area in which that vehicle or vessel is parked is reserved or otherwise unavailable for unauthorized vehicles or vessels and that the vehicle or vessel is subject to being removed at the owner's or operator's expense, any property owner or lessee, or person authorized by the property owner or lessee, prior to towing or removing any vehicle or vessel from private property without the consent of the owner or other legally authorized person in control of that vehicle or vessel, must post a notice meeting the following requirements:

a. The notice must be prominently placed at each driveway access or curb cut allowing vehicular access to the property, within 5 feet from the public right-of-way line. If there are no curbs or access barriers, the signs must be posted not less than one sign for each 25 feet of lot frontage.

b. The notice must clearly indicate, in not less than 2-inch high, light-reflective letters on a contrasting background, that unauthorized vehicles will be towed away at the owner's expense. The words "tow-away zone" must be included on the sign in not less than 4-inch high letters.

c. The notice must also provide the name and current telephone number of the person or firm towing or removing the vehicles or vessel.

d. The sign structure containing the required notices must be permanently installed with the words "tow-away zone" not less than 3 feet and not more than 6 feet above ground level and must be continuously maintained on the property for not less than 24 hours prior to the towing or removal of any vehicles or vessels.

e. The local government may require permitting and inspection of these signs prior to any towing or removal of vehicles or vessels being authorized.

f. A business with 20 or fewer parking spaces satisfies the notice requirements of this subparagraph by prominently displaying a sign stating "Reserved Parking for Customers Only Unauthorized Vehicles or Vessels Will be Towed Away At the Owner's Expense" in not less than 4-inch high, light-reflective letters on a contrasting background.

g. A property owner towing or removing vessels from real property must post notice, consistent with the requirements in subparagraphs a.–f., which apply to vehicles, that unauthorized vehicles or vessels will be towed away at the owner's expense/

A business owner or lessee may authorize the removal of a vehicle or vessel by a towing company when the vehicle or vessel is parked in such a manner that restricts the normal operation of business; and if a vehicle or vessel parked on a public right-of-way obstructs access to a private driveway the owner, lessee, or agent may have the vehicle or vessel removed by a towing com-

pany upon signing an order that the vehicle or vessel be removed without a posted tow-away zone sign.

6. Any person or firm that tows or removes vehicles or vessels and proposes to require an owner, operator, or person in control of a vehicle or vessel to pay the costs of towing and storage prior to redemption of the vehicle or vessel must file and keep on record with the local law enforcement agency a complete copy of the current rates to be charged for such services and post at the storage site an identical rate schedule and any written contracts with property owners, lessees, or persons in control of property which authorize such person or firm to remove vehicles or vessels as provided in this section.

7. Any person or firm towing or removing any vehicles from private property without the consent of the owner or other legally authorized person in control of the vehicles or vessels shall, on any trucks, wreckers as defined in s. 713.78(1)(c), or other vehicles or vessels used in the towing or removal, have the name, address, and telephone number of the company performing such service clearly printed in contrasting colors on the driver and passenger sides of the vehicle. The name shall be in at least 3-inch permanently affixed letters, and the address and telephone number shall be in at least 1-inch permanently affixed letters.

8. Vehicle entry for the purpose of removing the vehicle or vessel shall be allowed with reasonable care on the part of the person or firm towing the vehicle or vessel. Such person or firm shall be liable for any damage occasioned to the vehicle or vessel if such entry is not in accordance with the standard of reasonable care.

9. When a vehicle or vessel has been towed or removed pursuant to this section, it must be released to its owner or custodian within one hour after requested. Any vehicle or vessel owner or agent shall have the right to inspect the vehicle before accepting its return, and no release or waiver of any kind which would release the person or firm towing the vehicle or vessel from liability for damages noted by the owner or other legally authorized person at the time of the redemption may be required from any vehicle or vessel owner, custodian, or agent as a condition of release of the vehicle or vessel to its owner. A detailed, signed receipt showing the legal name of the company or person towing or removing the vehicle or vessel must be given to the person paying towing or storage charges at the time of payment, whether requested or not.

(b) These requirements are minimum standards and do not preclude enactment of additional regulations by any municipality or county including the right to regulate rates when vehicles or vessels are towed from private property.

(3) This section does not apply to law enforcement, firefighting, rescue squad, ambulance, or other emergency vehicles or vessels that are marked as such or to property owned by any governmental entity.

(4) When a person improperly causes a vehicle or vessel to be removed, such person shall be liable to the owner or lessee of the vehicle or vessel for the cost of removal, transportation, and storage; any damages resulting from the removal, transportation, or storage of the vehicle or vessel; attorney's fees; and court costs.

(5) (a) Any person who violates subparagraph (2)(a)2. or subparagraph (2)(a)6. commits a misdemeanor of the first degree, punishable as provided in s. 775.082 or s. 775.083. (b) Any person who violates subparagraph (2)(a)1. or subparagraph (2)(a)3,

subparagraph (2)(a)4., or subparagraph (2)(a)7, or subparagraph (2)(a)9. commits a felony of the third degree, punishable as provided in s. 775.082, s. 775.083, or s. 775.084.

Section 6. Except as otherwise expressly provided in this act, this act shall take effect July 1, 2005.

715.10 Disposition of Personal Property Landlord and Tenant Act; short title.—Sections 715.10-715.111 may be cited as the "Disposition of Personal Property Landlord and Tenant Act."

715.101 Application of ss. 715.10-715.111.—

(1) Sections 715.10-715.111 apply to all tenancies to which part I or part II of chapter 83 are applicable, and to tenancies after a writ of possession has been issued pursuant to s. 723.062.

(2) Sections 715.10-715.111 provide an optional procedure for the disposition of personal property which remains on the premises after a tenancy has terminated or expired and the premises have been vacated by the tenant through eviction, surrender, abandonment, or otherwise.

(3) Sections 715.10-715.111 do not apply to property which exists for the purpose of providing utility services and is owned by a utility, whether or not such property is actually in operation to provide such utility services.

(4) If the requirements of ss. 715.10-715.111 are not satisfied, nothing in ss. 715.10-715.111 affects the rights and liabilities of the landlord, the former tenant, or any other person.

715.102 Definitions of terms used in ss. 715.10-715.111.—As used in ss. 715.10-715.111, unless some other meaning is clearly indicated, the term:

(1) "Landlord" means any operator, keeper, lessor, or sublessor of furnished or unfurnished premises for rent, or her or his agent or successor-in-interest.

(2) "Owner" means any person other than the landlord who has any right, title, or interest in personal property.

(3) "Premises" includes any common areas associated therewith.

(4) "Reasonable belief" means the actual knowledge or belief a prudent person should have without making an investigation, including any investigation of public records; except that, when the landlord has specific information indicating that such an investigation would more probably than not reveal pertinent information and the cost of such an investigation would be reasonable in relation to the probable value of the personal property involved, the term "reasonable belief" includes the actual knowledge or belief a prudent person would have if such an investigation were made.

(5) "Tenant" includes any paying guest, lessee, or sublessee of any premises for rent, whether a dwelling unit or not.

715.103 Lost property.—Personal property which the landlord reasonably believes to have been lost shall be disposed of as otherwise provided by law. However, if the appropriate law enforcement agency or other government agency refuses to accept custody of property pursuant to chapter 705, the landlord may dispose of the property pursuant to ss. 715.10-715.111. The landlord is not liable to the owner of the property if she or he complies with this section and the other provisions of ss. 715.10-715.111.

715.104 Notification of former tenant of personal property remaining on premises after tenancy has terminated.—

(1) When personal property remains on the premises after a tenancy has terminated or expired and the premises have been vacated by the tenant, through eviction or otherwise, the landlord shall give written notice to such tenant and to any other person the landlord reasonably believes to be the owner of the property.

(2) The notice shall describe the property in a manner reasonably adequate to permit the owner of the property to identify it. The notice may describe all or a portion of the property, but the limitation of liability provided by s. 715.11 does not protect the landlord from any liability arising from the disposition of property not described in the notice, except that a trunk, valise, box, or other container which is locked, fastened, or tied in a manner which deters immediate access to its contents may be described as such without describing its contents. The notice shall advise the person to be notified that reasonable costs of storage may be charged before the property is returned, and the notice shall state where the property may be claimed and the date before which the claim must be made. The date specified in the notice shall be a date not fewer than 10 days after the notice is personally delivered or, if mailed, not fewer than 15 days after the notice is deposited in the mail.

(3) The notice shall be personally delivered or sent by first-class mail, postage prepaid, to the person to be notified at her or his last known address and, if there is reason to believe that the notice sent to that address will not be received by that person, also delivered or sent to such other address, if any, known to the landlord where such person may reasonably be expected to receive the notice.

715.105 Form of notice concerning abandoned property to former tenant.—

(1) A notice to the former tenant which is in substantially the following form satisfies the requirements of s. 715.104:

Notice of Right to Reclaim Abandoned Property

To: (Name of former tenant)

(Address of former tenant)

When you vacated the premises at (address of premises, including room or apartment number, if any) , the following personal property remained: (insert description of personal property) .

You may claim this property at (address where property may be claimed) .

Unless you pay the reasonable costs of storage and advertising, if any, for all the above-described property and take possession of the property which you claim, not later than (insert date not fewer than 10 days after notice is personally delivered or, if mailed, not fewer than 15 days after notice is deposited in the mail) , this property may be disposed of pursuant to s. 715.109.

(Insert here the statement required by subsection (2))

Dated:_____

(Signature of landlord)

(Type or print name of landlord)

(Telephone number)

(Address)

(2) The notice set forth in subsection (1) shall also contain one of the following statements:

(a) "If you fail to reclaim the property, it will be sold at a public sale after notice of the sale has been given by publication. You have the right to bid on the property at this sale. After the property is sold and the costs of storage, advertising, and sale are deducted, the remaining money will be paid over to the county. You may claim the remaining money at any time within 1 year after the county receives the money."

(b) "Because this property is believed to be worth less than $500, it may be kept, sold, or destroyed without further notice if you fail to reclaim it within the time indicated above."

715.106 Form of notice concerning abandoned property to owner other than former tenant.—

(1) A notice which is in substantially the following form given to a person who is not the former tenant and whom the landlord reasonably believes to be the owner of any of the abandoned personal property satisfies the requirements of s. 715.104:

Notice of Right to Reclaim Abandoned Property

To: (Name)

(Address)

When (name of former tenant) vacated the premises at (address of premises, including room or apartment number, if any) , the following personal property remained: (insert description of personal property) .

If you own any of this property, you may claim it at (address where property may be claimed) . Unless you pay the reasonable costs of storage and advertising, if any, and take possession of the property to which you are entitled, not later than (insert date not fewer than 10 days after notice is personally delivered or, if mailed, not fewer than 15 days after notice is deposited in the mail) , this property may be disposed of pursuant to s. 715.109.

(Insert here the statement required by subsection (2))

Dated:_____

(Signature of landlord)

(Type or print name of landlord)

(Telephone number)

(Address)

(2) The notice set forth in subsection (1) shall also contain one of the following statements:

(a) "If you fail to reclaim the property, it will be sold at a public sale after notice of the sale has been given by publication. You have the right to bid on the property at this sale. After the property is sold and the costs of storage, advertising, and sale are deducted, the remaining money will be paid over to the county. You may claim the remaining money at any time within 1 year after the county receives the money."

(b) "Because this property is believed to be worth less than $500, it may be kept, sold, or destroyed without further notice if you fail to reclaim it within the time indicated above."

715.107 Storage of abandoned property.—The personal property described in the notice either shall be left on the vacated premises or be stored by the landlord in a place of safekeeping until the landlord either releases the property pursuant to s. 715.108 or disposes of the property pursuant to s. 715.109. The landlord shall exercise reasonable care in storing the property, but she or he is not liable to the tenant or any other owner for any loss unless caused by the landlord's deliberate or negligent act.

715.108 Release of personal property.—

(1) The personal property described in the notice shall be released by the landlord to the former tenant or, at the landlord's option, to any person reasonably believed by the landlord to be its owner, if such tenant or other person pays the reasonable costs of storage and advertising and takes possession of the property not later than the date specified in the notice for taking possession.

(2) Where personal property is not released pursuant to subsection (1) and the notice has stated that the personal property will be sold at a public sale, the landlord shall release the personal property to the former tenant if she or he claims it prior to the time it is sold and pays the reasonable costs of storage, advertising, and sale incurred prior to the time the property is withdrawn from sale.

715.109 Sale or disposition of abandoned property.—

(1) If the personal property described in the notice is not released pursuant to s. 715.108, it shall be sold at public sale by competitive bidding. However, if the landlord reasonably believes that the total resale value of the property not released is less than $500, she or he may retain such property for her or his own use or dispose of it in any manner she or he chooses. Nothing in this section shall be construed to preclude the landlord or tenant from bidding on the property at the public sale. The successful bidder's title is subject to ownership rights, liens, and security interests which have priority by law.

(2) Notice of the time and place of the public sale shall be given by an advertisement of the sale published once a week for two consecutive weeks in a newspaper of general circulation where the sale is to be held. The sale must be held at the nearest suitable place to that where the personal property is held or stored. The advertisement must include a description of the goods, the name of the former tenant, and the time and place of the sale. The sale must take place at least 10 days after the first publication. If there is no newspaper of general circulation where the sale is to be held, the advertisement must be posted at least 10 days before the sale in not less than six conspicuous places in the neighborhood of the proposed sale. The last publication shall be at least 5 days before the sale is to be held. Notice of sale may be published before the last of the dates specified for taking possession of the property in any notice given pursuant to s. 715.104.

(3) The notice of the sale shall describe the property to be sold in a manner reasonably adequate to permit the owner of the property to identify it. The notice may describe all or a portion of the property, but the limitation of liability provided by s. 715.11 does not protect the landlord from any liability arising from the disposition of property not described in the notice, except that a trunk, valise, box, or other container which is locked, fastened, or tied in a manner which deters immediate access to its contents may be described as such without describing its contents.

(4) After deduction of the costs of storage, advertising, and sale, any balance of the proceeds of the sale which is not claimed by the former tenant or an owner other than such tenant shall be paid into the treasury of the county in which the sale took place not later than 30 days after the date of sale. The former tenant or other owner or other person having interest in the funds may claim the balance within 1 year from the date of payment to the county by making application to the county treasurer or other official designated by the county. If the county pays the balance or any part thereof to a claimant, neither the county nor any officer or employee thereof is liable to any other claimant as to the amount paid.

715.11 Nonliability of landlord after disposition of property.—

(1) Notwithstanding the provisions of s. 715.101, after the landlord releases to the former tenant property which remains on the premises after a tenancy is terminated, the landlord is not liable with respect to that property to any person.

(2) After the landlord releases property pursuant to s. 715.108 to a person who is not the former tenant and who is reasonably believed by the landlord to be the owner of the property, the landlord is not liable with respect to that property to:

(a) Any person to whom notice was given pursuant to s. 715.104; or

(b) Any person to whom notice was not given pursuant to s. 715.104 unless such person proves that, prior to releasing the property, the landlord believed or reasonably should have believed that such person had an interest in the property and also that the landlord knew or should have known upon reasonable investigation the address of such person.

(3) Where property is disposed of pursuant to s. 715.109, the landlord is not liable with respect to that property to:

(a) Any person to whom notice was given pursuant to s. 715.104; or

(b) Any person to whom notice was not given pursuant to s. 715.104 unless such person proves that, prior to disposing of the property pursuant to s. 715.109, the landlord believed or reasonably should have believed that such person had an interest in the property and also that the landlord knew or should have known upon reasonable investigation the address of such person.

715.111 Assessing costs of storage.—

(1) Costs of storage for which payment may be required under ss. 715.10-715.111 shall be assessed in the following manner:

(a) When a former tenant claims property pursuant to s. 715.108, she or he may be required to pay the reasonable costs of storage for all the personal property remaining on the premises at the termination of the tenancy, which costs are unpaid at the time the claim is made.

(b) When an owner other than the former tenant claims property pursuant to s. 715.108, she or he may be required to pay the reasonable costs of storage for only the property in which she or he claims an interest.

(2) In determining the costs to be assessed under subsection (1), the landlord may not charge more than one person for the same costs.

(3) If the landlord stores the personal property on the premises, the costs of storage shall be the fair rental value of the space reasonably required for such storage for the term of the storage.

APPENDIX C:
EVICTION FLOWCHARTS AND
LEGAL HOLIDAYS

On the next two pages are flowcharts that show each step in the eviction process. The first one is for an eviction for nonpayment of rent. The second one is for evictions based on the tenant's breach of some clause of the lease other than payment of rent or for the tenant's violation of some aspect of the *Landlord-Tenant Act*.

On the final page of this appendix is a list of the legal holidays in Florida. At one time it was imperative to know all of these dates because failure to exclude them in a three-day notice was fatal to an eviction. A recent change to the law states that the only holidays excluded in the three-day notice are those observed by the local court. This list is included so that you can be aware of any holidays that might be observed by your local court. To be sure, call the court administrator's office.

Eviction Flowchart—Nonpayment of Rent

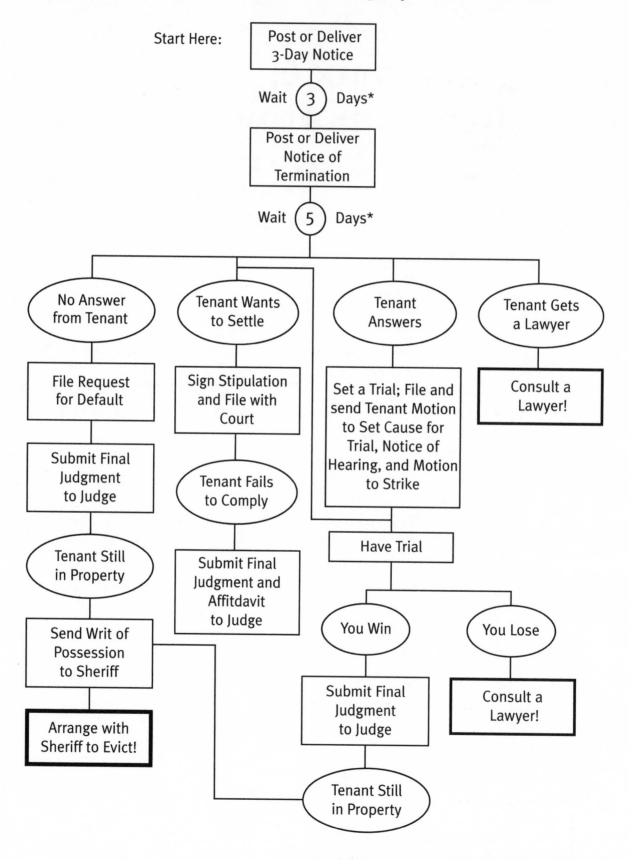

Start Here:

Post or Deliver 3-Day Notice

Wait (3) Days*

Post or Deliver Notice of Termination

Wait (5) Days*

No Answer from Tenant

Tenant Wants to Settle

Tenant Answers

Tenant Gets a Lawyer

File Request for Default

Sign Stipulation and File with Court

Set a Trial; File and send Tenant Motion to Set Cause for Trial, Notice of Hearing, and Motion to Strike

Consult a Lawyer!

Submit Final Judgment to Judge

Tenant Fails to Comply

Have Trial

Tenant Still in Property

Submit Final Judgment and Affitdavit to Judge

You Win

You Lose

Send Writ of Possession to Sheriff

Submit Final Judgment to Judge

Consult a Lawyer!

Arrange with Sheriff to Evict!

Tenant Still in Property

*Excluding Saturdays, Sundays, and legal holidays

Eviction Flowchart—Breach of Lease

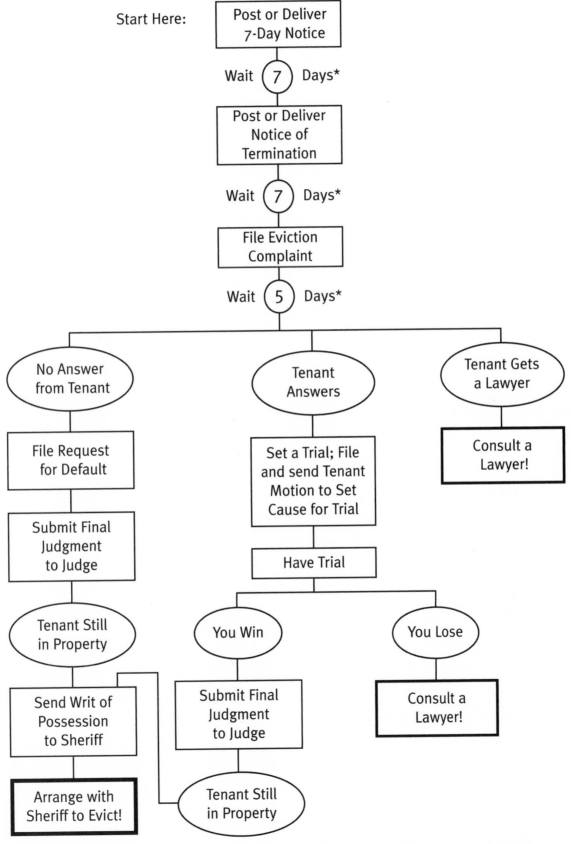

Start Here:

Post or Deliver
7-Day Notice

Wait (7) Days*

Post or Deliver
Notice of
Termination

Wait (7) Days*

File Eviction
Complaint

Wait (5) Days*

No Answer
from Tenant

Tenant
Answers

Tenant Gets
a Lawyer

File Request
for Default

Set a Trial; File
and send Tenant
Motion to Set
Cause for Trial

**Consult a
Lawyer!**

Submit Final
Judgment
to Judge

Have Trial

Tenant Still
in Property

You Win

You Lose

Send Writ of
Possession
to Sheriff

Submit Final
Judgment
to Judge

**Consult a
Lawyer!**

**Arrange with
Sheriff to Evict!**

Tenant Still
in Property

*Excluding Saturdays, Sundays, and legal holidays

Legal Holidays in Florida

(Florida Statutes Chapter 683)

Every Sunday	
New Year's Day	Jan. 1
Martin Luther King, Jr.'s Birthday	Jan. 15
Robert E. Lee's Birthday	Jan. 19
Abraham Lincoln's Birthday	Feb. 12
Susan B. Anthony's Birthday	Feb. 15
George Washington's Birthday	Third Mon. in Feb.
Good Friday	(varies)
Pascua Florida Day	April 2
Confederate Memorial Day	April 26
Memorial Day	Last Mon. in May
Jefferson Davis' Birthday	June 3
Flag Day	June 14
Independence Day	July 4
Labor Day	First Mon. in Sept.
Columbus Day and Farmers' Day	Second Mon. in Oct.
Veterans' Day	Nov. 11
General Election Day	(varies)
Thanksgiving Day	Fourth Thurs. in Nov.
Christmas Day	Dec. 25

Shrove Tuesday (in counties where carnival associations are organized to celebrate Mardi Gras)

Parade Day (in Hillsborough County)

Gasparilla Day (in Hillsborough County)

DeSoto Day (in Manatee County)

The chief judge of any circuit may designate Rosh Hashanah, Yom Kippur, and Good Friday as legal holidays for the courts within the circuit.

NOTE: *When a legal holiday falls on a Sunday, the next day is considered a legal holiday.*

APPENDIX D: BLANK FORMS

Use of the following forms is described in the text or is self-explanatory. If you do not understand any aspect of a form, seek advice from an attorney. Forms that have the words "The Florida Bar" at the bottom are the "simplified forms" approved by the Florida Supreme Court for use by paralegals and persons who wish to represent themselves.

Publisher's Note: Many of the blank forms found in this Appendix are replicas of the forms created by The Florida Bar. The format, look, and design of these forms are intended to match that of The Florida Bar forms and may contain differences or inconsistencies with other forms in the Appendix.

License: The forms in this book that contain the name of The Florida Bar in the lower left corner are in the public domain and may be copied by anyone. Other forms have been created by the author. Although this book is copyrighted, purchasers of the book are granted a license to copy the forms created by the author for their own personal use or use in their law practice.

Table of Forms

TENANT APPLICATION

Name_____ Date of Birth _____

Name_____ Date of Birth _____

Soc. Sec. Nos._____

Drivers' License Nos._____

Children & Ages_____

Present Landlord_____ Phone_____

Address _____ How Long?_____

Previous Landlord_____ Phone_____

Address_____

Second Previous Landlord_____ Phone_____

Address_____

Nearest Relative_____ Phone_____

Address_____

Employer_____ Phone_____

Address_____

Second Applicant's Employer_____ Phone_____

Address_____

Pets_____

Other persons who will stay at premises for more than one week_____

_____

Bank Name_____Acct. #_____

Bank Name_____Acct. #_____

Have you ever been evicted?_____

Have you ever been in litigation with a landlord?_____

The undersigned hereby attest that the above information is true.

_____

_____

This page intentionally left blank.

INSPECTION REPORT

Date: _____

Unit: _____

AREA	CONDITION			
	Move-In		Move-Out	
	Good	Poor	Good	Poor
Yard/garden				
Driveway				
Patio/porch				
Exterior				
Entry light/bell				
Living room/Dining room/Halls				
Floors/carpets				
Walls/ceilings				
Doors/locks				
Fixtures/light				
Outlets/switches				
Other				
Bedrooms				
Floors/carpets				
Walls/ceilings				
Doors/locks				
Fixtures/light				
Outlets/switches				
Other				
Bathrooms				
Faucets				
Toilet				
Sink/tub				
Floors/carpets				
Walls/ceiling				
Doors/locks				
Fixtures/lights				
Outlet/switches				
Other				
Kitchen				
Refrigerator				
Range				
Oven				
Dishwasher				
Sink/disposal				
Cabinets/counters				
Floors/carpets				
Walls/ceiling				
Doors/locks				
Fixtures/lights				
Outlets/switches				
Other				
Misc.				
Clostes/pantry				
Garage				
Keys				
Other				

_____   _____

          Tenant   Landlord

This page intentionally left blank.

PET AGREEMENT

THIS AGREEMENT is made pursuant to that certain Lease dated _____ between _____ as Landlord and _____ as Tenant.

In consideration of $_____ as nonrefundable cleaning payment and $_____ as additional security deposit paid by Tenant to Landlord, Tenant is allowed to keep the following pet(s): _____ on the premises _____ under the following conditions:

1. In the event the pet produces a litter, Tenant may keep them at the premises no longer than one month past weaning.

2. Tenant shall not engage in any commercial pet-raising activities.

3. No pets other than those listed above shall be kept on the premises without the further written permission of the Landlord.

4. Tenant agrees at all times to keep the pet from becoming a nuisance to neighbors and/or other tenants. This includes controlling the barking of the pet, if necessary, and cleaning any animal waste on and about the premises.

5. In the event the pet causes destruction of the property, becomes a nuisance, or Tenant otherwise violates this agreement, Landlord may terminate the Lease according to Florida law.

Date: _____, 20____

Landlord: Tenant:

_____   _____

_____   _____

This page intentionally left blank.

HOUSE OR DUPLEX LEASE

LANDLORD:_____   TENANT:_____

_____   _____

PROPERTY:_____

IN CONSIDERATION of the mutual covenants and agreements herein contained, Landlord hereby leases to Tenant, and Tenant hereby leases from Landlord the above-described property under the following terms:

    1. TERM. This lease shall be for a term of _____ beginning _____, 20____ and ending _____, 20____.

    2. RENT. The rent shall be $_____ per _____ and shall be due on or before the _____ day of each _____. In the event the rent is received more than three (3) days late, a late charge of $_____ shall be due. In the event a check bounces or an eviction notice must be posted, Tenant agrees to pay a $15.00 charge.

    3. PAYMENT. Payment must be received by Landlord on or before the due date at the following address: _____ or such place as designated by Landlord in writing. Tenant understands that this may require early mailing. In the event a check bounces, Landlord may require cash or certified funds.

    4. DEFAULT. In the event Tenant defaults under any terms of this lease, Landlord may recover possession as provided by Law and seek monetary damages.

    5. SECURITY. Landlord acknowledges receipt of the sum of $_____ as the last month's rent under this lease, plus $_____ as security deposit. In the event Tenant terminates the lease prior to its expiration date, said amounts are nonrefundable as a charge for Landlord's trouble in securing a new tenant, but Landlord reserves the right to seek additional damages if they exceed the above amounts.

    6. UTILITIES. Tenant agrees to pay all utility charges on the property except: _____.

    7. MAINTENANCE. Tenant has examined the property, acknowledges it to be in good repair and in consideration of the reduced rental rate, Tenant agrees to keep the premises in good repair and to do all minor maintenance promptly (under $_____ excluding labor) and provide extermination service.

    8. LOCKS. If Tenant adds or changes locks on the premises, Landlord shall be given copies of the keys. Landlord shall at all times have keys for access to the premises in case of emergencies.

    9. ASSIGNMENT. This lease may not be assigned by Tenant without the written consent of the Landlord.

    10. USE. Tenant shall not use the premises for any illegal purpose or any purpose which will increase the rate of insurance and shall not cause a nuisance for Landlord or neighbors. Tenant shall not create any environmental hazards on the premises.

    11. LAWN. Tenant agrees to maintain the lawn and shrubbery on the premises at Tenant's expense.

    12. LIABILITY. Tenant shall be responsible for insurance on his own property and agrees not to hold Landlord liable for any damages to Tenant's property on the premises.

    13. ACCESS. Landlord reserves the right to enter the premises for the purposes of inspection and to show to prospective purchasers.

    14. PETS. No pets shall be allowed on the premises except: _____, and there shall be a $_____ nonrefundable pet deposit.

    15. OCCUPANCY. The premises shall not be occupied by more than ____ adults and ____ children.

    16. TENANT'S APPLIANCES. Tenant agrees not to use any heaters, fixtures, or appliances drawing excessive current without consent of the Landlord.

17. PARKING. Tenant agrees that no parking is allowed on the premises except: _____
_____. No boats, recreation vehicles, or disassembled automobiles may be stored on the premises.

18. FURNISHINGS. Any articles provided to Tenant and listed on attached schedule are to be returned in good condition at the termination of this lease.

19. ALTERATIONS AND IMPROVEMENTS. Tenant shall make no alterations to the property without the written consent of the Landlord and any such alterations or improvements shall become the property of the Landlord.

20. ENTIRE AGREEMENT. This lease constitutes the entire agreement between the parties and may not be modified except in writing signed by both parties.

21. HARASSMENT. Tenant shall not do any acts to intentionally harass the Landlord or other tenants.

22. ATTORNEY'S FEES. In the event it becomes necessary to enforce this Agreement through the services of an attorney, Tenant shall be required to pay Landlord's attorney's fees.

23. SEVERABILITY. In the event any section of this Agreement shall be held to be invalid, all remaining provisions shall remain in full force and effect.

24. RECORDING. This lease shall not be recorded in any public records.

25. WAIVER. Any failure by Landlord to exercise any rights under this Agreement shall not constitute a waiver of Landlord's rights.

26. ABANDONMENT. In the event Tenant abandons the property prior to the expiration of the lease, Landlord may relet the premises and hold Tenant liable for any costs, lost rent, or damage to the premises. Lessor may dispose of any property abandoned by Tenant.

27. SUBORDINATION. Tenant's interest in the premises shall be subordinate to any encumbrances now or hereafter placed on the premises, to any advances made under such encumbrances, and to any extensions or renewals thereof. Tenant agrees to sign any documents indicating such subordination which may be required by lenders.

28. SURRENDER OF PREMISES. At the expiration of the term of this lease, Tenant shall immediately surrender the premises in as good condition as at the start of this lease.

29. LIENS. The estate of Landlord shall not be subject to any liens for improvements contracted by Tenant.

30. RADON GAS. Radon is a naturally occurring radioactive gas that, when it has accumulated in a building in sufficient quantities, may present health risks to persons who are exposed to it over time. Levels of radon that exceed federal and state guidelines have been found in buildings in Florida. Additional information regarding radon and radon testing may be obtained from your county public health unit.

31. SMOKE DETECTORS. Tenant shall be responsible for supplying smoke detectors, for keeping them operational, and for changing the battery when needed.

32. ABANDONED PROPERTY. BY SIGNING THIS RENTAL AGREEMENT THE TENANT AGREES THAT UPON SURRENDER OR ABANDONMENT, AS DEFINED BY CHAPTER 83, FLORIDA STATUTES, THE LANDLORD SHALL NOT BE LIABLE OR RESPONSIBLE FOR STORAGE OR DISPOSITION OF THE TENANT'S PERSONAL PROPERTY.

33. MISCELLANEOUS PROVISIONS. _____
_____
_____
_____.

WITNESS the hands and seals of the parties hereto as of this _____ day of _____, 20___.

LANDLORD: TENANT:

_____   _____

_____   _____

APARTMENT LEASE

LANDLORD:_____   TENANT:_____

_____   _____

PROPERTY:_____

IN CONSIDERATION of the mutual covenants and agreements herein contained, Landlord hereby leases to Tenant and Tenant hereby leases from Landlord the above-described property under the following terms:

    1. TERM. This lease shall be for a term of _____ beginning _____, 20___ and ending _____, 20___.

    2. RENT. The rent shall be $_____ per _____ and shall be due on or before the _____ day of each _____. In the event the rent is received more than three (3) days late, a late charge of $_____ shall be due. In the event a check bounces or an eviction notice must be posted, Tenant agrees to pay a $15.00 charge.

    3. PAYMENT. Payment must be received by Landlord on or before the due date at the following address: _____ or such place as designated by Landlord in writing. Tenant understands that this may require early mailing. In the event a check bounces, Landlord may require cash or certified funds.

    4. DEFAULT. In the event Tenant defaults under any terms of this lease, Landlord may recover possession as provided by Law and seek monetary damages.

    5. SECURITY. Landlord acknowledges receipt of the sum of $_____ as the last month's rent under this lease, plus $_____ as security deposit. In the event Tenant terminates the lease prior to its expiration date, said amounts are non-refundable as a charge for Landlord's trouble in securing a new tenant, but Landlord reserves the right to seek additional damages if they exceed the above amounts.

    6. UTILITIES. Tenant agrees to pay all utility charges on the property except: _____ _____.

    7. MAINTENANCE. Tenant has examined the property and acknowledges it to be in good repair. Tenant shall immediately repay any and all damage to the premises caused by Tenant or Tenant's guests. In the event of maintenance problems not caused by Tenant, they shall be immediately reported to Landlord or Landlord's agent.

    8. LOCKS. If Tenant adds or changes locks on the premises, Landlord shall be given copies of the keys. Landlord shall at all times have keys for access to the premises in case of emergencies.

    9. ASSIGNMENT. This lease may not be assigned by Tenant without the written consent of the Landlord.

    10. USE. Tenant shall not use the premises for any illegal purpose or any purpose which will increase the rate of insurance and shall not cause a nuisance for Landlord or neighbors. Tenant shall not create any environmental hazards on the premises.

    11. CONDOMINIUM. In the event the premises are a condominium unit, Tenant agrees to abide by all rules, regulations, and the declaration of condominium. Maintenance and recreation fees are to be paid by _____. This lease is subject to approval by the condominium association, and Tenant agrees to pay any fees necessary for such approval.

    12. LIABILITY. Tenant shall be responsible for insurance on his own property and agrees not to hold Landlord liable for any damages to Tenant's property on the premises.

    13. ACCESS. Landlord reserves the right to enter the premises for the purposes of inspection and to show to prospective purchasers.

    14. PETS. No pets shall be allowed on the premises except: _____, and there shall be a $_____ nonrefundable pet deposit.

    15. OCCUPANCY. The premises shall not be occupied by more than _____ adults and _____ children.

    16. TENANT'S APPLIANCES. Tenant agrees not to use any heaters, fixtures, or appliances drawing excessive current without consent of the Landlord.

    17. PARKING. Tenant agrees that no parking is allowed on the premises except:_____ _____. No boats, recreation vehicles, or disassembled automobiles may be stored on the premises.

18. FURNISHINGS. Any articles provided to Tenant and listed on attached schedule are to be returned in good condition at the termination of this lease.

19. ALTERATIONS AND IMPROVEMENTS. Tenant shall make no alterations to the property without the written consent of the Landlord and any such alterations or improvements shall become the property of the Landlord.

20. ENTIRE AGREEMENT. This lease constitutes the entire agreement between the parties and may not be modified except in writing signed by both parties.

21. HARASSMENT. Tenant shall not do any acts to intentionally harass the Landlord or other tenants.

22. ATTORNEY'S FEES. In the event it becomes necessary to enforce this Agreement through the services of an attorney, Tenant shall be required to pay Landlord's attorney's fees.

23. SEVERABILITY. In the event any section of this Agreement shall be held to be invalid, all remaining provisions shall remain in full force and effect.

24. RECORDING. This lease shall not be recorded in any public records.

25. WAIVER. Any failure by Landlord to exercise any rights under this Agreement shall not constitute a waiver of Landlord's rights.

26. ABANDONMENT. In the event Tenant abandons the property prior to the expiration of the lease, Landlord may relet the premises and hold Tenant liable for any costs, lost rent, or damage to the premises. Lessor may dispose of any property abandoned by Tenant.

27. SUBORDINATION. Tenants interest in the premises shall be subordinate to any encumbrances now or hereafter placed on the premises, to any advances made under such encumbrances, and to any extensions or renewals thereof. Tenant agrees to sign any documents indicating such subordination which may be required by lenders.

28. SURRENDER OF PREMISES. At the expiration of the term of this lease, Tenant shall immediately surrender the premises in as good condition as at the start of this lease.

29. LIENS. The estate of Landlord shall not be subject to any liens for improvements contracted by Tenant.

30. RADON GAS. Radon is a naturally occurring radioactive gas that, when it has accumulated in a building in sufficient quantities, may present health risks to persons who are exposed to it over time. Levels of radon that exceed federal and state guidelines have been found in buildings in Florida. Additional information regarding radon and radon testing may be obtained from your county public health unit.

31. SMOKE DETECTORS. Tenant shall be responsible for keeping smoke detectors operational and for changing battery when needed.

32. ABANDONED PROPERTY. BY SIGNING THIS RENTAL AGREEMENT THE TENANT AGREES THAT UPON SURRENDER OR ABANDONMENT, AS DEFINED BY CHAPTER 83, FLORIDA STATUTES, THE LANDLORD SHALL NOT BE LIABLE OR RESPONSIBLE FOR STORAGE OR DISPOSITION OF THE TENANT'S PERSONAL PROPERTY.

33. MISCELLANEOUS PROVISIONS. _____

_____

_____.

WITNESS the hands and seals of the parties hereto as of this _____ day of _____, 20___.

LANDLORD: TENANT:

_____   _____

_____   _____

RENTAL AGREEMENT

LANDLORD:_____   TENANT:_____

_____   _____

PROPERTY:_____

IN CONSIDERATION of the mutual covenants and agreements herein contained, Landlord hereby rents to Tenant and Tenant hereby rents from Landlord the above-described property under the following terms:

    1. TERM. This Rental Agreement shall be for a month-to-month tenancy that may be cancelled by either party upon giving notice to the other party at least fifteen days prior to the end of a month.

    2. RENT. The rent shall be $_____ per month and shall be due on or before the _____ day of each month. In the event the rent is received more than three (3) days late, a late charge of $_____ shall be due. In the event a check bounces or an eviction notice must be posted, Tenant agrees to pay a $15.00 charge.

    3. PAYMENT. Payment must be received by Landlord on or before the due date at the following address: _____ or such place as designated by Landlord in writing. Tenant understands that this may require early mailing. In the event a check bounces, Landlord may require cash or certified funds.

    4. DEFAULT. In the event Tenant defaults under any terms of this agreement, Landlord may recover possession as provided by Law and seek monetary damages.

    5. SECURITY. Landlord acknowledges receipt of the sum of $_____ as the last month's rent under this lease, plus $_____ as security deposit against rent or damages. In the event Tenant vacates the premises without giving proper notice, said amounts are nonrefundable as a charge for Landlord's trouble in securing a new tenant, but Landlord reserves the right to seek additional payment for any damages to the premises.

    6. UTILITIES. Tenant agrees to pay all utility charges on the property except: _____ _____.

_____

    7. MAINTENANCE. Tenant has examined the property, acknowledges it to be in good repair, and in consideration of the reduced rental rate, Tenant agrees to keep the premises in good repair and to do all minor maintenance promptly (under $_____ excluding labor) and provide extermination service.

    8. LOCKS. If Tenant adds or changes locks on the premises, Landlord shall be given copies of the keys. Landlord shall at all times have keys for access to the premises in case of emergencies.

    9. ASSIGNMENT. This agreement may not be assigned by Tenant without the written consent of the Landlord.

    10. USE. Tenant shall not use the premises for any illegal purpose or any purpose which will increase the rate of insurance and shall not cause a nuisance for Landlord or neighbors. Tenant shall not create any environmental hazards on the premises.

    11. LAWN. Tenant agrees to maintain the lawn and shrubbery on the premises at his expense.

    12. LIABILITY. Tenant shall be responsible for insurance on his own property and agrees not to hold Landlord liable for any damages to Tenant's property on the premises.

    13. ACCESS. Landlord reserves the right to enter the premises for the purposes of inspection and to show to prospective purchasers.

    14. PETS. No pets shall be allowed on the premises except: _____, and there shall be a $_____ nonrefundable pet deposit.

    15. OCCUPANCY. The premises shall not be occupied by more than ___ adults and ___ children.

    16. TENANT'S APPLIANCES. Tenant agrees not to use any heaters, fixtures, or appliances drawing excessive current without consent of the Landlord.

17. PARKING. Tenant agrees that no parking is allowed on the premises except: _____ _____. No boats, recreation vehicles, or disassembled automobiles may be stored on the premises.

18. FURNISHINGS. Any articles provided to tenant and listed on attached schedule are to be returned in good condition at the termination of this agreement.

19. ALTERATIONS AND IMPROVEMENTS. Tenant shall make no alterations to the property without the written consent of the Landlord, and any such alterations or improvements shall become the property of the Landlord.

20. ENTIRE AGREEMENT. This rental agreement constitutes the entire agreement between the parties and may not be modified except in writing signed by both parties.

21. HARASSMENT. Tenant shall not do any acts to intentionally harass the Landlord or other tenants.

22. ATTORNEY'S FEES. In the event it becomes necessary to enforce this agreement through the services of an attorney, Tenant shall be required to pay Landlord's attorney's fees.

23. SEVERABILITY. In the event any section of this agreement shall be held to be invalid, all remaining provisions shall remain in full force and effect.

24. RECORDING. This agreement shall not be recorded in any public records.

25. WAIVER. Any failure by Landlord to exercise any rights under this agreement shall not constitute a waiver of Landlord's rights.

26. SUBORDINATION. Tenant's interest in the premises shall be subordinate to any encumbrances now or hereafter placed on the premises, to any advances made under such encumbrances, and to any extensions or renewals thereof. Tenant agrees to sign any documents indicating such subordination which may be required by lenders.

27. SURRENDER OF PREMISES. At the expiration of the term of this agreement, Tenant shall immediately surrender the premises in as good condition as at the start of this agreement.

28. LIENS. The estate of Landlord shall not be subject to any liens for improvements contracted by Tenant.

29. RADON GAS. Radon is a naturally occurring radioactive gas that, when it has accumulated in a building in sufficient quantities, may present health risks to persons who are exposed to it over time. Levels of radon that exceed federal and state guidelines have been found in buildings in Florida. Additional information regarding radon and radon testing may be from your county public health unit.

30. SMOKE DETECTORS. Tenant shall be responsible for keeping smoke detectors operational and for changing battery when needed.

31. ABANDONED PROPERTY. BY SIGNING THIS RENTAL AGREEMENT THE TENANT AGREES THAT UPON SURRENDER OR ABANDONMENT, AS DEFINED BY CHAPTER 83, FLORIDA STATUTES, THE LANDLORD SHALL NOT BE LIABLE OR RESPONSIBLE FOR STORAGE OR DISPOSITION OF THE TENANT'S PERSONAL PROPERTY.

32. MISCELLANEOUS PROVISIONS. _____ _____ _____.

WITNESS the hands and seals of the parties hereto as of this ____ day of _____, 20____.

LANDLORD: TENANT:

_____   _____

_____   _____

AGREEMENT REGARDING ABANDONED PROPERTY
Under Florida Statutes §83.67(3)

This agreement is made between _____ as
Landlord and _____ as
Tenant of property described as _____.

Pursuant to Florida Statutes section 83.67(3) the undersigned Landlord and Tenant agree that BY SIGNING THIS AGREEMENT THE TENANT AGREES THAT UPON SURRENDER OR ABANDONMENT, AS DEFINED BY CHAPTER 83, FLORIDA STATUTES, THE LANDLORD SHALL NOT BE LIABLE OR RESPONSIBLE FOR STORAGE OR DISPOSITION OF THE TENANT'S PERSONAL PROPERTY.

Date:_____, 20_____   Landlord:

_____

_____

Tenant:

_____

_____

This page intentionally left blank.

Disclosure of Information on Lead-Based Paint and/or Lead-Based Paint Hazards

Lead Warning Statement

Housing built before 1978 may contain lead-based paint. Lead from paint, paint chips, and dust can pose health hazards if not managed properly. Lead exposure is especially harmful to young children and pregnant women. Before renting pre-1978 housing, lessors must disclose the presence of known lead-based paint and/or lead-based paint hazards in the dwelling. Lessees must also receive a federally approved pamphlet on lead poisoning prevention.

Lessor's Disclosure

(a) Presence of lead-based paint and/or lead-based paint hazards (check (i) or (ii) below):

    (i) _____ Known lead-based paint and/or lead-based paint hazards are present in the housing (explain).

    _____

    _____

    (ii) _____ Lessor has no knowledge of lead-based paint and/or lead-based paint hazards in the housing.

(b) Records and reports available to the lessor (check (i) or (ii) below):

    (i) _____ Lessor has provided the lessee with all available records and reports pertaining to lead-based paint and/or lead-based paint hazards in the housing (list documents below).

    _____

    _____

    (ii) _____ Lessor has no reports or records pertaining to lead-based paint and/or lead-based paint hazards in the housing.

Lessee's Acknowledgment (initial)

(c) _____ Lessee has received copies of all information listed above.

(d) _____ Lessee has received the pamphlet *Protect Your Family from Lead in Your Home.*

Agent's Acknowledgment (initial)

(e) _____ Agent has informed the lessor of the lessor's obligations under 42 U.S.C. 4852(d) and is aware of his/her responsibility to ensure compliance.

Certification of Accuracy

The following parties have reviewed the information above and certify, to the best of their knowledge, that the information they have provided is true and accurate.

_____	_____	_____	_____
Lessor	Date	Lessor	Date
_____	_____	_____	_____
Lessee	Date	Lessee	Date
_____	_____	_____	_____
Agent	Date	Agent	Date

This page intentionally left blank.

Renovation Notice — *For use in notifying tenants of renovations in common areas of multi-family housing.*

The following renovation activities will take place in the following locations:

_____

Activity *(e.g., sanding, window replacement)*

_____

Location *(e.g., lobby, recreation center)*

The expected starting date is _____ and the expected ending date is _____. Because this is an older building built before 1978, some of the paint disturbed during the renovation may contain lead. You may obtain a copy of the pamphlet, *Protect Your Family From Lead in Your Home*, by telephoning me at _____. Please leave a message and be sure to include your name, phone number and address. I will either mail you a pamphlet or slide one under your door.

_____   _____
Date   Printed name of renovator

                                           _____
                                           Signature of renovator

Record of Tenant Notification Procedures — *Procedures Used For Delivering Notices to Tenants of Renovations in Common Areas*

Project Address:

_____

Street   (apt. #)

_____

City   State   Zip Code

_____

Owner of multi-family housing   Number of dwelling units

_____

Method of delivering notice forms *(e.g. delivery to units, delivery to mailboxes of units)*

_____

Name of person delivering notices

_____

Signature of person delivering notices   Date of Delivery

This page intentionally left blank.

Confirmation of Receipt of Lead Pamphlet

I have received a copy of the pamphlet, *Protect Your Family From Lead in Your Home*, informing me of the potential risk of the lead hazard exposure from reno-vation activity to be performed in my dwelling unit. I received this pamphlet before the work began.

_____   _____
Printed name of recipient   Date

_____
Signature of recipient

Self-Certification Option (for tenant-occupied dwellings only) —
If the lead pamphlet was delivered but a tenant signature was not obtainable, you may check the appropriate box below.

☐ Refusal to sign — I certify that I have made a good faith effort to deliver the pamphlet, *Protect your Family From Lead In Your Home,* to the rental dwelling unit listed below at the date and time indicated and that the occupant refused to sign the confirmation of receipt. I further certify that I have left a copy of the pamphlet at the unit with the occupant.

☐ Unavailable for signature — I certify that I have made a good faith effort to deliver the pamphlet, *Protect Your Family From Lead In Your Home,* to the rental dwelling unit listed below and that the occupant was unavailable to sign the confirmation of receipt. I further certify that I have left a copy of the pam-phlet at the unit by sliding it under the door.

_____   _____
Printed name of person certifying   Attempted delivery dates and times
lead pamphlet delivery

_____
Signature of person certifying
lead pamphlet delivery

_____
_____
_____
Unit Address

Note Regarding Mailing Option — *As an alternative to delivery in person, you may mail the lead pamphlet to the owner and/or tenant. Pamphlet must be mailed at least 7 days before renovation (Document with a certificate of mailing from the post office).*

This page intentionally left blank.

NOTICE OF HOLDING SECURITY DEPOSIT

To:_____

From:_____

Pursuant to Florida Statutes §83.49(2) this notice is to advise you that your security deposit is being held as follows:

1. The account is at the following depository: _____

_____

2. The funds are:

    ☐ in a separate account solely holding security deposits

    ☐ in an account commingled with landlord's funds

3. The account is:

    ☐ interest-bearing

    ☐ not interest-bearing

4. Florida statutes provide as follows:

§83.49(3) (a) Upon the vacating of the premises for termination of the lease, if the landlord does not intend to impose a claim on the security deposit, the landlord shall have fifteen(15) days to return the security deposit together with interest if otherwise required, or the landlord shall have thirty (30) days to give the tenant written notice by certified mail to the tenant's last known mailing address of his or her intention to impose a claim on the deposit and the reason for imposing the claim. The notice shall contain a statement in substantially the following form:

This is a notice of my intention to impose a claim for damages in the amount of $_____ upon your security deposit, due to _____. It is sent to you as required by s. 83.49(3), Florida Statutes. You are hereby notified that you must object in writing to this deduction from your security deposit within fifteen(15) days from the time you receive this notice or I will be authorized to deduct my claim from your security deposit. Your objection must be sent to (landlord's address).

If the landlord fails to give the required notice within the thirty-day period, he or she forfeits the right to impose a claim upon the security deposit.

(b) Unless the tenant objects to the imposition of the landlord's claim or the amount thereof within fifteen (15) days after receipt of the landlord's notice of intention to impose a claim, the landlord may then deduct the amount of his or her claim and shall remit the balance of the deposit to the tenant within thirty (30) days after the date of the notice of intention to impose a claim for damages.

(c) If either party institutes an action in a court of competent jurisdiction to adjudicate the party's right to the security deposit, the prevailing party is entitled to receive his or her court costs plus a reasonable fee for his or her attorney. The court shall advance the cause on the calendar.

(d) Compliance with this section by an individual or business entity authorized to conduct business in this state, including Florida-licensed real estate brokers and salespersons, shall constitute compliance with all other relevant Florida Statutes pertaining to security deposits held pursuant to a rental agreement or other landlord-tenant relationship. Enforcement personnel shall look solely to this section to determine compliance. This section prevails over any conflicting provisions in chapter 475 and in other sections of the Florida Statutes and shall operate to permit licensed real estate brokers to disburse security deposits and deposit money without having to comply with the notice and settlement procedures contained in s. 475.25(1)(d).

This page intentionally left blank.

AMENDMENT TO LEASE/RENTAL AGREEMENT

The undersigned parties to that certain agreement dated _____,
20____ on the premises known as _____,
hereby agree to amend said agreement as follows:

WITNESS the hands and seals of the parties hereto this _____ day of _____,20____.

Landlord: Tenant:

_____   _____

_____   _____

This page intentionally left blank.

INSPECTION REQUEST

Date:

To:

It will be necessary to enter your dwelling unit for the purpose of _____ _____ _____. If possible, we would like access on _____ at _____o'clock ____.m.

In the event this is not convenient, please call to arrange another time.

Sincerely,

_____

Address:

Phone:

This page intentionally left blank.

STATEMENT FOR REPAIRS

Date:

To:

It has been necessary to repair damage to the premises that you occupy, which was caused by you or your guests. The costs for repairs were as follows:

This amount is your responsibility under the terms of the lease and Florida law and should be forwarded to us at the address below.

Sincerely,

_____

Address:

Phone:

This page intentionally left blank.

NOTICE OF CHANGE OF TERMS

Date:

To:

Dear _____,

    You are hereby notified that effective _____ the terms of your rental agreement will be changed as follows:

    If you elect to terminate your tenancy prior to that date kindly provide fifteen (15) days notice as provided by law.

Sincerely,

_____

Address:

Phone:

This page intentionally left blank.

LETTER TO VACATING TENANT

Date:

To:

Dear _____

    This letter is to remind you that your ☐ lease ☐ oral rental agreement will expire on _____, 20_____. Please be advised that we do not intend to renew or extend it.

    The keys should be delivered to us at the address below on or before the end of the lease along with your forwarding address. We will inspect the premises for damages, deduct any amounts necessary for repairs, and refund any remaining balance as required by law.

Sincerely,

_____

Address:

Phone:

This page intentionally left blank.

ANNUAL LETTER—CONTINUATION OF TENANCY

Date:

To:

Dear _____,

    This letter is to remind you that your lease will expire on _____, 20_____. Please advise us within _____ days as to whether you intend to renew your lease. If so, we will prepare a new lease for your signature(s).

    If you do not intend to renew your lease, the keys should be delivered to us at the address below on or before the end of the lease along with your forwarding address. We will inspect the premises for damages, deduct any amounts necessary for repairs, and refund any remaining balance as required by law.

    If we have not heard from you as specified above, we will assume that you will be vacating the premises and will arrange for a new tenant to move in at the end of your term.

Sincerely,

_____

Address:

Phone:

This page intentionally left blank.

NOTICE OF TERMINATION OF AGENT

Date:

To:

    You are hereby advised that _____ is no longer our agent effective _____, 20____. On and after this date he or she is no longer authorized to collect rent, accept notices, or make any representations or agreements regarding the property.

    Rent should thereafter be paid to us directly unless you are instructed otherwise in writing.

    If you have any questions you may contact us at the address or phone number below.

Sincerely,

_____

Address:

Phone:

This page intentionally left blank.

NOTICE OF APPOINTMENT OF AGENT

Date:

To:

    You are hereby advised that effective _____, 20____, our agent for collection of rent and other matters regarding the property will be _____. However, no terms of the written lease may be modified or waived without our written signature(s).

    If you have any questions you may contact us at the address or phone number below.

Sincerely,

_____

Address:

Phone:

This page intentionally left blank.

NOTICE OF INTENTION TO IMPOSE CLAIM ON SECURITY DEPOSIT

To: _____

     Tenant's Name

_____

     Address

_____

     City, State, Zip Code

Date: _____, 20_____

     This is a notice of my intention to impose a claim for damages in the amount of $_____ upon your security deposit due to _____

_____.

     [insert amount of damages]

     [insert damage done to premises or other reason for claiming security deposit]

It is sent to you as required by §83.49(3), Florida Statutes. You are hereby notified that you must object in writing to this deduction from your security deposit within fifteen (15) days from the time you receive this notice, or I will be authorized to deduct my claim from your security deposit. Your objection must be sent to

_____.

     [insert Landlord's address]

Landlord's Name _____

Address _____

Phone Number _____

Approved for use under rule 10-2.1(a) of
the Rules Regulating the Florida Bar

The Florida Bar 1993

This form was completed
with the assistance of:
Name:
Address:
Telephone Number:

This page intentionally left blank.

THREE-DAY NOTICE

To: _____

     Tenant's Name

     _____

     Address

     _____

     City, State, Zip Code

From: _____

Date: _____, 20____

You are hereby notified that you are indebted to me in the sum of $_____

                                                          [insert amount owed by Tenant]

for the rent and use of the premises_____

                                   [insert address of leased premises, including county]

Florida, now occupied by you and that I demand payment of the rent or possession of the premises within three days (excluding Saturday, Sunday, and legal holidays) from the date of delivery of this notice, to-wit: on or before the ____ day of _____, 20____ [insert the date which is three days from the delivery of this notice, excluding the date of delivery, Saturday, Sunday, and legal holidays].

_____

Signature

_____

Name of Landlord/Property Manager
[Circle one]

_____

Address

_____

City, State, Zip Code

_____

Phone Number

Approved for use under rule 10-2.1(a) of
the Rules Regulating the Florida Bar

The Florida Bar 1993

This form was completed
with the assistance of:
Name:
Address:
Telephone Number:

This page intentionally left blank.

SEVEN-DAY NOTICE

To: _____

      Tenant's Name

    _____

      Address

    _____

      City, State, Zip Code

From: _____

Date: _____, 20_____

    You are hereby notified that you are not complying with your lease in that_____
_____. Demand is hereby made that you remedy
            [insert noncompliance]
the noncompliance within seven days of receipt of this notice or your lease shall be deemed terminated, and you shall vacate the premises upon such termination. If this same conduct or conduct
of a similar nature is repeated within twelve months, your tenancy is subject to termination without you being given an opportunity to cure the noncompliance.

                               _____

                               Landlord's Name _____

                               Address _____

                               _____

                               Phone Number _____

This form was completed
with the assistance of:
Name:
Address:
Telephone Number:

This page intentionally left blank.

NOTICE OF TERMINATION

To: _____

      Tenant's Name

      _____

      Address

      _____

      City, State, Zip Code

From: _____

Date: _____, 20_____

Dear _____:

          [Tenant's Name]

      You are hereby notified that your lease is terminated immediately. You shall have seven (7) days from delivery of this letter to vacate the premises. This action is taken because:

      _____

      Landlord's Name _____

      Address _____

      _____

      Phone Number _____

This form was completed
with the assistance of:
Name:
Address:
Telephone Number:

This page intentionally left blank.

NOTICE OF NON-RENEWAL

To: _____

     Tenant's Name

     _____

     Address

     _____

     City, State, Zip Code

From: _____

Date: _____, 20____

Dear _____,

     [Tenant's Name]

     You are notified that your tenancy will not be renewed at the end of the present term. You will be expected to vacate the premises on or before _____, 20____. In the event that you do not vacate the premises by said date, legal action may be taken in which you may be held liable for double rent, court costs, and attorney's fees.

_____

Landlord's Name _____

Address _____

_____

Phone Number _____

This form was completed
with the assistance of:
Name:
Address:
Telephone Number:

This page intentionally left blank.

CIVIL COVER SHEET

The civil cover sheet and the information contained herein neither replace nor supplement the filing and service of pleadings or other papers as required by law. This form is required for the use of the Clerk of Court for the purpose of reporting judicial workload data pursuant to Florida Statute 25.075.

NAME OF COURT_____

I. CASE STYLE

_____ *

PLAINTIFF/PETITIONER

* CASE #_____

VS. *

* DIVISION _____

*

_____

DEFENDANT/RESPONDENT

_____

II. TYPE OF CASE (Place an X in one box only. If the case fits more than one type of case, select the most definite.)

DOMESTIC RELATIONS

[] Simplified Dissolution
[] Dissolution
[] Support - IV-D
[] Support - Non IV-D
[] URESA - IV-D
[] URESA - Non IV-D
[] Domestic Violence
[] Other Domestic Relations

TORTS

[] Professional
  Malpractice
[] Products Liability
[] Auto Negligence
[] Other Negligence

OTHER CIVIL

[] Contracts
[] Condominium
[] Real Property/
  Foreclosure
[] Eminent Domain
[] Other

III. IS JURY TRIAL DEMANDED IN COMPLAINT?   [] YES   [] NO

DATE: _____

_____
SIGNATURE OF ATTORNEY OR PARTY
INITIATING ACTION

ADDRESS: _____

_____

PHONE: _____

This page intentionally left blank.

IN THE COUNTY COURT, IN AND FOR
_____COUNTY, FLORIDA

CASE NO.: _____

[Insert case number assigned
by Clerk of the Court]

_____,

[Insert name of Landlord]

Plaintiff,

vs.

**COMPLAINT FOR EVICTION
AND DAMAGES**

_____,

[Insert name of Tenant]

Defendant.

_____

Plaintiff,_____, sues Defendant, _____, and alleges:
[insert name of Landlord]   [insert name of Tenant]

COUNT I
Tenant Eviction

1. This is an action to evict a tenant from real property in _____
_____ County, Florida.

[insert county in which the rental property is located]

2. Plaintiff owns the following described real property in said County: _____
_____.

[insert legal or street description of rental property including, if applicable, unit number]

3. Defendant has possession of the property under a/an (oral/written) agreement to pay
rent of $_____ payable _____.
        [insert rental amount]   [insert terms of rental payments, i.e., weekly, monthly, etc.]
A copy of the written agreement, if any, is attached as Exhibit "A."

4. Defendant failed to pay the rent due _____, 20_____.

[insert date of payment Tenant has failed to make]

5. Plaintiff served Defendant with a notice on _____, 20 _____, to pay

[insert date of notice]

the rent or deliver possession but Defendant refuses to do either. A copy of the notice is attached as Exhibit "B."

WHEREFORE, Plaintiff demands judgment for possession of the property against Defendant.

COUNT II
Damages

6. This is an action for damages that do not exceed $15,000.

7. Plaintiff restates those allegations contained in paragraphs 1 through 5 above.

8. Defendant owes Plaintiff $_____ that is due with interest

[insert past due rent amount]

since _____, 20____.

[insert date of last rental payment tenant failed to make]

WHEREFORE, Plaintiff demands judgment for damages against Defendant.

_____

Landlord's Name _____

Address _____

_____

Phone Number _____

This form was completed
with the assistance of:
Name:
Address:
Telephone Number:

IN THE COUNTY COURT, IN AND FOR
_____COUNTY, FLORIDA

CASE NO.: _____

[Insert case number assigned
by Clerk of the Court]

_____,

[Insert name of Landlord]

Plaintiff,

vs.

_____,

[Insert name of Tenant]

Defendant.

_____

COMPLAINT FOR EVICTION

Plaintiff, _____, sues Defendant, _____, and alleges:

[insert name of Landlord]   [insert name of Tenant]

1. This is an action to evict a tenant from real property in _____
_____, County, Florida.

[insert county in which the rental property is located]

2. Plaintiff owns the following described real property in said County: _____
_____.

[insert legal or street description of rental property including, if applicable, unit number]

3. Defendant has possession of the property under a/an (oral/written) agreement to pay rent
of $_____ payable _____.

[insert rental amount]   [insert terms of rental payments, i.e., weekly, monthly, etc.]

A copy of the written agreement, if any, is attached as Exhibit "A."

4. Defendant failed to pay the rent due _____, 20_____.

[insert date of payment Tenant failed to make]

5. Plaintiff served Defendant with a notice on _____, 20_____, to

[insert date of notice]

pay the rent or deliver possession but Defendant refuses to do either. A copy of the notice is attached as Exhibit "B."

WHEREFORE, Plaintiff demands judgment for possession of the property against Defendant.

_____

Signature

_____

Name of Landlord/Property Manager
[Circle one]

_____

Address

_____

City, State, Zip Code

_____

Phone Number

This form was completed
with the assistance of:
Name:
Address:
Telephone Number:

IN THE COUNTY COURT, IN AND FOR
_____COUNTY, FLORIDA

CASE NO.: _____

[Insert case number assigned
by Clerk of the Court]

_____,

[Insert name of Landlord]

Plaintiff,

vs.

_____,

[Insert name of Tenant]

Defendant.

_____

**COMPLAINT FOR EVICTION
FOR FAILURE TO COMPLY
WITH LEASE (OTHER THAN
FAILURE TO PAY RENT)**

Plaintiff, _____, sues Defendant, _____, and alleges:

[insert name of Landlord]   [insert name of Tenant]

1. This is an action to evict a tenant from real property in _____

_____, County, Florida.

[insert county in which the rental property is located]

2. Plaintiff owns the following described real property in said County: _____

_____.

[insert legal or street description of rental property including, if applicable, unit number]

3. Defendant has possession of the property under a/an (oral/written) agreement to pay rent

of $_____ payable _____.

[insert rental amount]   [insert terms of rental payments, i.e., weekly, monthly, etc.]

A copy of the written agreement, if any, is attached as Exhibit "A."

4. Plaintiff served Defendant with a notice on _____, 20_____, giving

[insert date of notice]

written notice to the Defendant that the Defendant was in violation of his rental agreement. A copy
of said notice, setting forth the violations of the rental agreement, is attached hereto as Exhibit "B."

5. Defendant has failed to correct or discontinue the conduct set forth in the above-mentioned notice.

WHEREFORE, Plaintiff demands judgment for possession of the property against Defendant.

Landlord's Name _____

Address_____

This form was completed
with the assistance of:
Name:
Address:
Telephone Number:

IN THE COUNTY COURT, IN AND FOR
_____COUNTY, FLORIDA

CASE NO.: _____
[Insert case number assigned
by Clerk of the Court]

_____,
[Insert name of Landlord]
                Plaintiff,

vs.

_____,
[Insert name of Tenant]
                Defendant.

_____

**COMPLAINT FOR EVICTION—
HOLDOVER TENANT**

Plaintiff, _____, sues Defendant, _____, and alleges:
      [insert name of Landlord]   [insert name of Tenant]

COUNT I

1. This is an action to evict a tenant from real property in _____
_____ County, Florida.
[insert county in which the rental property is located]

2. Plaintiff owns the following described real property in said County: _____
_____.
[insert legal or street description of rental property including, if applicable, unit number]

3. Defendant has possession of the property under a/an (oral/written) agreement to which terminated
on _____, 20_____. A copy of the written agreement, if any, is attached as Exhibit "A."

4. Defendant failed to vacate the premises at the end of said agreement.

COUNT II

5. This is an action for double rent.

6. Defendant(s) owe Plaintiff the sum of $_____ for each day Defendant(s) remain(s) in the
premises since the termination of the tenancy.

WHEREFORE, Plaintiff demands judgment for possession of the property and rent owed against Defendant(s).

_____

Landlord's Name _____

Address _____

_____

Phone Number _____

This form was completed
with the assistance of:
Name:
Address:
Telephone Number:

This page intentionally left blank.

VERIFICATION OF COMPLAINT

STATE OF FLORIDA   )
)
COUNTY OF _____   )

The undersigned, being the Plaintiff in the foregoing complaint, being first duly sworn, deposes and says:

    1. That the allegations in the attached Complaint for Eviction are true.

    2. That the Defendant(s) are not in the military service of the United States.

_____
Plaintiff

Sworn to and subscribed before me by _____ who is

personally known to me or produced _____ as

identification on this ____ day of _____, 20____.

_____
Notary Public
My commission expires:

(Attach a copy of this form to your Complaint)

This page intentionally left blank.

IN THE COUNTY COURT, IN AND FOR
_____COUNTY, FLORIDA

CASE NO.: _____

[Insert case number assigned
by Clerk of the Court]

_____,

[Insert name of Landlord]

Plaintiff,

vs.

_____,

[Insert name of Tenant]

Defendant.

_____

**EVICTION SUMMONS—
RESIDENTIAL**

TO: _____

Defendant(s)

_____

_____

PLEASE READ CAREFULLY

You are being sued by _____ to require you to move out of the place where you are living for the reasons given in the attached complaint.

You are entitled to a trial to decide whether you can be required to move, but you MUST do ALL of the things listed below. You must do them within FIVE (5) days (not including Saturday, Sunday, or any legal holiday observed by the clerk of the court) after the date these papers were given to you or to a person who lives with you or were posted at your home.

THE THINGS YOU MUST DO ARE AS FOLLOWS:

(1) Write down the reason(s) why you think you should not be forced to move. The written reason(s) must be given to the court clerk at _____, _____.

[insert name of county]   [insert address of courthouse]

(2) Mail or give a copy of your written reason(s) to:

_____.

[insert Landlord's name and address]

(3) Give the court clerk the rent that is due as set forth in the landlord's complaint or as determined by the Court. YOU MUST PAY THE CLERK THE RENT EACH TIME IT BECOMES DUE UNTIL THE LAWSUIT IS OVER. Whether you win or lose the lawsuit, the judge may pay this rent to the landlord. Pay to the clerk of the court the amount of rent that the attached complaint claims to be due and any rent that becomes due until the lawsuit is over. If you believe that the amount claimed in the complaint is incorrect, you should file with the clerk of the court a motion to have the court determine the amount to

be paid. If you file a motion, you must attach to the motion any documents supporting your position and mail or give a copy of the motion to the plaintiff/plaintiff's attorney.

(4) If you and the landlord do not agree on the amount of rent owed, give the court clerk the money you say you owe. Then, before the trial, you must ask the judge to set up a hearing to decide what amount should be given to the court clerk. If you file a motion to have the court determine the amount of rent to be paid to the clerk of the court, you must immediately contact the office of the judge to whom the case is assigned to schedule a hearing to decide what amount should be paid to the clerk of the court while the lawsuit is pending.

IF YOU DO NOT DO ALL OF THESE THINGS SPECIFIED ABOVE WITHIN 5 WORKING DAYS AFTER THE DATE THAT THESE PAPERS WERE GIVEN TO YOU OR TO A PERSON WHO LIVES WITH YOU OR WERE POSTED AT YOUR HOME, YOU MAY BE EVICTED WITHOUT A HEARING OR FURTHER NOTICE.

(5) If the attached complaint also contains a claim for money damages (such as unpaid rent), you must respond to that claim separately. You must write down the reasons why you believe that you do not owe the money claimed. The written reasons must be given to the clerk of the court at the address specified in paragraph (1) above, and you must mail or give a copy of your written reasons to the plaintiff/plaintiff's attorney at the address specified in paragraph (2) above. THIS MUST BE DONE WITHIN TWENTY (20) DAYS AFTER THE DATE THESE PAPERS WERE GIVEN TO YOU OR TO A PERSON WHO LIVES WITH YOU OR WERE POSTED AT YOUR HOME. This obligation is separate from the requirement of answering the claim for eviction within five (5) working days after these papers were given to you or to a person who lives with you or were posted at your home.

THE STATE OF FLORIDA:
To Each Sheriff of the State: You are commanded to serve this summons and a copy of the complaint in this lawsuit on the above-named defendant.
DATED on _____, 20_____
Clerk of the Court
By:_____
As Deputy Clerk

NOTIFICACION DE DESALOJO/RESIDENCIAL

A: _____
Demandado(s)

_____

_____

SIRVASE LEER CON CUIDADO
Usted esta siendo demandado por _____ para exigirle que desaloje el lugar donde reside por los motivos que se expresan en la demanda adjunta. Usted tiene derecho a ser sometido a juicio para determinar si se le puede exigir que se mude, pero ES NECESARIO que haga TODO lo que se le pide a continuacion en un plazo de 5 dias (no incluidos los sabados, domingos, ni

dias feriados) a partir de la fecha en que estos documentos se le entregaron a usted o a una persona que vive con usted, o se colocaron en su casa.

USTED DEBERA HACER LO SIGUIENTE:

(1) Escribir el (los) motivo(s) por el (los) cual(es) cree que no se le debe obligar a mudarse. El (Los) motivo(s) debera(n) entregarse por escrito al secretario del tribunal en el Edificio de los Tribunales de Condado de _____, Florida.

(2) Enviar por correo o darle su(s) motivo(s) por escrito a:

_____

Demandante/Abogado del Demandante

_____

_____

Direccion

(3) Pagarle al secretario del tribunal el monto del alquiler que la demanda adjunta reclama como adeudado, así como cualquier alquiler pagadero hasta que concluya el litigio. Si usted considera que el monto reclamado en la demanda es incorrecto, debera presentarle al secretario del tribunal una mocion para que el tribunal determine el monto que deba pagarse. Si usted presenta una mocion, debera adjuntarle a esta cualesquiera documentos que respalden su posicion, y enviar por correo o entregar una copia de la misma al demandante/abogado del demandante.

(4) Si usted presenta una mocion para que el tribunal determine el monto del alquiler que deba pagarse al secretario del tribunal, debera comunicarse de inmediato con la oficina del juez al que se le haya asignado el caso para que programe una audiencia con el fin de determinar el monto que deba pagarse al secretario del tribunal mientras el litigio este pendiente.

SI USTED NO LLEVA A CABO LAS ACCIONES QUE SE ESPECIFICAN ANTERIORMENTE EN UN PLAZO DE 5 DIAS LABORABLES A PARTIR DE LA FECHA EN QUE ESTOS DOCUMENTOS SE LE ENTREGARON A USTED O A UNA PERSONA QUE VIVE CON USTED, O SE COLOQUEN EN SU CASA, SE LE PODRA DESALOJAR SIN NECESIDAD DE CELEBRAR UNA AUDIENCIA NI CURSARSELE OTRO AVISO.

(5) Si la demanda adjunta tambien incluye una reclamacion por danos y perjuicios pecunarios (tales como el incumplimiento de pago del alquiler), usted debera responder a dicha reclamacion por separado. Debera exponer por escrito los motivos por los cuales considera que usted no debe la suma reclamada, y entregarlos al secretario del tribunal en la direccion que se especifica en el parrafo (1) anterior, asi como enviar por correo o entregar una copia de los mismos al demandante/abogado del demandante en la direccion que se especifica en el parrafo (2) anterior. ESTO DEBERA LLEVARSE A CABO EN UN PLAZO DE 20 DIAS A PARTIR DE LA FECHA EN QUE ESTOS DOCUMEN-TOS SE LE ENTREGARON A USTED O A UNA PERSONA QUE VIVE CON USTED, O SE COLOQUEN EN SU CASA. Esta obligacion es aparte del requisito de responder a la demanda de desalojo en un plazo de 5 días a partir de la fecha en que estos documentos se le entregaron a usted o a una persona que vive con usted, o se coloquen en su casa.

CITATION D'EVICTION/RESIDENTIELLE

A _____

Defendeur(s)

_____

_____

LISEZ ATTENTIVEMENT

Vous êtes poursuivi par _____ pour exiger que vous evacuez les lieux de votre residence pour les raisons enumerées dans la plainte ci-dessous. Vous avez droit a un procés pour determiner si vous devez demenager, mais vous devez, au prealable, suivre les instructions enumerées ci-dessous, pendant les 5 jours (non compris le samedi, le dimanche, ou un jour ferie) à partir de la date ou ces documents ont été donnes à vous ou à la personne vivant avec vous, ou ont été affichés à votre residence.

LISTE DES INSTRUCTIONS A SUIVRE:

(1) Enumerer par écrit les raisons pour lesquelles vous pensez ne pas avoir à demenager. Elles doivent être remises au clerc du tribunal a _____ County Courthouse _____, Florida.

(2) Envoyer ou donner une copie au:

_____

Plaignant/Avocat du Plaignant

_____

Adresse

(3) Payer au clerc du tribunal le montant des loyers dus comme établi dans la plainte et le montant des loyers dus jusqu'à la fin du procés. Si vous pensez que le montant établi dans la plainte est incorrect, vous devez presenter au clerc du tribunal une demande en justice pour determiner la somme a payer. Pour cela vous devez attacher à la demande tous les documents soutenant votre position et faire parvenir une copie de la demande au plaignant/avocat du plaignant.

(4) Si vous faites une demande en justice pour determiner la somme à payer au clerc du tribunal, vous devrez immédiatement prevenir le bureau de juge qui presidera au proces pour fixer la date de l'audience qui decidera quelle somme doit être payée au clerc du tribunal pendant que le procés est en cours.

SI VOUS NE SUIVEZ PAS CES INSTRUCTIONS À LA LETTRE DANS LES 5 JOURS QUE SUIVENT LA DATE OU CES DOCUMENTS ONT ÉTÉ REMIS A VOUS OU A LA PERSONNE HABITANT AVEC VOUS, OU ONT ÉTÉ AFFICHES À VOTRE RESIDENCE, VOUS POUVEZ ÊTRE EXPULSES SANS AUDIENCE OU SANS AVIS PREALABLE.

(5) Si la plainte ci-dessus contient une demande pour dommages pecuniaires, tels des loyers arrieres, vous devez y repondre separement. Vous devez enumerer par écrit les raisons pour lesquelles vous estimez ne pas devoir le montant demande. Ces raisons écrites doivent être données au clerc du tribunal à l'adresse specifiée dans le paragraphe (1) et une copie de ces raisons donnée ou envoyée au plaignant\avocat du plaignant à l'adresse specifiée dans le paragraphe (2). Cela doit être fait dans les 20 jours suivant la date ou ces documents ont été presentes à vous ou à la personne habitant avec vous, ou affiches à votre residence. Cette obligation ne fait pas partie des instructions à suivre en reponse au procés d'eviction dans les 5 jours suivant la date ou ces documents ont été presentes à vous ou à la personne habitant avec vous, ou affiches à votre residence.

IN THE COUNTY COURT, IN AND FOR

_____COUNTY, FLORIDA

CASE NO.: _____

[Insert case number assigned
by Clerk of the Court]

_____,

[Insert name of Landlord]

Plaintiff,

vs.

**SUMMONS—
ACTION FOR BACK RENT AND DAMAGES**

_____,

[Insert name of Tenant]

Defendant.

_____

Each Defendant is further required to serve written defenses to the demand or Back Rent and All Other Damages to the Premises contained in said Complaint upon the above-named _____ at the above-named address within 20 days after service of

[insert Landlord's name]

this Summons upon the Defendant, exclusive of the day of Service, and to file the original of said written defenses with the Clerk of said court either before service on _____

[insert Landlord's name]

or thereafter. If you fail to do so, a default will be entered against Defendant for the relief demanded in that portion of the Complaint.

WITNESS my hand and seal of said Court this ____ day of _____, 20____.

[COURT SEAL]

CLERK OF COURT

By:_____

Deputy Clerk

Approved for use under rule 10-2.1(a) of
the Rules Regulating the Florida Bar

The Florida Bar 1993

This form was completed
with the assistance of:
Name:
Address:
Telephone number:

This page intentionally left blank.

IN THE COUNTY COURT, IN AND FOR
_____COUNTY, FLORIDA

CASE NO.: _____

[Insert case number assigned
by Clerk of the Court]

_____,

[Insert name of Landlord]

Plaintiff,

vs.

_____,

[Insert name of Tenant]

Defendant.

_____

**MOTION FOR CLERK'S DEFAULT—
RESIDENTIAL EVICTION**

Plaintiff moves for entry of a default against _____ for

[name]

failure to respond as required by law plaintiff's complaint for residential eviction.

_____

Name_____

Address_____

_____

Telephone Number_____

DEFAULT—RESIDENTIAL EVICTION

A default is entered in this action against the Defendant for eviction for failure to respond as required by law.

DATE:_____   CLERK OF THE COURT

By:_____

Deputy Clerk

cc: _____

[Insert name of Landlord]

_____

[Insert name and address of Tenant]

Approved for use under rule 10-2.1(a) of
the Rules Regulating the Florida Bar

The Florida Bar 1993

This form was completed
with the assistance of:
Name:
Address:
Telephone number:

This page intentionally left blank.

form 34 ◆ 235

IN THE COUNTY COURT, IN AND FOR
_____COUNTY, FLORIDA

CASE NO.: _____

[Insert case number assigned
by Clerk of the Court]

_____,

[Insert name of Landlord]

                    Plaintiff,

vs.

_____,

[Insert name of Tenant]

               Defendant.

_____

**MOTION FOR CLERK'S DEFAULT—
DAMAGES (RESIDENTIAL EVICTION)**

Plaintiff moves for entry of a default against _____, for
                                            [name]

damages for failing to respond as required by law plaintiff's complaint for damages.

_____

Name_____

Address_____

_____

Telephone Number_____

DEFAULT—DAMAGES

A default is entered in this action against the Defendant for eviction for failure to respond as required by law.

DATE:_____

CLERK OF THE COURT

By:_____

Deputy Clerk

cc: _____

[Insert name of Landlord]

_____

[Insert name and address of Tenant]

Approved for use under rule 10-2.1(a) of
the Rules Regulating the Florida Bar

The Florida Bar 1993

This form was completed
with the assistance of:
Name:
Address:
Telephone number:

This page intentionally left blank.

IN THE COUNTY COURT, IN AND FOR
_____COUNTY, FLORIDA

CASE NO.: _____

[Insert case number assigned
by Clerk of the Court]

_____,

[Insert name of Landlord]

Plaintiff,

vs.

_____,

[Insert name of Tenant]

Defendant.

_____

**MOTION FOR DEFAULT JUDGMENT—
RESIDENTIAL EVICTION**

Plaintiff asks the court to enter a Default Final judgment against _____,

[name]

Defendant, for residential eviction and says:

1.   Plaintiff filed a complaint alleging grounds for residential eviction of Defendant.

2.   A default was entered by the Clerk of this Court on _____.

[date]

WHEREFORE, Plaintiff asks this Court to enter a Final judgment For Residential Eviction against Defendant.

_____

Name_____

Address_____

_____

Telephone Number_____

cc: _____

[Insert name and address of Tenant]

Approved for use under rule 10-2.1(a) of
the Rules Regulating the Florida Bar

The Florida Bar 1993

This form was completed
with the assistance of:
Name:
Address:
Telephone number:

This page intentionally left blank.

IN THE COUNTY COURT, IN AND FOR

_____COUNTY, FLORIDA

CASE NO.: _____

[Insert case number assigned
by Clerk of the Court]

_____,

[Insert name of Landlord]

Plaintiff,

vs.

_____,

[Insert name of Tenant]

Defendant.

_____

**MOTION FOR DEFAULT
FINAL JUDGMENT—
DAMAGES (RESIDENTIAL EVICTION)**

Plaintiff asks the court to enter a Default Final judgment against _____,

[name]

Defendant, for damages and says:

   1.   Plaintiff filed a complaint for damages against the Defendant.

   2.   Defendant has failed to timely file an answer, and a Default has been entered by the Clerk of
this Court on _____.

                        [date]

   3.   In support of this Motion, Plaintiff submits the attached Affidavit of Damages.

   WHEREFORE, Plaintiff asks this Court to enter a Final judgment against Defendant.

   I CERTIFY that I ___ mailed, ___ telefaxed and mailed, or ___ hand delivered a copy of this motion
and attached affidavit to the Defendant at _____
_____.

[insert address at which tenant was served and telefax number if sent by telefax]

_____

Name_____

Address_____

_____

Telephone Number_____

Approved for use under rule 10-2.1(a) of
the Rules Regulating the Florida Bar

The Florida Bar 1993

This form was completed
with the assistance of:
Name:
Address:
Telephone Number:

This page intentionally left blank.

IN THE COUNTY COURT, IN AND FOR

_____COUNTY, FLORIDA

CASE NO.: _____

[Insert case number assigned
by Clerk of the Court]

_____,

[Insert name of Landlord]

Plaintiff,

vs.

_____,

[Insert name of Tenant]

Defendant.

_____

AFFIDAVIT OF DAMAGES

STATE OF FLORIDA   )

COUNTY OF   )

BEFORE ME, the undersigned authority, personally appeared _____

[name]

who being first duly sworn, says:

1.   I am ____ the Plaintiff or ___ the Plaintiff's agent (check appropriate response) in this case and am authorized to make this affidavit.

2.   This affidavit is based on my own personal knowledge.

3.   Defendant has possession of the property, which is the subject of this eviction under an agreement to pay rent of $_____per_____.

                   [rental amount]   [week, month, or other payment period]

4.   Defendant has not paid the rent due since _____.

                                    [date of payment tenant has failed to make]

5.   Defendant owes Plaintiff $ _____ as alleged in the complaint plus interest.

                            [past due rent amount]

6.   Defendant owes Plaintiff $_____ as alleged in the com-

[amount of other damages]

plaint plus interest.

_____

Name_____

Acknowledged before me on _____, by _____, who:

[date]   [name]

_____ is personally known to me/ _____ produced _____ as identification, and who

_____ did/ _____ did not take an oath.

[document]

_____

NOTARY PUBLIC-STATE OF FLORIDA

Name: _____

Commission No.: _____

My Commission Expires: _____

I CERTIFY that I _____ mailed, _____ telefaxed and mailed, or _____ hand delivered a copy of this motion and attached affidavit to the Defendant at _____

_____.

[insert address at which tenant was served and telefax number if sent by telefax]

This form was completed
with the assistance of:
Name:
Address:
Telephone Number:

IN THE COUNTY COURT, IN AND FOR

_____COUNTY, FLORIDA

CASE NO.: _____

_____,

[Insert name of Landlord]

Plaintiff,

vs.

NONMILITARY AFFIDAVIT

_____,

[Insert name of Tenant]

Defendant.

STATE OF FLORIDA   )

COUNTY OF   )

_____, being first duly sworn, states under penalty of perjury:

____ 1.   That I know of my own personal knowledge that the respondent is not on active duty in the armed forces of the United States.

____ 2.   That I have inquired of the armed forces of the United States and the U.S. Public Health Service to determine whether the respondent, _____, is a member of the armed services and am attaching certificates stating that the respondent is not now in the armed forces.

DATED: _____

_____

Signature of Affiant

Name_____

Address_____

_____

Telephone No._____

Acknowledged before me on _____, 20___, by _____, who
            [date]   [name]

____ is personally known to me ____/ produced _____ as identification, and who
                                                              [document]

____ did/ ____ did not take an oath.

_____

NOTARY PUBLIC-STATE OF FLORIDA

Name: _____

Commission No.: _____

My Commission Expires: _____

I CERTIFY that I have ____ mailed, ____ telefaxed and mailed, or ____ hand delivered a copy of this motion on _____ to: Attorney for opposing party/Pro se party at the name and address, telefax number below:

Name _____

Address _____

Telefax No. _____

Approved for use under rule 10-2.1(a) of
the Rules Regulating the Florida Bar

This form was completed
with the assistance of:
Name:
Address:
Telephone Number:

The Florida Bar 1993

This page intentionally left blank.

IN THE COUNTY COURT, IN AND FOR

_____COUNTY, FLORIDA

CASE NO.: _____

[Insert case number assigned
by Clerk of the Court]

_____,

[Insert name of Landlord]

                        Plaintiff,

vs.

_____,

[Insert name of Tenant]

                        Defendant.

_____

**FINAL JUDGMENT—
EVICTION**

THIS ACTION came before the Court upon Plaintiff's Complaint for eviction. On the evidence presented, it is

ADJUDGED that Plaintiff, _____, recover from

[insert Landlord's name]

Defendant, _____, possession of the real property described

[insert Tenant's name]

as follows: _____

[insert legal or street description of rental premises including, if applicable, unit number]

and $ _____ as court costs, for which let Writs of Possession and Execution now issue.

ORDERED in_____, _____

[insert city in which court is located]   [insert county in which court is located]

COUNTY, FLORIDA on _____, _____.

_____

County Judge

cc: _____

[Insert name of Landlord]

_____

[Insert name of Tenant]

Approved for use under rule 10-2.1(a) of
the Rules Regulating the Florida Bar

The Florida Bar 1993

This form was completed
with the assistance of:
Name:
Address:
Telephone Number:

This page intentionally left blank.

IN THE COUNTY COURT, IN AND FOR
_____COUNTY, FLORIDA

CASE NO.: _____

[Insert case number assigned
by Clerk of the Court]

_____,

[Insert name of Landlord]

_____

_____

[Insert address of Landlord]

                                    Plaintiff,

vs.

_____,

[Insert name of Tenant]

_____

_____

[Insert address of Tenant]

                                    Defendant.

_____

**FINAL JUDGMENT—
DAMAGES**

THIS ACTION came before the Court upon Plaintiff's Complaint for unpaid rent. On the evidence presented, it is

ADJUDGED that Plaintiff, _____, recover from

[insert Landlord's name]

Defendant, _____, the sum of $_____ with

[insert Tenant's name]

costs in the sum of $ _____, making a total of $ _____, that shall bear interest at the legal rate pursuant to section 55.03, Florida Statutes for which let execution now issue.

ORDERED in_____, _____

[insert city in which court is located]   [insert county in which court is located]

COUNTY, FLORIDA on _____, _____.

_____

County Judge

cc: _____

[Insert name of Landlord]

_____

[Insert name of Tenant]

Approved for use under rule 10-2.1(a) of
the Rules Regulating the Florida Bar

The Florida Bar 1998

This form was completed
with the assistance of:
Name:
Address:
Telephone Number:

This page intentionally left blank.

IN THE COUNTY COURT, IN AND FOR
_____COUNTY, FLORIDA

CASE NO.: _____

[Insert case number assigned
by Clerk of the Court]

_____,

[Insert name of Landlord]
                            Plaintiff,

vs.

_____,   **NOTICE OF HEARING**

[Insert name of Tenant]

                         Defendant.

_____

To: _____

          Tenant's Name

          _____

          Address

          _____

          City, State, Zip Code

PLEASE TAKE NOTICE that on the _____ day of _____, _____, at _____ o'clock ___.m. or as soon thereafter as can be heard, the undersigned will bring on to be heard Plaintiff's Motion to Strike and Motion for Default before the Honorable _____, one of the judges of the above Court in his/her Chambers in Room _____ in the Courthouse at _____, in _____ County, Florida.

Time set aside: _____.

PLEASE GOVERN YOURSELF ACCORDINGLY.

DATED this _____ day of _____, _____.

     I HEREBY CERTIFY that a copy hereof is being furnished by regular U.S. Mail on this date to the above-mentioned addressee.

_____

Plaintiff

_____

Address

_____

_____

Phone

This page intentionally left blank.

IN THE COUNTY COURT, IN AND FOR
_____COUNTY, FLORIDA

CASE NO.: _____

[Insert case number assigned
by Clerk of the Court]

_____,

[Insert name of Landlord]

Plaintiff,

vs.

_____,   **MOTION TO STRIKE**

[Insert name of Tenant]

Defendant.

_____

COMES NOW the Plaintiff and moves this Court to Strike the Answer of Defendant, and in support of his Motion states as follows:

The Defenses contained in Defendant's Answer fail to state a defense, legal or equitable, to Plaintiff's complaint to Remove Tenant, more particularly:

a.   This is an action for possession of real property as authorized and governed by Chapter 83 of the Florida Statutes.

b.   The Defendant's Defenses do not allege that the Defendant paid or tendered payment of the amount of rent when due or within three (3) days after delivery of written demand for rent or possession by the Plaintiff as provided by Florida Statutes 83.56(3).

c.   The Defendant's Defenses do not allege that the Plaintiff accepted, or agreed to accept, payment of rent at any time after expiration of the three (3) day period contemplated by Florida Statutes 83.56(3).

d.   The Plaintiff has terminated the rental agreement in accordance with Florida Statutes 83.56(3) and is entitled to possession of the premises as provided by Florida Statutes 83.56.

e.   Defendants have not deposited the rent alleged to be due into the registry of the court.

I HEREBY CERTIFY that a copy of the foregoing has been sent by U.S. MAIL to _____(Defendant), at _____,
Florida, this _____ day of _____, _____.

_____

Plaintiff

_____

_____

Address

This page intentionally left blank.

IN THE COUNTY COURT, IN AND FOR
_____COUNTY, FLORIDA

CASE NO.: _____

[Insert case number assigned
by Clerk of the Court]

_____,

[Insert name of Landlord]

                        Plaintiff,

vs.

_____,   **MOTION FOR DEFAULT**

[Insert name of Tenant]

                        Defendant.

_____

      Plaintiff moves for entry of a default against _____, for

                                          [name]

damages for failing to respond as required by law plaintiff's complaint.

                    _____

                    Name _____

                    Address _____

                    _____

                    Telephone Number _____

DEFAULT

      A default is entered in this action against the Defendant for eviction for failure to respond
as required by law.

      DATE:_____

                                  _____

                                  County Judge

cc: _____

       [Insert name of Landlord]

    _____

       [Insert name and address of Tenant]

                            This form was completed
                            with the assistance of:
                            Name:
                            Address:
                            Telephone Number:

This page intentionally left blank.

IN THE COUNTY COURT, IN AND FOR
_____COUNTY, FLORIDA

CASE NO.: _____
[Insert case number assigned
by Clerk of the Court]

_____,

[Insert name of Landlord]
Plaintiff,

vs.

_____,   **STIPULATION**

[Insert name of Tenant]
Defendant.

_____

     The parties to this action hereby stipulate as follows:

     1. The defendant acknowledges the sum of $_____ to be due and owing to the plaintiffs.

     2. In partial payment of the above debt, the defendant(s) agree(s) to immediately pay to the plaintiff(s) the amount of $_____, and the balance of the above debt will be paid as follows:

$_____ due on _____ $_____ due on _____

$_____ due on _____ $_____ due on _____

     In addition to the above-stated amounts, the defendant, as a further condition hereof, agrees to pay to the plaintiffs the sum of $_____ on the ___ day of each month, in cash, representing periodic installments payable under the rental agreement between the parties for rent of the subject residential premises.

     3. If all of the foregoing sums are paid as set out above, in full, in cash, and when due, this action shall be dismissed with prejudice, and each party does hereby release the other by a general release as if set out here in full.

     4. If any of the above sums are not paid as set out above, the plaintiffs shall be entitled to a Writ of Possession to be executed forthwith upon the filing of an Affidavit of Non-Payment. Defendant hereby waives a hearing on plaintiffs' application for an order of tenant removal in such case.

     If defendant should default in any of the above payments, and defendant abandons possession of the dwelling or is lawfully evicted by reason of such default, it is agreed that plaintiffs shall be entitled to a money judgment for any of such payments as are in default at the time of defendant's abandonment or eviction. Defendant waives notice and hearing on plaintiffs' application for such money judgment.

Dated: _____, _____.

_____   _____

Plaintiff   Defendant

_____   _____

Plaintiff   Defendant

This page intentionally left blank.

IN THE COUNTY COURT, IN AND FOR
_____COUNTY, FLORIDA

CASE NO.: _____
[Insert case number assigned
by Clerk of the Court]

_____,

[Insert name of Landlord]

Plaintiff,

vs.

_____,   **MOTION TO SET CAUSE FOR TRIAL**

[Insert name of Tenant]

Defendant.

_____

The Plaintiff _____ state that this action is at
issue and ready to be set for trial and request the date for trial be set by the Court.
The estimated time for trial is 30 minutes.

I HEREBY CERTIFY that a copy of the foregoing has been sent by regular U.S. Mail to
_____.

_____
Plaintiff
Address: _____

_____
Phone: _____

ORDER

THIS CAUSE coming on to be heard upon Motion to Set Cause for Trial, it is ORDERED
that this cause, being the issue, be and it is hereby set for trial before the Honorable
_____ in the Courthouse in _____, Florida on
the _____ day of _____, _____ at _____ o'clock _____.m. in Room _____.
DONE AND ORDERED in Chambers in _____, _____
County, Florida, this _____ day of _____, _____.

_____
COUNTY JUDGE

Copies to: Plaintiff
               Defendant

This page intentionally left blank.

IN THE COUNTY COURT, IN AND FOR
_____COUNTY, FLORIDA

CASE NO.: _____

[Insert case number assigned
by Clerk of the Court]

_____,

[Insert name of Landlord]

Plaintiff,

vs.

_____,   **PLAINTIFF'S NOTICE FOR TRIAL**

[Insert name of Tenant]

Defendant.

_____

PLEASE TAKE NOTICE that the above captioned action is at issue and is set for trial before the honorable _____, Judge of the County Court, on _____, the _____ day of _____, _____, at _____ o'clock ____.m., in room _____ of the _____ County Courthouse at _____.

_____

Plaintiff

Address: _____

_____

Phone: _____

I hereby certify that a copy of this Notice has been furnished to the defendant by hand delivery this _____ day of _____, _____.

_____

Plaintiff

This page intentionally left blank.

IN THE COUNTY COURT, IN AND FOR
_____COUNTY, FLORIDA

CASE NO.: _____

[insert case number assigned
by Clerk of the Court]

_____,

[Insert name of Landlord]

Plaintiff,

vs.

WRIT OF POSSESSION

_____,

[Insert name of Tenant]

Defendant.

_____

STATE OF FLORIDA
TO THE SHERIFF OF _____ COUNTY, FLORIDA:

[insert county in which rental property is located]

YOU ARE COMMANDED to remove all persons from the following described property in
_____, County, Florida: _____

[insert county in which rental property is located]   [insert legal or street

_____

description of rental premises including, if applicable, unit number]

and to put _____ in possession of it.

[insert Landlord's name]

DATED on _____ day of _____, 20_____.

Clerk, County Court

[SEAL]

By:_____
Deputy Clerk

Approved for use under rule 10-2.1(a) of
the Rules Regulating the Florida Bar

The Florida Bar 1993

This form was completed
with the assistance of:
Name:
Address:
Telephone Number:

This page intentionally left blank.

IN THE COUNTY COURT, IN AND FOR
_____COUNTY, FLORIDA

CASE NO.: _____

[Insert case number assigned
by Clerk of the Court]

_____,

[Insert name of Landlord]

                  Plaintiff,

vs.

_____,

[Insert name of Tenant]

                  Defendant.

_____

                         **MOTION TO DISBURSE FUNDS
                         FROM THE COURT REGISTRY**

The Plaintiff requests that the Court order the clerk to disburse the rent payments paid into the court registry in this cause and in support would show:

1. This is an action for possession of real property based upon nonpayment of rent.

2. Plaintiff's expenses for debt service, taxes, insurance, utilities, and maintenance on the property are continuing to accrue on a daily basis, and Plaintiff's sole source of income to meet those expenses is the rent from the premises. Unless plaintiff receives the rent payments now being posted into the registry of the court, plaintiff will have to borrow funds from other sources to meet his obligations.

3. Plaintiff requests that he be allowed to apply ex parte for an order of disbursement on the first business day following deposit of continuing rent in this action.

I hereby certify that a copy of the foregoing has been furnished to defendant by _____ this ____ day of _____, _____.

                              _____

                              Plaintiff

                              Address: _____

                              _____

                              Phone: _____

                              _____

                              County Judge

Copies to: Plaintiff

                Defendant

This page intentionally left blank.

IN THE COUNTY COURT, IN AND FOR

_____COUNTY, FLORIDA

CASE NO.: _____

(Insert case number assigned
by Clerk of the Court)

_____,

[Insert name of Landlord]

                         Plaintiff,

vs.   **ORDER DISBURSING FUNDS FROM**

_____,   **THE COURT REGISTRY**

[Insert name of Tenant]

                         Defendant.

_____

THIS CAUSE coming on to be heard upon Motion to Release Funds from the Court Registry, it is ORDERED that the funds being held by the clerk in this cause be released to Plaintiff forthwith.

     DONE AND ORDERED in Chambers in_____, _____ County, Florida, this _____ day of _____, 20_____.

_____

County Judge

Copies to: Plaintiff
            Defendant

This page intentionally left blank.

FINAL DISPOSITION FORM

I. CASE STYLE

(Name of Court)_____

Plaintiff   _____   Case #: _____

vs.   Judge: _____

Defendant   _____

II. MEANS OF FINAL DISPOSITION (Place an "x" in one box only)

❏ Dismissed Before Hearing

❏ Dismissed After Hearing

❏ Disposed by Default

❏ Disposed by Judge

❏ Disposed by Non-Jury Trial

❏ Disposed by Jury Trial

❏ Other

DATE_____   **SIGNATURE OF PARTY OR ATTORNEY FOR PARTY INITIATING ACTION:**

_____

This page intentionally left blank.

NOTICE

To:_____

_____

_____

Re: Your Check No._____

Criminal remedies:

Pursuant to Florida Statutes, section 832.07:

You are hereby notified that a check numbered_____ in the face amount of $_____, issued by you on_____, _____ drawn upon _____(bank) and payable to _____ has been dishonored. Pursuant to Florida law, you have seven days from receipt of this notice to tender payment in cash of the full amount of the check plus a service charge of $25, if the face value does exceeds $50 but does not exceed $300, $40, if the face value exceeds $300, or five percent of the face amount of the check, whichever is greater, the total being $_____ and _____ cents. Unless this amount is paid in full within the time specified above, the holder of such check may turn over the dishonored check and all other available information relating to this incident to the state attorney for criminal prosecution. You may be additionally liable in a civil action for triple the amount of the check, but in no case less than $50, together with the amount of the check, a service charge, court costs, reasonable attorney fees, and incurred bank fees, as provided in section 68.065.

Civil remedies:

Pursuant to Florida Statutes, section 68.065:

You are hereby notified that a check numbered_____ in the face amount of $_____, issued by you on_____, _____ drawn upon _____(bank) and payable to _____ has been dishonored. Pursuant to Florida law, you have thirty days from receipt of this notice to tender payment in cash of the full amount of the check plus a service charge of $25, if the face value does exceeds $50 but does not exceed $300, $40, if the face value exceeds $300, or five percent of the face amount of the check, whichever is greater, the total being $_____ and _____ cents. Unless this amount is paid in full within the thirty-day period, the holder of the check or instrument may file a civil action against you for three times the amount of the check, but in no case less than $50, in addition to the payment of the check plus any court costs, reasonable attorney fees, and any bank fees incurred by the payee taking this action.

Payment should be made to: _____

_____

_____

Sent by Certified Mail, return receipt requested.

This page intentionally left blank.

NOTICE OF RIGHT TO RECLAIM ABANDONED PROPERTY
(Property of former tenant valued under $500)

TO:_____

_____

_____

WHEN YOU VACATED THE PREMISES AT _____
APT. ____, THE FOLLOWING PERSONAL PROPERTY REMAINED:

YOU MAY CLAIM THIS PROPERTY _____
_____. UNLESS YOU PAY THE REASON-
ABLE COSTS OF STORAGE AND ADVERTISING, IF ANY, FOR ALL THE
ABOVE-DESCRIBED PROPERTY AND TAKE POSSESSION OF THE PROPERTY WHICH
YOU CLAIM NO LATER THAN _____, _____.* THIS PROPERTY
MAY BE DISPOSED OF PURSUANT TO S. 715.109.

BECAUSE THE PROPERTY IS BELIEVED TO BE WORTH LESS THAN $500, IT MAY BE
KEPT, SOLD, OR DESTROYED WITHOUT FURTHER NOTICE IF YOU FAIL TO RECLAIM
IT WITHIN THE TIME INDICATED ABOVE.

Dated:_____   _____

                                Landlord_____
                                Telephone:_____
                                Address:_____

                                _____

Insert date not fewer than ten days after notice is personally delivered or, if mailed, not fewer than fifteen days after notice is deposited in the mail.

This page intentionally left blank.

NOTICE OF RIGHT TO RECLAIM ABANDONED PROPERTY
(Property of person other than tenant valued under $500)

TO:_____

_____

_____

WHEN _____ VACATED THE PREMISES AT
_____ APT. _____,
THE FOLLOWING PERSONAL PROPERTY REMAINED:

IF YOU OWN ANY OF THIS PROPERTY, YOU MAY CLAIM THIS PROPERTY
AT:_____.

UNLESS YOU PAY THE REASONABLE COSTS OF STORAGE AND ADVERTISING, IF
ANY, FOR ALL THE ABOVE-DESCRIBED PROPERTY AND TAKE POSSESSION OF THE
PROPERTY WHICH YOU ARE ENTITLED NO LATER THAN _____,
_____.* THIS PROPERTY MAY BE DISPOSED OF PURSUANT TO S. 715.109.

BECAUSE THE PROPERTY IS BELIEVED TO BE WORTH LESS THAN $500, IT MAY BE
KEPT, SOLD, OR DESTROYED WITHOUT FURTHER NOTICE IF YOU FAIL TO RECLAIM
IT WITHIN THE TIME INDICATED ABOVE.

Dated:_____   _____

                               Landlord_____
                               Telephone:_____
                               Address:_____

                               _____

*Insert date not fewer than ten days after notice is personally delivered or, if mailed, not fewer
than fifteen days after notice is deposited in the mail.

This page intentionally left blank.

NOTICE OF RIGHT TO RECLAIM ABANDONED PROPERTY
(Property of former tenant valued over $500)

TO:_____

_____

_____

WHEN YOU VACATED THE PREMISES AT _____

_____ APT. _____, THE FOLLOWING PERSONAL

PROPERTY REMAINED:

YOU MAY CLAIM THIS PROPERTY AT: _____

_____.

UNLESS YOU PAY THE REASONABLE COSTS OF STORAGE AND ADVERTISING, IF ANY, FOR ALL THE ABOVE-DESCRIBED PROPERTY AND TAKE POSSESSION OF THE PROPERTY WHICH YOU CLAIM NO LATER THAN _____, _____.* THIS PROPERTY MAY BE DISPOSED OF PURSUANT TO S. 715.109.

IF YOU FAIL TO RECLAIM THE PROPERTY, IT WILL BE SOLD AT A PUBLIC SALE AFTER NOTICE OF THE SALE HAS BEEN GIVEN BY PUBLICATION. YOU HAVE THE RIGHT TO BID ON THE PROPERTY AT THIS SALE. AFTER THE PROPERTY IS SOLD AND THE COSTS OF STORAGE, ADVERTISING, AND SALE ARE DEDUCTED, THE REMAINING MONEY WILL BE PAID OVER TO THE COUNTY. YOU MAY CLAIM THE REMAINING MONEY AT ANY TIME WITHIN ONE YEAR AFTER THE COUNTY RECEIVES THE MONEY.

Dated:_____

_____

Landlord_____

Telephone:_____

Address:_____

_____

Insert date not fewer than ten days after notice is personally delivered or, if mailed, not fewer than fifteen days after notice is deposited in the mail.

This page intentionally left blank.

NOTICE OF RIGHT TO RECLAIM ABANDONED PROPERTY
(Property of person other than tenant valued over $500)

TO:_____

_____

_____

WHEN _____ VACATED THE
PREMISES AT _____
APT. _____, THE FOLLOWING PERSONAL PROPERTY REMAINED:

IF YOU OWN ANY OF THIS PROPERTY, YOU MAY CLAIM THIS PROPERTY AT
_____.
UNLESS YOU PAY THE REASONABLE COSTS OF STORAGE AND ADVERTISING, IF
ANY, FOR ALL THE ABOVE-DESCRIBED PROPERTY AND TAKE POSSESSION OF THE
PROPERTY WHICH YOU ARE ENTITLED NO LATER THAN _____,
_____.* THIS PROPERTY MAY BE DISPOSED OF PURSUANT TO S. 715.109.

IF YOU FAIL TO RECLAIM THE PROPERTY, IT WILL BE SOLD AT A PUBLIC SALE
AFTER NOTICE OF THE SALE HAS BEEN GIVEN BY PUBLICATION. YOU HAVE THE
RIGHT TO BID ON THE PROPERTY AT THIS SALE. AFTER THE PROPERTY IS SOLD
AND THE COSTS OF STORAGE, ADVERTISING, AND SALE ARE DEDUCTED, THE
REMAINING MONEY WILL BE PAID OVER TO THE COUNTY. YOU MAY CLAIM THE
REMAINING MONEY AT ANY TIME WITHIN ONE YEAR AFTER THE COUNTY
RECEIVES THE MONEY.

Dated:_____

Landlord_____
Telephone:_____
Address:_____

_____

*Insert date not fewer than ten days after notice is personally delivered or, if mailed, not fewer
than fifteen days after notice is deposited in the mail.

This page intentionally left blank.

IN THE COUNTY COURT, IN AND FOR
_____COUNTY, FLORIDA

CASE NO.: _____

[Insert case number assigned
by Clerk of the Court]

_____,

[insert name of Landlord]   Plaintiff,

vs.

SATISFACTION OF JUDGMENT

_____,

[insert name of Tenant]   Defendant.
_____

This document is signed by _____, [insert: "individually" or "as agent of Plaintiff corporation"] _____ on _____,

_____.

Plaintiff, _____, acknowledges full payment of the judgment signed by the Judge on _____, _____. Plaintiff agrees that Defendant(s) do(es) not owe the Plaintiff any more monies for the judgment.

_____   _____
        [Witness]   [Plaintiff]

_____
        [Witness]

Acknowledged before me on _____, by _____, who

_____ is personally known to me/ _____ produced _____ as identification, and who
_____ did/ _____ did not take an oath.

_____
            [date]

_____
         [document]

_____

NOTARY PUBLIC-STATE OF FLORIDA

Name: _____

Commission No.: _____

My Commission Expires: _____

Approved for use under rule 10-2.1(a) of
the Rules Regulating the Florida Bar

The Florida Bar 1993

This form was completed
with the assistance of:
Name:
Address:
Telephone Number:

This page intentionally left blank.

PROPERTY MANAGEMENT AGREEMENT

THIS AGREEMENT is made on _____, 20_____ between _____ _____ as Owner and _____ _____ as Manager, of the Property, known as _____ _____

WHEREAS Owner wishes to hire Manager to take over the day to day management of the Property and Manager wishes to take over such duties,

THEREFORE, in consideration of the mutual agreements contained herein, the parties agree as follows:

1. Authority. Manager is hereby appointed exclusive agent with power and authority to lease and manage the Property.

2. Term. This agreement shall be for a term of _____ months, beginning _____, 20____ and ending, _____, 20____.

3. Duties. Manager shall rent, manage, and control the property using its best efforts to find and keep tenants. Manager shall negotiate all leases on terms agreed by Owner. Manager shall contract for all necessary repairs to the property. Manager shall collect all rents and remit to Owner after payment of _____. Payments shall be made to Owner of net amounts, less $_____ kept on deposit for expenses, at least once every _____ days.

4. Leases. Manager shall execute all leases and rental agreements:
    ____ in Manager's name as landlord.
    ____ in Owner's name. Manager is hereby appointed as attorney-in-fact to execute such agreements.

Manager shall have authority to serve any legal notices on tenants and to take any legal action as is permitted by law to enforce leases, evict tenants or collect money owed.

5. Compensation. The manager shall be paid as follows: _____ _____.

6. Sale of Property. In the event of a bona fide sale of the property, Owner may terminate this contract upon giving thirty-days notice.

_____   _____
Owner   Manager

INDEX

commercially reasonable manner, 109

common areas, 16, 36, 40, 41

Complaint, 83

Complaint for Eviction and Damages, 101

condominiums, 2, 8, 14, 19, 23, 112

contracts of sale, 4

cooperatives, 2, 23

countersuits, 95

court procedures, 82

credit reporting agencies, 12

crimes, 45, 46

D

damage deposits, 19

damages, 27, 32, 55, 60, 103
    amount, 102
    interest, 102
    money, 90, 101
    other, 103
    punitive, 95

death, 76

defendant index, 12

defenses, 90, 93, 104
    equitable, 93

Department of Business Regulation, 4, 112

Department of Housing and Urban
    Development (HUD), 6

Department of Legal Affairs, 5

Department of Motor Vehicles, 109

depositions, 88

destruction of the premises, 58, 68

discovery, 94

discrimination, 12, 13, 14, 16

distress for rent, 106

Division of Hotels and Motels, 4

dogs, 44

duplexes, 20, 23, 37, 39, 41, 46

E

educational facilities, 2

efficiencies, 18

eminent domain, 20

employment rentals, 68

Environmental Protection Agency (EPA), 5, 40

evictions, 77, 80, 83, 94, 97, 101, 102, 112
    grounds, 79
    settling, 78

exterminations, 36

F

Fair Debt Collection Act, 73, 81

Fair Housing Act, 13, 14

fictitious names, 7, 91

Final Judgment, 86, 87, 103

fires, 58

fixtures, 20

foreclosures, 49

fourteen-day notice, 73

fraud, 25

fuel, 36

G

garbage, 36
    removal, 36, 39

geriatric facilities, 2

good faith, 7

H

handicapped persons, 12, 13, 14, 15

harassment, 96

HIV, 16

holding over, 59

holidays, 86, 87

home health care facilities, 5

hospices, 5

hot water, 36, 39

hotels, 2, 4, 33

hurricanes, 58

I

illegality, 25

implied warranty of habitability, 38

impossibility, 25

W

SPHINX® PUBLISHING'S STATE TITLES
Up-to-Date for Your State

California Titles
How to File for Divorce in CA (5E)	$26.95
How to Settle & Probate an Estate in CA (2E)	$28.95
How to Start a Business in CA (2E)	$21.95
How to Win in Small Claims Court in CA (2E)	$18.95
Landlords' Legal Guide in CA (2E)	$24.95
Make Your Own CA Will	$18.95
Tenants' Rights in CA	$21.95

Florida Titles
How to File for Divorce in FL (8E)	$28.95
How to Form a Corporation in FL (6E)	$24.95
How to Form a Limited Liability Co. in FL (3E)	$24.95
How to Form a Partnership in FL	$22.95
How to Make a FL Will (7E)	$16.95
How to Probate and Settle an Estate in FL (5E)	$26.95
How to Start a Business in FL (7E)	$21.95
How to Win in Small Claims Court in FL (7E)	$18.95
Land Trusts in Florida (6E)	$29.95
Landlords' Rights and Duties in FL (10E)	$22.95

Georgia Titles
How to File for Divorce in GA (5E)	$21.95
How to Start a Business in GA (4E)	$21.95

Illinois Titles
Child Custody, Visitation and Support in IL	$24.95
How to File for Divorce in IL (3E)	$24.95
How to Make an IL Will (3E)	$16.95
How to Start a Business in IL (4E)	$21.95
Landlords' Legal Guide in IL	$24.95

Maryland, Virginia and the District of Columbia Titles
How to File for Divorce in MD, VA, and DC	$28.95
How to Start a Business in MD, VA, or DC	$21.95

Massachusetts Titles
How to Form a Corporation in MA	$24.95
How to Start a Business in MA (4E)	$21.95
Landlords' Legal Guide in MA (2E)	$24.95

Michigan Titles
How to File for Divorce in MI (4E)	$24.95
How to Make a MI Will (3E)	$16.95
How to Start a Business in MI (4E)	$24.95

Minnesota Titles

How to File for Divorce in MN	$21.95
How to Form a Corporation in MN	$24.95
How to Make a MN Will (2E)	$16.95

New Jersey Titles

How to File for Divorce in NJ	$24.95
How to Start a Business in NJ	$21.95

New York Titles

Child Custody, Visitation and Support in NY	$26.95
File for Divorce in NY	$26.95
How to Form a Corporation in NY (2E)	$21.95
How to Make a NY Will (3E)	$16.95
How to Start a Business in NY (2E)	$18.95
How to Win in Small Claims Court in NY (3E)	$18.95
Tenants' Rights in NY	$21.95

North Carolina and South Carolina Titles

How to File for Divorce in NC (3E)	$22.95
How to Make a NC Will (3E)	$16.95
How to Start a Business in NC or SC	$24.95
Landlords' Rights & Duties in NC	$21.95

Ohio Titles

How to File for Divorce in OH (3E)	$24.95
How to Form a Corporation in OH	$24.95
How to Make an OH Will	$16.95

Pennsylvania Titles

Child Custody, Visitation and Support in PA	$26.95
How to File for Divorce in PA (4E)	$24.95
How to Form a Corporation in PA	$24.95
How to Make a PA Will (2E)	$16.95
How to Start a Business in PA (3E)	$21.95
Landlords' Legal Guide in PA	$24.95

Texas Titles

Child Custody, Visitation and Support in TX	$22.95
How to File for Divorce in TX (4E)	$24.95
How to Form a Corporation in TX (3E)	$24.95
How to Make a TX Will (3E)	$16.95
How to Probate and Settle an Estate in TX (4E)	$26.95
How to Start a Business in TX (4E)	$21.95
How to Win in Small Claims Court in TX (2E)	$16.95
Landlords' Legal Guide in TX	$24.95

SPHINX® PUBLISHING ORDER FORM

BILL TO:

SHIP TO:

Phone #

Terms

F.O.B. Chicago, IL

Ship Date

Charge my: ☐ VISA ☐ MasterCard ☐ American Express

Credit Card Number

Expiration Date

☐ **Money Order or Personal Check**

Qty	ISBN	Title	Retail	Ext.
		SPHINX PUBLISHING NATIONAL TITLES		
___	1-57248-363-6	101 Complaint Letters That Get Results	$18.95	___
___	1-57248-361-X	The 529 College Savings Plan (2E)	$18.95	___
___	1-57248-483-7	The 529 College Savings Plan Made Simple	$7.95	___
___	1-57248-460-8	The Alternative Minimum Tax	$14.95	___
___	1-57248-349-0	The Antique and Art Collector's Legal Guide	$24.95	___
___	1-57248-347-4	Attorney Responsibilities & Client Rights	$19.95	___
___	1-57248-482-9	The Childcare Answer Book	$12.95	___
___	1-57248-382-2	Child Support	$18.95	___
___	1-57248-487-X	Cómo Comprar su Primera Casa	$8.95	___
___	1-57248-488-8	Cómo Conseguir Trabajo en los Estados Unidos	$8.95	___
___	1-57248-148-X	Cómo Hacer su Propio Testamento	$16.95	___
___	1-57248-462-4	Cómo Negociar su Crédito	$8.95	___
___	1-57248-463-2	Cómo Organizar un Presupuesto	$8.95	___
___	1-57248-147-1	Cómo Solicitar su Propio Divorcio	$24.95	___
___	1-57248-373-3	The Complete Adoption and Fertility Legal Guide	$24.95	___
___	1-57248-166-8	The Complete Book of Corporate Forms	$24.95	___
___	1-57248-383-0	The Complete Book of Insurance	$18.95	___
___	1-57248499-3	The Complete Book of Personal Legal Forms	$24.95	___
___	1-57248-500-0	The Complete Credit Repair Kit	$19.95	___
___	1-57248-458-6	The Complete Hiring and Firing Handbook	$18.95	___
___	1-57248-353-9	The Complete Kit to Selling Your Own Home	$18.95	___
___	1-57248-229-X	The Complete Legal Guide to Senior Care	$21.95	___
___	1-57248-498-5	The Complete Limited Liability Company Kit	$21.95	___
___	1-57248-391-1	The Complete Partnership Book	$24.95	___
___	1-57248-201-X	The Complete Patent Book	$26.95	___
___	1-57248-480-2	The Mortgage Answer Book	$14.95	___
___	1-57248-369-5	Credit Smart	$18.95	___
___	1-57248-163-3	Crime Victim's Guide to Justice (2E)	$21.95	___
___	1-57248-481-0	The Easy Will and Living Will Kit	$16.95	___
___	1-57248-251-6	The Entrepreneur's Internet Handbook	$21.95	___
___	1-57248-235-4	The Entrepreneur's Legal Guide	$26.95	___
___	1-57248-346-6	Essential Guide to Real Estate Contracts (2E)	$18.95	___
___	1-57248-160-9	Essential Guide to Real Estate Leases	$18.95	___
___	1-57248-375-X	Fathers' Rights	$19.95	___
___	1-57248-450-0	Financing Your Small Business	$17.95	___
___	1-57248-459-4	Fired, Laid Off or Forced Out	$14.95	___
___	1-57248-502-7	The Frequent Traveler's Guide	$14.95	___
___	1-57248-331-8	Gay & Lesbian Rights	$26.95	___
___	1-57248-139-0	Grandparents' Rights (3E)	$24.95	___
___	1-57248-475-6	Guía de Inmigración a Estados Unidos (4E)	$24.95	___
___	1-57248-187-0	Guía de Justicia para Víctimas del Crimen	$21.95	___
___	1-57248-253-2	Guía Esencial para los Contratos de Arrendamiento de Bienes Raices	$22.95	___
___	1-57248-334-2	Homeowner's Rights	$19.95	___
___	1-57248-164-1	How to Buy a Condominium or Townhome (2E)	$19.95	___
___	1-57248-197-7	How to Buy Your First Home (2E)	$14.95	___
___	1-57248-384-9	How to Buy a Franchise	$19.95	___
___	1-57248-472-1	How to File Your Own Bankruptcy (6E)	$21.95	___
___	1-57248-343-1	How to File Your Own Divorce (5E)	$26.95	___
___	1-57248-390-3	How to Form a Nonprofit Corporation (3E)	$24.95	___
___	1-57248-345-8	How to Form Your Own Corporation (4E)	$26.95	___

Qty	ISBN	Title	Retail	Ext.
___	1-57248-232-X	How to Make Your Own Simple Will (3E)	$18.95	___
___	1-57248-479-9	How to Parent with Your Ex	$12.95	___
___	1-57248-379-2	How to Register Your Own Copyright (5E)	$24.95	___
___	1-57248-394-6	How to Write Your Own Living Will (4E)	$18.95	___
___	1-57248-156-0	How to Write Your Own Premarital Agreement (3E)	$24.95	___
___	1-57248-504-3	HR for Small Business	$14.95	___
___	1-57248-230-3	Incorporate in Delaware from Any State	$26.95	___
___	1-57248-158-7	Incorporate in Nevada from Any State	$24.95	___
___	1-57248-474-8	Inmigración a los EE.UU. Paso a Paso (2E)	$24.95	___
___	1-57248-400-4	Inmigración y Ciudadanía en los EE.UU. Preguntas y Respuestas	$16.95	___
___	1-57248-453-5	Law 101	$16.95	___
___	1-57248-374-1	Law School 101	$16.95	___
___	1-57248-377-6	The Law (In Plain English)® for Small Business	$19.95	___
___	1-57248-476-4	The Law (In Plain English)® for Writers	$16.95	___
___	1-57248-223-0	Legal Research Made Easy (3E)	$21.95	___
___	1-57248-449-7	The Living Trust Kit	$21.95	___
___	1-57248-165-X	Living Trusts and Other Ways to Avoid Probate (3E)	$24.95	___
___	1-57248-486-1	Making Music Your Business	$18.95	___
___	1-57248-186-2	Manual de Beneficios para el Seguro Social	$18.95	___
___	1-57248-220-6	Mastering the MBE	$16.95	___
___	1-57248-455-1	Minding Her Own Business, 4E	$14.95	___
___	1-57248-480-2	The Mortgage Answer Book	$14.95	___
___	1-57248-167-6	Most Val. Business Legal Forms You'll Ever Need (3E)	$21.95	___
___	1-57248-388-1	The Power of Attorney Handbook (5E)	$22.95	___
___	1-57248-332-6	Profit from Intellectual Property	$28.95	___
___	1-57248-329-6	Protect Your Patent	$24.95	___
___	1-57248-376-8	Nursing Homes and Assisted Living Facilities	$19.95	___
___	1-57248-385-7	Quick Cash	$14.95	___
___	1-57248-350-4	El Seguro Social Preguntas y Respuestas	$16.95	___
___	1-57248386-5	Seniors' Rights	$19.95	___
___	1-57248-217-6	Sexual Harassment: Your Guide to Legal Action	$18.95	___
___	1-57248-378-4	Sisters-in-Law	$16.95	___
___	1-57248-219-2	The Small Business Owner's Guide to Bankruptcy	$21.95	___
___	1-57248-395-4	The Social Security Benefits Handbook (4E)	$18.95	___
___	1-57248-216-8	Social Security Q&A	$12.95	___
___	1-57248-328-8	Starting Out or Starting Over	$14.95	___
___	1-57248-525-6	Teen Rights (and Responsibilities) (2E)	$14.95	___
___	1-57248-457-8	Tax Power for the Self-Employed	$17.95	___
___	1-57248-366-0	Tax Smarts for Small Business	$21.95	___
___	1-57248-236-2	Unmarried Parents' Rights (2E)	$19.95	___
___	1-57248-362-8	U.S. Immigration and Citizenship Q&A	$18.95	___
___	1-57248-387-3	U.S. Immigration Step by Step (2E)	$24.95	___
___	1-57248-392-X	U.S.A. Immigration Guide (5E)	$26.95	___
___	1-57248-178-0	¡Visas! ¡Visas! ¡Visas!	$9.95	___
___	1-57248-177-2	The Weekend Landlord	$16.95	___
___	1-57248-451-9	What to Do — Before "I DO"	$14.95	___
___	1-57248-225-7	Win Your Unemployment Compensation Claim (2E)	$21.95	___

Total for this page ___

To order, call Sourcebooks at 1-800-432-7444 or FAX (630) 961-2168 (Bookstores, libraries, wholesalers—please call for discount)

Prices are subject to change without notice.

Find more legal information at: **www.SphinxLegal.com**

SPHINX® PUBLISHING ORDER FORM

Qty	ISBN	Title	Retail	Ext.
____	1-57248-330-X	The Wills, Estate Planning and Trusts Legal Kit	$26.95	____
____	1-57248-473-X	Winning Your Personal Injury Claim (3E)	$24.95	____
____	1-57248-333-4	Working with Your Homeowners Association	$19.95	____
____	1-57248-380-6	Your Right to Child Custody, Visitation and Support (3E)	$24.95	____
____	1-57248-505-1	Your Rights at Work	$14.95	____

CALIFORNIA TITLES
Qty	ISBN	Title	Retail	Ext.
____	1-57248-489-6	How to File for Divorce in CA (5E)	$26.95	____
____	1-57248-464-0	How to Settle and Probate an Estate in CA (2E)	$28.95	____
____	1-57248-336-9	How to Start a Business in CA (2E)	$21.95	____
____	1-57248-194-3	How to Win in Small Claims Court in CA (2E)	$18.95	____
____	1-57248-246-X	Make Your Own CA Will	$18.95	____
____	1-57248-397-0	Landlords' Legal Guide in CA (2E)	$24.95	____
____	1-57248-241-9	Tenants' Rights in CA	$21.95	____

FLORIDA TITLES
Qty	ISBN	Title	Retail	Ext.
____	1-57248-396-2	How to File for Divorce in FL (8E)	$28.95	____
____	1-57248-356-3	How to Form a Corporation in FL (6E)	$24.95	____
____	1-57248-490-X	How to Form a Limited Liability Co. in FL (4E)	$24.95	____
____	1-57071-401-0	How to Form a Partnership in FL	$22.95	____
____	1-57248-456-X	How to Make a FL Will (7E)	$16.95	____
____	1-57248-354-7	How to Probate and Settle an Estate in FL (5E)	$26.95	____
____	1-57248-339-3	How to Start a Business in FL (7E)	$21.95	____
____	1-57248-204-4	How to Win in Small Claims Court in FL (7E)	$18.95	____
____	1-57248-381-4	Land Trusts in Florida (7E)	$29.95	____
____	1-57248-491-8	Landlords' Rights and Duties in FL (10E)	$22.95	____

GEORGIA TITLES
Qty	ISBN	Title	Retail	Ext.
____	1-57248-340-7	How to File for Divorce in GA (5E)	$21.95	____
____	1-57248-493-4	How to Start a Business in GA (4E)	$21.95	____

ILLINOIS TITLES
Qty	ISBN	Title	Retail	Ext.
____	1-57248-244-3	Child Custody, Visitation, and Support in IL	$24.95	____
____	1-57248-206-0	How to File for Divorce in IL (3E)	$24.95	____
____	1-57248-170-6	How to Make an IL Will (3E)	$16.95	____
____	1-57248-265-9	How to Start a Business in IL (4E)	$21.95	____
____	1-57248-252-4	Landlords' Legal Guide in IL	$24.95	____

MARYLAND, VIRGINIA AND THE DISTRICT OF COLUMBIA
Qty	ISBN	Title	Retail	Ext.
____	1-57248-240-0	How to File for Divorce in MD, VA, and DC	$28.95	____
____	1-57248-359-8	How to Start a Business in MD, VA, or DC	$21.95	____

MASSACHUSETTS TITLES
Qty	ISBN	Title	Retail	Ext.
____	1-57248-115-3	How to Form a Corporation in MA	$24.95	____
____	1-57248-466-7	How to Start a Business in MA (4E)	$21.95	____
____	1-57248-398-9	Landlords' Legal Guide in MA (2E)	$24.95	____

MICHIGAN TITLES
Qty	ISBN	Title	Retail	Ext.
____	1-57248-467-5	How to File for Divorce in MI (4E)	$24.95	____
____	1-57248-182-X	How to Make a MI Will (3E)	$16.95	____
____	1-57248-468-3	How to Start a Business in MI (4E)	$18.95	____

MINNESOTA TITLES
Qty	ISBN	Title	Retail	Ext.
____	1-57248-142-0	How to File for Divorce in MN	$21.95	____
____	1-57248-179-X	How to Form a Corporation in MN	$24.95	____
____	1-57248-178-1	How to Make a MN Will (2E)	$16.95	____

NEW JERSEY TITLES
Qty	ISBN	Title	Retail	Ext.
____	1-57248-239-7	How to File for Divorce in NJ	$24.95	____
____	1-57248-448-9	How to Start a Business in NJ	$21.95	____

NEW YORK TITLES
Qty	ISBN	Title	Retail	Ext.
____	1-57248-193-5	Child Custody, Visitation and Support in NY	$26.95	____
____	1-57248-351-2	File for Divorce in NY	$26.95	____
____	1-57248-249-4	How to Form a Corporation in NY (2E)	$24.95	____
____	1-57248-401-2	How to Make a NY Will (3E)	$16.95	____
____	1-57248-469-1	How to Start a Business in NY (3E)	$21.95	____
____	1-57248-198-6	How to Win in Small Claims Court in NY (2E)	$18.95	____
____	1-57248-122-6	Tenants' Rights in NY	$21.95	____

NORTH CAROLINA AND SOUTH CAROLINA TITLES
Qty	ISBN	Title	Retail	Ext.
____	1-57248-185-4	How to File for Divorce in NC (3E)	$22.95	____
____	1-57248-371-7	How to Start a Business in NC or SC	$24.95	____
____	1-57248-091-2	Landlords' Rights & Duties in NC	$21.95	____

OHIO TITLES
Qty	ISBN	Title	Retail	Ext.
____	1-57248-503-5	How to File for Divorce in OH (3E)	$24.95	____
____	1-57248-174-9	How to Form a Corporation in OH	$24.95	____
____	1-57248-173-0	How to Make an OH Will	$16.95	____

PENNSYLVANIA TITLES
Qty	ISBN	Title	Retail	Ext.
____	1-57248-242-7	Child Custody, Visitation and Support in PA	$26.95	____
____	1-57248-495-0	How to File for Divorce in PA (4E)	$24.95	____
____	1-57248-358-X	How to Form a Corporation in PA	$24.95	____
____	1-57248-094-7	How to Make a PA Will (2E)	$16.95	____
____	1-57248-357-1	How to Start a Business in PA (3E)	$21.95	____
____	1-57248-245-1	Landlords' Legal Guide in PA	$24.95	____

TEXAS TITLES
Qty	ISBN	Title	Retail	Ext.
____	1-57248-171-4	Child Custody, Visitation, and Support in TX	$22.95	____
____	1-57248-399-7	How to File for Divorce in TX (4E)	$24.95	____
____	1-57248-470-5	How to Form a Corporation in TX (3E)	$24.95	____
____	1-57248-255-9	How to Make a TX Will (3E)	$16.95	____
____	1-57248-496-9	How to Probate and Settle an Estate in TX (4E)	$26.95	____
____	1-57248-471-3	How to Start a Business in TX (4E)	$21.95	____
____	1-57248-111-0	How to Win in Small Claims Court in TX (2E)	$16.95	____
____	1-57248-355-5	Landlords' Legal Guide in TX	$24.95	____

SubTotal This page ____

SubTotal previous page ____

Shipping — $5.00 for 1st book, $1.00 each additional ____

Illinois residents add 6.75% sales tax ____

Connecticut residents add 6.00% sales tax ____

Total ____

To order, call Sourcebooks at 1-800-432-7444 or FAX (630) 961-2168 (Bookstores, libraries, wholesalers—please call for discount)
Prices are subject to change without notice.
Find more legal information at: **www.SphinxLegal.com**